THE WARREN BUFFETT WAY

THIRD EDITION

ROBERT G. HAGSTROM

WILEY

THE WARREN BUFFETT WAY

THIRD EDITION

Authorized reprint by Wiley India Pvt. Ltd., 4435-36/7, Ansari Road, Daryaganj, New Delhi – 110002.

Cover image: © Bloomberg via Getty Images
Cover design: Paul McCarthy

Reprint: 2017

Printed at: Sanat Printers, Kundli, Haryana.

ISBN: 978-81-265-4643-5

Contents

Table [illegible] Berkshire Hathaway 1991 Common Stock Portfolio

Number of Shares	Company	Cost	Market Value
46,700,000	The Coca-Cola Company	$1,023,920	$3,747,675
6,850,000	GEICO Corporation	45,713	1,363,150
24,000,000	The Gillette Company	600,000	1,347,000
3,000,000	Capital Cities/ABC, Inc.	517,500	1,300,500
2,495,200	Federal Home Loan Mortgage Corp.	77,245	343,090
1,727,765	The Washington Post Company	9,731	336,050
31,247,000	Guinness plc	264,782	296,755
5,000,000	Wells Fargo & Company	289,431	290,000
	Total common stocks	$2,828,322	$9,024,220

Source: Berkshire Hathaway 1991 Annual Report.

Note: Dollar amounts are in thousands.

Table [illegible] Berkshire Hathaway 1992 Common Stock Portfolio

Number of Shares	Company	Cost	Market Value
93,400,000	The Coca-Cola Company	$1,023,920	$3,911,125
34,250,000	GEICO Corporation	45,713	2,226,250
3,000,000	Capital Cities/ABC, Inc.	517,500	1,523,500
24,000,000	The Gillette Company	600,000	1,365,000
16,196,700	Federal Home Loan Mortgage Corp.	414,527	783,515
6,358,418	Wells Fargo & Company	380,983	485,624
4,350,000	General Dynamics	312,438	450,769
1,727,765	The Washington Post Company	9,731	396,954
38,335,000	Guinness plc	333,019	299,581
	Total common stocks	[illegible]	$11,442,318

Source: Berkshire Hathaway 1992 Annual Report.

Note: Dollar amounts are in thousands.

Foreword: The Exception

What accounts for Warren Buffett's exceptional investment success? That's one of the questions I'm asked most often. It's also the question I want to explore in this foreword.

When I studied for my MBA at the University of Chicago in the late 1960s, I was exposed to a new theory of finance that had been developed, largely there, in the preceding few years. One of the most important components of the "Chicago School" of thought was the Efficient Market Hypothesis. According to that hypothesis, the combined efforts of millions of intelligent, motivated, objective, and informed investors cause information to immediately be reflected in market prices such that assets will provide a fair risk-adjusted return, no more and no less. Prices are never so low or so high that they can be taken advantage of, and thus no investors can be capable of consistently identifying opportunities to benefit. It's this hypothesis that gives rise to the Chicago School's best-known dictum: You can't beat the market.

The Efficient Market Hypothesis supplies the intellectual basis for that conclusion, and there are lots of empirical data showing that, despite all their efforts, most investors don't beat the market. That's a pretty strong case for the inability to outperform.

It's not that no investors beat the market. Every once in a while some do, and just as many underperform; market efficiency isn't so strong a force that it's impossible for individual investors' returns to deviate from the market's return. It's merely asserted that no one can do it to a sufficient degree and consistently enough to disprove the Efficient Market Hypothesis. There are outliers, as in most processes, but their superior returns are described as being based on randomness and thus ephemeral. When I grew up, there was a saying that "If you put enough chimpanzees in a room with typewriters, eventually one of them will write the Bible." That is, when randomness is present, just about anything can happen once in a while. However, as my mother used to say, "It's the exception that proves the rule." A general rule may not hold 100 percent, but the fact that exceptions are so rare attests to its basic truth. Every day, millions of investors, amateur and professional alike, prove you can't beat the market.

And then there's Warren Buffett.

Warren and a few other legendary investors—including Ben Graham, Peter Lynch, Stan Druckenmiller, George Soros, and Julian Robertson—have performance records that fly in the face of the Chicago School. In short, they've outperformed by a big enough margin, for long enough periods of time, with large enough amounts of money, that the advocates of market efficiency are forced onto the defensive. Their records show that exceptional investors can beat the market through skill, not chance.

Especially in Warren's case, it's hard to argue with the evidence. On his office wall, he displays a statement, typed by him, showing that he started The Buffett Partnership in 1956 with $105,000. Since then, he has attracted additional capital and earned returns on it such that Berkshire Hathaway now has investments totaling $143 billion and a net worth of $202 billion. He's kicked the hell out of the indices for many years. And in the process, he's become the second wealthiest man in America. This last achievement wasn't based on dynastic real estate assets or a unique technological invention, as with so many on Forbes's lists, but on applying hard work and skill in investment markets that are open to everyone.

What's responsible for Warren Buffett's singular accomplishments? In my view these are the keys:

- **He's super-smart.** One of the many *bon mots* attributed to Warren is the following: "If you have an IQ of 160, sell

30 points. You don't need them." As Malcolm Gladwell pointed out in the book *Outliers*, you don't have to be a genius to achieve great success, just smart enough. Beyond that, incremental intelligence doesn't necessarily add to your chances. In fact, there are people so smart that they can't get out of their own way, or can't find the path to success (and happiness) in the real world. A high IQ isn't enough to make someone a great investor; if it were, college professors would probably be the richest people in America. It's important to also to be business-oriented and have "savvy" or "street smarts."

I have a sneaking suspicion that Warren's IQ is well above 130 . . . *and* that he hasn't made any effort to dispose of those "non-essential" extra points. His ability to cut to the core of a question, to reach a well-founded conclusion, and to hold that conclusion even if things initially go against him are all key elements in who he is and what he's accomplished. In short, he's fiercely analytical.

He's also incredibly quick. It doesn't take him weeks or months to reach a conclusion. He also doesn't need a cadre of analysts pushing numbers. He doesn't feel the need to know and consider every data point: just the ones that matter. And he has a great sense for which they are.

- **He's guided by an overarching philosophy.** Many investors think they're smart enough to master anything, or at least they act that way. Further, they believe the world is constantly changing, and you have to be eclectic and change your approach to adapt, racing to stay up with the latest wonder. The trouble with this is that no one really can know everything, it's hard to constantly retool and learn new tricks, and this mindset prevents the development of specialized expertise and helpful shortcuts.

Warren, on the other hand, knows what he doesn't know, sticks to what he does know, and leaves the rest for others. This is essential, since as Mark Twain said, "It ain't what you don't know that gets you into trouble. It's what you know for sure that just ain't so." Warren only invests in industries he understands and feels comfortable with. He emphasizes fairly prosaic fields and avoids, for example, high tech companies. He famously passes on things that are outside his philosophy and ken. Importantly, he can live with the possibility that the things he passes on will make money for others and he'll be left looking on as they do. (Most people can't.)

- **He's mentally flexible.** The fact that it's important to have a guiding philosophy doesn't mean it's never good to change. It can be desirable to adapt to significantly changed circumstances. It's even possible to come across a better philosophy. The key lies in knowing when to change and when to hold fast.

  Early in his career, Warren adopted the approach of his great teacher, Ben Graham. It's called "deep value"—buying castoffs when they're being given away, especially when companies can be bought for less than their net cash. It has sometimes been derided as "picking up cigar butts." After a while, however, with urging from his partner, Charlie Munger, he switched to emphasizing high-quality companies with protective "moats" and pricing power, led by outstanding people, at reasonable (but not necessarily giveaway) prices.

  It was long an aspect of Warren's approach to eschew companies that were capital-intensive, but he was able to overcome that bias to buy the Burlington Northern Santa Fe railway and take advantage of its economic sensitivity coming out of the 2008 financial collapse, and the outlook for increasing rail carriage.

  A philosophy should supply guidance but not rigidity. This—like many other things in investing—is a tough dilemma to master. Warren doesn't shrink from the challenge, neither changing with every new fad nor letting his thinking get stuck in cement.

- **He's unemotional.** Many of the obstacles to investment success relate to human emotion; the main reason for the failure of the Efficient Market Hypothesis is that investors rarely satisfy the requirement of objectivity. Most become greedy, confident, and euphoric when prices are high, causing them to celebrate their winners and buy more rather than take profits. And they get depressed and fearful when prices are low, causing them to sell assets at bargain prices and invariably discouraging them from buying. And perhaps worst of all, they have a terrible tendency to judge how they're doing based on how others are doing, and to let envy of others' success force them to take additional risk for the simple reason that others are doing so. Envy is enough to make people follow the crowd, even into investments they know nothing about.

Warren appears absolutely immune to these emotional influences. He doesn't get overjoyed when things appreciate, or downcast when they don't, and for him success is clearly defined by himself, not the masses or the media. He doesn't care whether others think he's right, or whether his investment decisions promptly make him look right. (He was written off as "past his prime" early in 2000 because of his failure to participate in what turned out to be the tech bubble, but he never changed his spots.) He only cares what he (and Charlie Munger) thinks . . . and whether his shareholders make money.

- **He's contrarian and iconoclastic.** Whereas the typical investor thinks he should follow the herd, despite its susceptibility to the errors of emotion, the best investors behave in a contrarian fashion, diverging from the herd at the key moments. But it's not enough to do the opposite of what others are doing. You have to understand what they're doing; understand why it's wrong; know what to do instead; have the nerve to act in a contrary fashion (that is, to adopt and hold what Yale's David Swensen calls "uncomfortably idiosyncratic positions"); and be willing to look terribly wrong until the ship turns and you're proved right. That last element can feel like it's taking forever; as the old saying goes, "Being too far ahead of your time is indistinguishable from being wrong." Take it all together and it's clear that this isn't easy.

It's obvious that Warren is highly capable of contrarian behavior. In fact, he revels in it. He once wrote me that he had seen high yield bonds when the market priced them like flowers and he had seen them when they were considered weeds. "I liked them better when they were weeds." The contrarian prefers to buy things when they're out of favor. Warren does it like no one else.

- **He's counter-cyclical.** Investing consists of dealing with the future, and yet many of the best estors accept that they can't predict what the macro future holds in terms of economic developments, interest rates and market fluctuations. If we can't excel at the thing that most people want to hang their hat on, what can we do? In my view, there are great gains to be had from behaving counter-cyclically.

  It's emotionally easy to invest when the economy is improving, companies are reporting higher earnings, asset prices are rising, and risk bearing is being rewarded. But buying appreciated assets doesn't hold the key to superior investment results. Rather, the greatest bargains are accessed by buying when the economy and companies are suffering: that's more likely to be the climate in which asset prices understate their merits. However, this, too, is not easy.

  Warren has repeatedly demonstrated his ability—in fact his preference—for investing at the bottom of the cycle, when optimism is in short supply. His investments of $5 billion each in 10 percent preferred stock of Goldman Sachs and General Electric at the depths of the 2008 financial crisis, and his purchase of economically sensitive Burlington Northern for $34 billion in 2009, are emblematic of this. The wisdom of these investments is obvious today in retrospect, but how many acted as boldly when fear of a financial collapse was rampant?
- **He has a long-term focus and is unconcerned with volatility.** Over my 45 years in the business, investors' time horizons have gotten shorter and shorter. This is likely the result of increased media attention to investment results (there was none in the 1960s), its contagion to investors and their clients, and the striving for yearly gains introduced by hedge

funds' annual incentive fees. But as other people allow nonsensical biases to affect their thoughts and actions, we can profit from avoiding them. Thus, most investors' excessive concern with quarterly and annual results creates profit opportunities for those who think in terms of longer periods.

Warren has famously said that his "holding period is forever," and that he "prefers a lumpy 15 percent a year over a smooth 12 percent." This allows him to stick with great ideas for long periods of time, compounding his gains and allowing profits to build up untaxed, rather than turning over the portfolio every year and paying taxes at short-term rates. It also helps him avoid getting shaken out in times of volatility, and instead lets him take advantage of them. In fact, rather than insist on liquidity and take advantage of the ability to exit from investments, Warren's actions make clear that he is happy making investments he could never shed.

- **He's unafraid to bet big on his best ideas.** Diversification has long played a leading part in so-called prudent investment management. In short, it reduces the likelihood of large individual losses (and of being sued for having had too much in a losing position). But while it reduces the pain caused by losing investments, a high degree of diversification correspondingly reduces the potential gain from winners.

As in many things, Warren takes a divergent view of diversification: "The strategy we've adopted precludes our following standard diversification dogma. Many pundits would therefore say the strategy must be riskier than that employed by more conventional investors. We believe that a policy of portfolio concentration may well decrease risk if it raises, as it should, both the intensity with which an investor thinks about a business and the comfort-level he must feel with its economic characteristics before buying into it."

Warren understands that great ideas come along only on rare occasion, so he keeps the bar high, only invests in great ideas, and bets big when he sees one. Thus, he commits significantly to the companies and people he believes in;

he doesn't hold anything just because others do and he's worried it may perform well without his being represented; and he refuses to diversify into things he thinks less of just to mitigate the impact of errors— that is, to practice what he calls "de-worstification." It's obvious that all of these things are essential if you're to have a chance at great results. But that doesn't keep them from being the exception in portfolio management, not the rule.

- **He's willing to be inactive.** Too many investors act as if there's always something great to do. Or perhaps they think they have to give the impression that they're smart enough to always be able to find a brilliant investment. But great investment opportunities are exceptional . . . and by definition, that means they're not available every day.

  Warren is famously willing to be inactive for long periods of time, turning down deal after deal until the right one comes along. He's famous for his analogy to one of baseball's greatest hitters, Ted Williams, standing at the plate with his bat on his shoulder and waiting for the perfect pitch; it exemplifies his insistence on making investments only when they're compelling. Who would argue that the supply of good deals is steady, or that it's always an equally good time to invest?

- **Finally, he's not worried about losing his job.** Very few investors are able to take all the actions they think are right. Many are constrained in terms of their ability to buy assets that are illiquid, controversial or unseemly; sell appreciating assets that "everyone" is sure will go further; and concentrate their portfolios in their few best ideas. Why? Because they fear the consequences of being wrong.

  "Agents" who manage money for others worry that acting boldly will expose them to the risk of being fired by their employers or terminated by their clients. Thus, they moderate their actions, doing only that which is considered prudent and uncontroversial. That's the tendency that caused John Maynard Keynes to observe, "Worldly wisdom teaches that it is better for reputation to fail conventionally than to succeed unconventionally." But that tendency introduces an important conundrum: if you're unwilling to take a position so bold that it can embarrass you if it fails, it's correspondingly impossible to take a position that can make a real difference if it works out well. Great investors are able to follow up their intellectual conclusions with action; in short, they dare to be great.

Warren obviously doesn't have to worry about being let go by his employer. His position is as close to permanent as there is, as is his capital. There are no clients able to withdraw their capital, mandating the sale of assets at bargain prices as befalls the typical money manager during market crashes. This simple fact plays a significant part in any great investor's success, and I'm sure it's no coincidence that Warren set things up this way, transitioning from a hedge fund structure to Berkshire Hathaway's corporate form. He wouldn't have it any other way.

Of course, Warren Buffett shares many other attributes of outstanding investors. He's focused, disciplined, and purposeful; he's hard working; he's highly numerate and logical; he's a voracious collector of information, through both reading and networking with people he respects; and at this point, he invests because he enjoys solving the complex intellectual problem that it represents, not to gain fame or make money. Those latter things are the by-product of his efforts, but not his goal, I'm sure.

In theory, many others could have done what Warren Buffett did over the last 60 years. The attributes listed above are rare, but not unique. And each one makes compelling sense; who would take the other side of any of these propositions? It's just that few people are able to demonstrate all of them in action. It's the combination of all of them—and the addition of that intangible "something" that makes a special person special—that has enabled Warren to succeed so exceptionally by applying The Warren Buffett Way.

Howard Marks
July 2013

Foreword to the Second Edition

When Robert Hagstrom first published *The Warren Buffett Way* in 1994, it quickly became a phenomenon. To date [2004], more than 1.2 million copies have been sold. The book's popularity is a testimony to the accuracy of its analysis and the value of its advice.

Any time the subject is Warren Buffett, it is easy to become overwhelmed by the sheer size of the numbers. Whereas most investors think in terms of hundreds or perhaps thousands, Buffett moves in a world of millions and billions. But that does not mean he has nothing to teach us. Quite the opposite. If we look at what he does and has done, and are able to discern the underlying thinking, we can model our decisions on his.

That is the profound contribution of Robert's book. He closely studied Warren Buffett's actions, words, and decisions for a number of years, and then set about analyzing them for common threads. For this book, he distilled those common threads into 12 tenets, timeless principles that guide Buffett's investment philosophy through all circumstances and all markets. In just the same way, they can guide any investor.

The enduring value of Robert's work is due to this clear focus—although the book talks about investment techniques, it is fundamentally about investment principles. And principles do not change. I can almost hear Warren saying, with his wry smile, "That's why they call them principles."

The past 10 years have given us a vivid demonstration of that basic truth. In those 10 years, the trends of the stock market changed several times over. We witnessed a high-flying bubble that made many people rich, and then a steep crash into a protracted, painful bear market before the market finally hit bottom in the spring of 2003 and started to turn back up.

All along the way, Warren Buffett's investment approach never changed. He has continued to follow the same principles outlined in this book:

- Think of buying stocks as buying fractional interests in whole businesses.
- Construct a focused, low-turnover portfolio.
- Invest in only what you can understand and analyze.
- Demand a margin of safety between the purchase price and the company's long-term value.

Berkshire Hathaway investors, as usual, reap the benefits of that steady approach. Since the recovery began in 2003, Berkshire Hathaway stock is up about $20,000 per share, more than 30 percent, far surpassing the returns of the overall market over the comparable period.

There is a chain of thinking for value investors that begins with Benjamin Graham, through Warren Buffett and his contemporaries, to the next generation of practitioners such as Robert Hagstrom. Buffett, Graham's best-known disciple, frequently advises investors to study Graham's book *The Intelligent Investor.* I often make the same recommendation myself. And I am convinced that Robert's work shares with that classic book one critical quality: The advice may not make you rich, but it is highly unlikely to make you poor. If understood and intelligently implemented, the techniques and principles presented here should make you a better investor.

Bill Miller
Chairman and Chief Investment Officer, LMM, LLC
October 2004

Foreword to the First Edition

One weekday evening early in 1989, I was home when the telephone rang. Our middle daughter, Annie, then 11, was first to the phone. She told me that Warren Buffett was calling. I was convinced this had to be a prank. The caller started by saying, "This is Warren Buffett from Omaha [as if I might confuse him with some other Warren Buffett]. I just finished your book, I loved it, and I would like to quote one of your sentences in the Berkshire annual report. I have always wanted to do a book, but I never have gotten around to it." He spoke very rapidly with lots of enthusiasm and must have said 40 words in 15 or 20 seconds, including a couple of laughs and chuckles. I instantly agreed to his request and I think we talked for five or ten minutes. I remember he closed by saying, "If you ever visit Omaha and don't come by and see me, your name will be mud in Nebraska."

Clearly not wanting my name to be mud in Nebraska, I took him up on his offer about six months later. Warren Buffett gave me a personal tour of every square foot of the office (which did not take long, as the whole operation could fit inside less than half of a tennis court), and I said hello to all 11 employees. There was not a computer or a stock quotation machine to be found.

After about an hour we went to a local restaurant where I followed his lead and had a terrific steak and my first Cherry Coke in 30 years. We talked about jobs we had as children, baseball, and bridge, and exchanged stories about companies in which we had held investments in the past. Warren discussed or answered questions about each stock and operation that Berkshire (he never called his company Berkshire Hathaway) owned.

Why has Warren Buffett been the best investor in history? What is he like as an individual, a shareholder, a manager, and an owner of entire companies? What is so unique about the Berkshire Hathaway annual report, why does he donate so much effort to it, and what can someone learn from it? To attempt to answer those questions, I talked with him directly, and reread the last five annual reports and his earliest reports as chairman (the 1971 and 1972 reports each had only two pages of text). In addition, I had discussions with nine individuals who have been actively involved with Warren Buffett in varied relationships and from different viewpoints during the past four to over 30 years: Jack Byrne, Robert Denham, Don Keough, Carol Loomis, Tom Murphy, Charlie Munger, Carl Reichardt, Frank Rooney, and Seth Schofield.

In terms of his personal qualities, the responses were quite consistent. Warren Buffett is, first of all, very content. He loves everything he does, dealing with people and reading mass quantities of annual and quarterly reports and numerous newspapers and periodicals. As an investor he has discipline, patience, flexibility, courage, confidence, and decisiveness. He is always searching for investments where risk is eliminated or minimized. In addition, he is very adept at probability and as an oddsmaker. I believe this ability comes from an inherent love of simple math computations, his devotion and active participation in the game of bridge, and his long experience in underwriting and accepting high levels of risk in insurance and in reinsurance. He is willing to take risks where the odds of total loss are low and upside rewards are substantial. He lists his failures and mistakes and does not apologize. He enjoys kidding himself and compliments his associates in objective terms.

Warren Buffett is a great student of business and a wonderful listener, and able to determine the key elements of a company or a complex issue with high speed and precision. He can make a decision not to invest in something in as little as two minutes and conclude that it is time to make a major purchase in just a few days of research. He is always prepared, for as he has said in an annual report, "Noah did not start building the Ark when it was raining."

As a manager he almost never calls a division head or the chief executive of a company but is delighted at any time of the day or night for them to call him to report something or to seek counsel. After investing in a stock or purchasing an entire operation, he becomes a cheerleader and sounding board: "At Berkshire we don't tell .400 hitters how to swing," using an analogy to baseball management.

Two examples of Warren Buffett's willingness to learn and adapt himself are public speaking and computer usage. In the 1950s Warren invested $100 in a Dale Carnegie course "not to prevent my knees from knocking when public speaking but to do public speaking while my knees are knocking." At the Berkshire annual meeting in front of more than 2,000 people, Warren Buffett sits on a stage with Charlie Munger, and, without notes, lectures and responds to questions in a fashion that would please Will Rogers, Ben Graham, King Solomon, Phil Fisher, David Letterman, and Billy Crystal. To be able to play more bridge, early in 1994 Warren learned how to use a computer so he could join a network where you can play with other individuals from their locations all over the country. Perhaps in the near future he will begin to use some of the hundreds of data retrieval and information services on companies that are available on computers today for investment research.

Warren Buffett stresses that the critical investment factor is determining the intrinsic value of a business and paying a fair or bargain price. He doesn't care what the general stock market has done recently or will do in the future. He purchased over $1 billion of Coca-Cola in 1988 and 1989 after the stock had risen over fivefold the prior six years and over five-hundredfold the previous 60 years. He made four times his money in three years and plans to make a lot more the next five, 10, and 20 years with Coke. In 1976 he purchased a very major position in GEICO when the stock had declined from $61 to $2 and the general perception was that the stock was definitely going to zero.

How can the average investor employ Warren Buffett's methods? Warren Buffett never invests in businesses he cannot understand or that are outside his "circle of competence." All investors can, over time, obtain and intensify their circle of competence in an industry where they are professionally involved or in some sector of business they enjoy researching. One does not have to be correct very many times in a lifetime, as Warren states that 12 investment decisions in his 40-year career have made all the difference.

Risk can be reduced greatly by concentrating on only a few holdings if it forces investors to be more careful and thorough in their research. Normally more than 75 percent of Berkshire's common stock holdings are represented by only five different securities. One of the principles demonstrated clearly several times in this book is to buy great businesses when they are having a temporary problem or when the stock market declines and creates bargain prices for outstanding franchises. Stop trying to predict the direction of the stock market, the economy, interest rates, or elections, and stop wasting money on individuals who do this for a living. Study the facts and the financial condition, value the company's future outlook, and purchase when everything is in your favor. Many people invest in a way similar to playing poker all night without ever looking at their cards.

Very few investors would have had the knowledge and courage to purchase GEICO at $2 or Wells Fargo or General Dynamics when they were depressed, as there were numerous learned people saying those companies were in substantial trouble. However, Warren Buffett also purchased stock of Capital Cities/ABC, Gillette, Washington Post, Affiliated Publications, Freddie Mac, or Coca-Cola (which have produced over $6 billion of profits for Berkshire Hathaway, or 60 percent of the $10 billion of shareholders' equity); these were all well-run companies with strong histories of profitability, and were dominant business franchises.

In addition to his own shareholders, Warren Buffett uses the Berkshire annual report to help the general public become better investors. On both sides of his family he is descended from newspaper editors, and his Aunt Alice was a public school teacher for more than 30 years. Warren Buffett enjoys both teaching and writing about business in general and investing in particular. He taught on a volunteer basis when he was 21 at the University of Nebraska in Omaha. In 1955, when he was working in New York City, he taught an adult education course on the stock market at Scarsdale High School. For 10 years in the late 1960s and 1970s he gave a free lecture course at Creighton University. In 1977 he served on a committee headed by Al Sommer, Jr., to advise the Securities and Exchange Commission on corporate disclosure. After that involvement, the scale of the Berkshire annual report changed dramatically with the 1977 report written in late 1977 and early 1978. The format became more similar to the partnership reports he had produced from 1956 to 1969.

Since the early 1980s, the Berkshire annual reports have informed shareholders of the performance of the holdings of the company and new investments, have updated the status of the insurance and the reinsurance industry, and (since 1982) have listed acquisition criteria about businesses Berkshire would like to purchase. The report is generously laced with examples, analogies, stories, and metaphors containing the dos and don'ts of proper investing in stocks.

Warren Buffett has established a high standard for the future performance of Berkshire by setting an objective of growing intrinsic value by 15 percent a year over the long term, something few people, and no one from 1956 to 1993 besides himself, have ever done. He has stated it will be a difficult standard to maintain due to the much larger size of the company, but there are always opportunities around and Berkshire keeps lots of cash ready to invest and it grows every year. His confidence is somewhat underlined by the final nine words of the June 1993 annual report on page 60: "Berkshire has not declared a cash dividend since 1967."

Warren Buffett has stated that he has always wanted to write a book on investing. Hopefully that will happen someday. However, until that event, his annual reports are filling that function in a fashion somewhat similar to the nineteenth-century authors who wrote in serial form: Edgar Allan Poe, William Makepeace Thackeray, and Charles Dickens. The Berkshire Hathaway annual reports from 1977 through 1993 are 17 chapters of that book. And also in the interim we now have *The Warren Buffett Way*, in which

Robert Hagstrom outlines Buffett's career and presents examples of how his investment technique and methods evolved as well as the important individuals in that process. The book also details the key investment decisions that produced Buffett's unmatched record of performance. Finally, it contains the thinking and the philosophy of an investor who has consistently made money using the tools available to every citizen no matter one's level of wealth.

PETER S. LYNCH
October 1994

Introduction

My father, Philip A. Fisher, looked with great pride on Warren Buffett's adoption of some of his views and on their long and friendly relationship. If my father had been alive to write this introduction, he would have jumped at the chance to share some of the good feelings he experienced over the decades from his acquaintance with one of the very few men whose investment star burned so brightly as to make his dim by comparison. My father genuinely liked Warren Buffett and was honored that Buffett embraced some of his ideas. My father died at 96—exactly three months before I received an unexpected letter asking if I would write about my father and Warren Buffett. This introduction has helped me to connect some dots and provide some closure regarding my father and Mr. Buffett. For readers of *The Warren Buffett Way*, I hope I can provide a very personal look into an important piece of investment history and some thoughts on how to best use this wonderful book.

There is little I will say about Mr. Buffett since that is the subject of this book and Robert Hagstrom covers that ground with grace and insight. It's well known that my father was an important influence on Warren Buffett and, as Mr. Hagstrom writes, my father's influence figured more prominently in Buffett's thinking in recent years. For his part, as my father became acquainted with Warren Buffett, he grew to admire qualities in him that he felt were essential to investing success but are rare among investment managers.

When Warren Buffett visited my father 40 years ago, in a world with relatively primitive information tools by today's standards, my father had his own ways of gathering information. He slowly built a circle of acquaintances over the decades—investment professionals he respected and who knew him well enough to understand what he was and wasn't interested in, and who might share good ideas with him. Toward that end, he concluded that he would meet any young investment professional once. If he was impressed, he might see that person again and build a relationship. He rarely saw anyone twice. Very high standards! In his mind, if you didn't get an "A," you got an "F." And once he had judged against someone, he simply excluded that person, forever. One shot at building a relationship. Time was scarce.

Warren Buffett as a young man was among the very, very few who impressed my father sufficiently in his first meeting to merit a second meeting and many more meetings after that. My father was a shrewd judge of character and skill. Unusually so! He based his career on judging people. It was one of his best qualities and a major reason why he put so much emphasis on qualitative judgment of business management in his stock analysis. He was always very proud he had picked Warren Buffett as an "A" before Buffett had won his much-deserved fame and acclaim.

The relationship between Warren Buffett and my father survived my father's occasional lapses when he would mistakenly call Mr. Buffett "Howard" (Warren's father's name). This is an unusual story that has never been told and perhaps says much about both my father and Warren Buffett.

My father was a small man with a big mind that raced intensely. While kindly, he was nervous, often agitated, and personally insecure. He was also very, very much a creature of habit. He followed daily catechisms rigorously because they made him more secure. And he loved to sleep, because when he slept, he wasn't nervous or insecure. So when he couldn't stop his mind from racing at night, which was often, he played memory games instead of counting sheep. One sleep game he played was memorizing the names and districts of all the members of Congress until he drifted off.

Starting in 1942, he memorized the name of Howard Buffett and associated it with Omaha, over and over again, night after night, for more than a decade. His brain mechanically linked the words "Omaha," "Buffett," and "Howard" as a related series long before he met Warren Buffett. Later, as Warren's career began to build and his star rose, it was still fully two decades before my father could fully disentangle Buffett and Omaha from "Howard." That annoyed my father because he couldn't control his mind and because he was fond of Warren Buffett and valued their relationship. Father knew exactly who Warren Buffett was, but in casual conversation he often said something like "That bright young Howard Buffett from Omaha." The more he said it, the harder it became to eliminate it from his phraseology. A man of habit habitually vexed.

Early one morning when they were to meet, my father was intent on sorting out "Howard" from "Warren." Still, at one point in the conversation, my father referred to Warren as "Howard." If Warren noticed, he gave no sign and certainly did not correct my father. This occurred sporadically throughout the 1970s. By the 1980s, my father finally had purged the word "Howard" from any sentence referencing Buffett. He was actually proud when he left "Howard" behind for good. Years later, I asked him if he ever explained this to Warren. He said he hadn't because it embarrassed him so much.

Their relationship survived because it was built on much stronger stuff. I think one of the kernels of their relationship was their shared philosophy in associating with people of integrity and skill. When Mr. Buffett says in regard to overseeing Berkshire Hathaway managers, "We don't tell .400 hitters how to swing," that is almost straight from Phil Fisher's playbook. Associate with the best, don't be wrong about that, and then don't tell them what to do.

Over the years, my father was very impressed with how Mr. Buffett evolved as an investor without compromising any of his core principles. Every decade, Mr. Buffett has done things no one would have predicted from reading about his past, and done them well. Within professional investing, most people learn in craft-like form some particular style of investing and then never change. They buy low price-earnings (P/E) stocks or leading tech names or whatever. They build that craft and then never change, or change only marginally. In contrast, Warren Buffett consistently took new approaches, decade after decade—so that it was impossible to predict what he might do next. You could not have predicted his 1970s franchise orientation from his original strict value bent. You could not have predicted his 1980s consumer products orientation at above-market average P/Es from his previous approaches. His ability to change—and to do it successfully—could be a book unto itself. When most people attempt to evolve as he has, they fail. Mr. Buffett didn't fail, my father believed, because he never lost sight of who he was. He always remained true to himself.

My father was never physically far for very long from Rudyard Kipling's famous poem, "If." In his desk, by his nightstand, in his den—always close. He read it over and over and quoted it often to me. I keep it by my desk as part of keeping him close to me. Being insecure but undaunted, he would tell you in Kipling-like fashion to be very serious about your career and your investments, but do not take yourself too seriously. He would urge you to contemplate others' criticisms of you, but never consider them your judge. He would urge you to challenge yourself, but not judge yourself too extremely either way and, when in your eyes you've failed, force yourself to try again. And he would urge you to do the next thing, yet unfathomed.

It is that part about Mr. Buffett, his knack for evolving consistently with his values and past—doing the next thing unfathomed—that my father most admired. Moving forward unfettered by the past restraints, utterance, convention, or pride. Buffett, to my father's way of thinking, embodied some of the qualities immortalized by Kipling.

Unfortunately, there will always be a small percentage of society, but a large absolute number, of small-minded envious miscreants who can't create a life of their own. Instead they love to throw mud. The purpose of life for these misguided souls is to attempt to create pain where they can't otherwise create gain. By the time a successful career concludes, mud will have been thrown at almost everyone of any accomplishment. And if any can stick, it will. My insecure father always expected mud to be thrown at everyone, himself included, but for those he admired, he hoped it would not stick. And when mud was thrown, he would expect those he admired, in Kipling-like fashion, to contemplate the criticism or allegation without feeling judged by it. Always through Kipling's eyes!

Through a longer career than most, Warren Buffett has acquitted himself remarkably—little mud has been thrown at him and none has stuck. A testament indeed. Kipling would be pleased, as was my father. It goes back to Mr. Buffett's core values—he always knows exactly who he is and what he is about. He isn't tormented by conflicts of interest that can undermine his principles and lead to less-than-admirable behaviors. There was no mud to throw so no mud stuck. And that is the prime part of Warren Buffett you should try to emulate. Know who you are.

I am writing this introduction in part to suggest to you how to use this book. Throughout my career, people have asked me why I don't do things more like my father did or why I don't do things more like Mr. Buffett. The answer is simple. I am myself, not them. I have to use my own comparative advantages. I'm not as shrewd a judge of people as my father and I'm not the genius Buffett is.

It is important to use this book to learn, but don't use this book to be like Warren Buffett. You can't be Warren Buffett and, if you try, you will suffer. Use this book to understand Buffett's ideas and then take those ideas and integrate them into your own approach to investing. It is only from your own ideas that you create greatness. The insights in this book are useful only when you ingest them into your own persona rather than trying to twist your persona to fit the insights. (A twisted persona is a lousy investor unless you're twisted naturally.) Regardless, I guarantee that you cannot be Warren Buffett no matter what you read or how hard you try. You have to be yourself.

That is the greatest lesson I got from my father, a truly great teacher at many levels—not to be him or anyone else, but to be the best I could evolve into, never quitting the evolution. The greatest lesson you can glean from Warren Buffett? To learn from him without desiring to be like him. If you're a young reader, the greatest investment lesson is to find who you really are. If you're an older reader, the greatest lesson is that you really are much younger than you think you are and you should act that way—a rare gift. Were that not possible, then Mr. Buffett wouldn't still be ably evolving at what for most people is postretirement age. Think of Warren Buffett as a teacher, not a role model, and think of this book as the single best explanation of his teachings, well stated and easily learned. You can learn an enormous amount from this book, and that can be the foundation for developing your own successful investment philosophy.

Kenneth L. Fisher
July 2013

Preface

In June 1984, I enrolled in a training program at Legg Mason Wood Walker in Baltimore, Maryland. For two weeks I listened to presentations on investing, market analysis, compliance, and selling techniques. I was expected to start my career as an investment broker soon, but I couldn't shake the feeling that I had made a terrible mistake.

Legg Mason was a value shop, and its training program emphasized the classic works on value investing, including Benjamin Graham and David Dodd's *Security Analysis* and Graham's *The Intelligent Investor*. Each day, the firm's veteran brokers would stop by and share their insights on stocks and the market. They handed us a *Value Line Investment Survey* of their favorite stock. Each company possessed the same attributes: a low price-to-earnings ratio, a low price-to-book ratio, and a high dividend yield. More often than not, the company was also deeply out of favor with the market, as evidenced by the long period the stock had underperformed the market. Over and over again, we were told to avoid the high-flying popular growth stocks and instead focus on the downtrodden, where the risk-reward ratio was much more favorable.

I understood the logic of the value investment approach; the math was not difficult. *Value Line* gave us an easy snapshot of a company's balance sheet and income statement dating back 20 years. On top was a graph of the company's stock price marching in lockstep with each year's results. But no matter how many times I looked at a company's spreadsheet, I felt something was missing.

On Thursday afternoon, the day before our training program ended, my instructor handed me a photocopy of a 1983 annual report from Berkshire Hathaway, a company I had never heard of, written by Warren Buffett, a guy I had never heard of. We were told to read the Chairman's Letter and then be prepared to discuss it the next morning.

In my hotel room that night, I quickly thumbed through the Berkshire annual report and noticed, to my disappointment, there were no pictures or graphs. The Chairman's Letter to shareholders, alone, was nearly 20 pages long. Resigned, I plopped down in my chair and began to read. It is hard to describe what happened next, but over the course of the evening, my entire view of investing changed.

For two weeks I had stared at numbers, ratios, and formulas, but now I was reading about companies and the people who ran them. Buffett introduced me to the 80-year-old Rose Blumkin, an immigrant from Russia who was generating $100 million in sales at Nebraska Furniture Mart. I became acquainted with Stan Lipsey, publisher of the *Buffalo News*, and Chuck Higgins at See's Candies, and learned about the economics of running a newspaper and the competitive advantages of a confectionery business. Buffett then discussed the operating results of Berkshire's insurance businesses, including the National Indemnity Company and the one-third interest in GEICO. But Buffett didn't just rattle off the numbers; he walked me through the nuances of the insurance business, including yearly premiums written, loss reserves, combined ratios, and the tax advantages of structured settlements. If that weren't enough, Buffett also gave shareholders an easy-to-understand tutorial on how a company's intrinsic value could exceed its book value by the magic of economic goodwill.

The next morning I walked back into the training program, changed. The *Value Line* sheets with their endless string of numbers were still there, but those numerical skeletons had suddenly grown muscle, skin, and purpose. In a word, the companies had come alive. Instead of seeing just numbers, I began to think about companies, the people who were running the businesses, and the products and services that ultimately generated the numbers that filled a spreadsheet.

When I entered production the following week, I was filled with a sense of purpose. There was no doubt in my mind what I was going to do. I was going to invest my clients' money in Berkshire Hathaway and in the stocks that Berkshire bought for its own portfolio. Each time Buffett would drop a breadcrumb, I would pick it up and buy it for my clients. If Buffett bought a stock, I would call the company, request its annual report, and study it intently, trying to figure out what he saw that others had missed. Before the advent of the Internet, you could send a check for $25 to the Securities and Exchange Commission and it would photocopy any annual report you wanted. I sent away for all the Berkshire Hathaway annual reports. Along the way, I collected all the newspaper and magazine articles written about Buffett. Anything and everything Buffett or Berkshire did, I would get a copy, read it, and file it. I was like a kid following a ballplayer.

A few years later, Carol Loomis wrote an article for *Fortune* magazine titled "The Inside Story of Warren Buffett" (April 11, 1998). Marshall Loeb, then managing editor of *Fortune*, thought it was time to write a full profile of Buffett, and he knew Carol was the perfect writer. Up until that time, the only inside look you could get about Buffett came from his Chairman's Letters and his once-a-year appearance at Berkshire's annual meeting in Omaha. But those who were aware that Carol Loomis also edited Berkshire's annual reports knew that if anyone could write an inside story on Buffett she would be the one. I raced to the newsstand to grab what I was sure would be the last copy available.

Carol said she wanted to write a different type of story, one that emphasized Buffett not just as an investor but also as an "extraordinary businessman." She did not disappoint. It was a beautifully written 7,000-word article that indeed gave the Buffett faithful a more intimate look at the man now dubbed the Wizard of Omaha. Carol gave us many insights, but none more ground-shaking for me than three little sentences tucked neatly inside the article.

"What we do is not beyond anybody else's competence," said Buffett. "I feel the same way about managing that I do about investing: It's just not necessary to do extraordinary things to get extraordinary results."

Now I am sure many who read this chalked it up to Buffett's Midwestern humility. Buffett is not a braggart. But neither does he mislead. I was sure he would not have made this statement if he did not believe it to be true. And if it were true, as I believed it was, it meant there was the possibility of uncovering a road map or, better yet, a treasure map that would describe how Buffett thinks about investing in general and stock selection specifically. This was my motivation for writing *The Warren Buffett Way.*

Reading Berkshire Hathaway annual reports for two decades, the annual reports of the companies Berkshire purchased, and the many articles written about Buffett helped me gain an understanding of how Buffett thinks about common stock investing. The single most important insight I gained was the knowledge that Buffett, whether he is purchasing common stocks or wholly owned businesses, approaches each transaction in the same way. Whether he is buying a public or a private company, Buffett goes through the same process, in more or less the same sequence. He thinks about the business, the people who run the business, the economics of the business, and then the value of the business, and in each case he lays what he learns against his own benchmarks. I labeled them investment tenets and divided them into four categories: business tenets, management tenets, financial tenets, and market tenets. The goal of *The Warren Buffett Way* was to take the major companies that Buffett had purchased for Berkshire Hathaway and discover whether they were, in fact, aligned with the tenets reflected in his writings and speeches. What would be valuable, in my opinion, and what would be valuable to investors was a thorough examination of his thoughts and strategies aligned with the purchases that Berkshire made over the years, all compiled in one source. To that end, I believe we were successful.

I had never met Warren Buffett before writing the first edition of the book. I did not consult with him while developing it. Consultation surely would have been an added bonus, but I was fortunate enough to draw from his own extensive writings on the subject of investing. Throughout the book I have employed extensive quotes from Berkshire Hathaway's annual reports, specifically the Chairman's Letters. Mr. Buffett granted me permission to use the copyrighted material, but only after he had an opportunity to review the book. However, this permission in no way implies tha he cooperated on the book or that he made available to me secrets or strategies that are not already available from his writings. Almost everything Warren Buffett does is public, but it was loosely noted.

The principal challenge I faced in writing the book was to prove or disprove Buffett's confession that "what [I] do is not beyond anybody else's competence." Some critics argue that, despite his success, Warren Buffett's idiosyncrasies prevent his investment approach from being widely adopted. I disagree. Buffett is idiosyncratic—it is a source of his success—but I will argue that his methodology, once understood, is applicable to both individual and institutional investors alike. It is the goal of this book to help investors employ the strategies that I believe made Warren Buffett successful.

Still there are skeptics. The major pushback we have received over the years is that reading a book about Warren Buffett will not ensure that you will be able to generate the same investment returns that Buffett achieved. First, I never insinuated that by reading the book an individual could achieve the same investment returns as Buffett. Second, I was puzzled why anyone would think so. It seemed to me that if you bought a book about how to play golf like Tiger Woods, you shouldn't expect to become Tiger's equal on the golf course. You read the book because you believe there are some tips in the book that will help improve your game. The same is true of *The Warren Buffett Way*. If, by reading this book, you pick up some lessons that help improve your investment results, then the book is a success. Considering how poorly most people perform in the stock market, achieving some improvement will not be a herculean task.

Buffett and Charlie Munger, the vice chairman of Berkshire and Buffett's intellectual sparring partner, were once asked about the possibility that their two great minds would educate a new generation of investors. That, of course, is exactly what they have been doing for the past 40 years. Berkshire Hathaway's annual reports are famous for their clarity, absence of mumbo jumbo, and superb educational value. Anyone fortunate enough to attend a Berkshire Hathaway annual meeting knows how illuminating they can be.

… knowledge is a journey. On his own journey, Warren … much of the wisdom of others, starting with Benjamin …d Phil Fisher. To that, he would add the many business … he learned from his partner, Charlie Munger. Collectively …ese experiences have helped shape a mosaic of investment understanding that Buffett, in turn, generously shares with others—that is, to others who are willing to do their own homework and learn all they can, with a fresh, vigorous, open mind.

At the 1995 Berkshire Hathaway annual meeting, Charlie Munger said, "It's extraordinary how resistant some people are to learning anything." Buffett added, "What's really astounding is how resistant they are even when it's in their self-interest to learn." Then, in a more reflective tone, Buffett continued, "There is an incredible resistance to thinking or changing. I quoted Bertrand Russell one time, saying, 'Most men would rather die than think. Many have.' And in a financial sense, that's very true."

In the 20 years since I wrote *The Warren Buffett Way*, the noise in the stock market has continued to rise. And just when you think it can't get any louder, it turns into a deafening screech. Television commentators, financial writers, analysts, and market strategists are over-talking each other, all vying for investors' attention. The Internet is an information marvel. Everyone agrees. But it has also given free access, or should I say a free platform, to anyone with a financial opinion. As a result, we are all awash in financial advice.

Yet, despite an avalanche of information, investors continually struggle to earn a profit. Some are hard-pressed to even continue. Stock prices skyrocket for little reason, then plummet just as quickly. People who have turned to the stock market to invest for their children's education or even their own retirement are bewildered. There appears to be neither rhyme nor reason to the market, only folly.

Far above the market madness stand the wisdom and counsel of Warren Buffett. In an environment that seems to favor the speculator over the investor, Buffett's advice has proven, time and again, to be a safe harbor for millions of lost investors. Occasionally misaligned investors will yell out, "But it's different this time!" and occasionally they will be right. Politics springs surprises, the economy reacts, and the stock market reverberates in a slightly different tone. New companies are born while others mature. Industries evolve and adapt. Change is constant, but the investment principles outlined in this book have endured. "That is why they are called principles," Buffett once quipped.

Here is a succinct and powerful lesson from the 1996 annual report: "Your goal as an investor should be simply to purchase, at a rational price, a part interest in an easily understood business whose earnings are virtually certain to be materially higher, five, ten, and twenty years from now. Over time, you will find only a few companies that meet those standards—so when you see one that qualifies, you should buy a meaningful amount of stock."

Whatever level of funds you have available for investing, whatever industry or company you are interested in, you cannot find a better touchstone than that.

ROBERT G. HAGSTROM
Villanova, Pennsylvania
October 2013

CHAPTER 1

A Five-Sigma Event

THE WORLD'S GREATEST INVESTOR

"Brace yourself," Buffett said, with a sly grin. He was sitting in a Manhattan living room on a spring morning with one of his dearest and oldest friends, Carol Loomis. A *New York Times* best-selling author and an award-winning journalist, Carol is senior editor-at-large at *Fortune* magazine, where she has worked since 1954, and is considered to be the magazine's resident expert on Warren Buffett. It is well known among the Buffett faithful that she has also been editing Berkshire Hathaway's annual reports since 1977.

On that spring day in 2006, Buffett told Carol that he had changed his thinking about how and when he was going to give away his fortune in Berkshire Hathaway stock. Like most people, Carol knew that Buffett, after a small allocation to his three children, was going to leave 99 percent of his wealth to charity, but it was always thought it would go to the Buffett Foundation established by his late wife, Susan. Now he was telling Carol he had changed his mind. "I know what I want to do," he said, "and it makes sense to get going."[1]

So, shortly before lunch, on June 26, 2006, Warren Buffett, who was then the second richest man in the world, stepped up to the microphone inside the New York Public Library. The audience—hundreds of the wealthiest people in the city—greeted him with a standing ovation. After a few brief words, Buffett reached inside his jacket pocket and pulled out five letters. Each one announced the disposition of his fortune, and only awaited his signature. The first three letters were easy; he just signed "Dad" and then handed them to his children: daughter Suze, eldest son Howard, and second son Peter. The fourth letter was turned over to a representative of his late wife's charitable foundation. Together, these four letters promised to give away a combined $6 billion.[2]

The fifth letter was the surprise. Buffett signed it and handed it to the wife of the only man on the planet who was richer than himself, Bill Gates. With that last letter, Buffett pledged over $30 billion in Berkshire Hathaway stock to the world's largest philanthropic organization, the Bill and Melinda Gates Foundation. It was by far the single greatest amount of money ever given away, miles bigger than the contributions by Andrew Carnegie ($7.2 billion when adjusted to current dollars), John D. Rockefeller ($7.1 billion), or John D. Rockefeller Jr. ($5.5 billion).

In the days that followed, there were countless questions. Was Buffett ill, perhaps even dying? "No, absolutely not," he said. "I feel terrific." Did his wife's passing have anything to do with his decision? "Yes, it does," confessed Buffett. It was well known that Susie would have inherited Buffett's fortune for the Buffett Foundation. "She would have enjoyed the process," he said. "She was a little afraid of it, in terms of scaling up. But she would have liked doing it, and would have been very good at it."[3]

But after his wife's death, Buffett changed his thinking. He realized that the Bill and Melinda Gates Foundation was a terrific organization, already scaled to handle the billions of dollars Buffett was going to send its way. They "wouldn't have to go through the real grind of getting to a megasize like the Buffett Foundation would—and they could productively use my money now," he said. "What can be more logical, in whatever you want done, than finding someone better equipped than you are to do it?"[4]

It was quintessential Buffett. Rationality prevailed. At Berkshire Hathaway, Buffett reminds us there are scores of managers running businesses that do a much better job of running their operations than he ever could. Likewise, the Bill and Melinda Gates

Foundation would do a better job of managing his philanthropy than he could do himself.

Bill Gates said of his friend, "Warren will be remembered not only as the greatest investor, but the world's greatest investor for good."[5] This will most certainly be true. But it is important to remember that the good his philanthropic generosity will do was made possible in the first place by his unparalleled investing skill. When Buffett handed the letter and check for $30 billion to Melinda Gates, I immediately thought back to another check he had written 50 years earlier—for $100, his initial investment in the Buffett Partnership, Ltd.

Buffett has always claimed he won the ovarian lottery. He figures the odds of him being born in 1930 in the United States were about 30:1. He admits he couldn't run fast and would never have been a good football player. Neither, despite his talents at plucking a ukulele, would he ever become a concert violinist. But he was "wired in a particular way" that would allow him "to thrive in a big capitalist economy with a lot of action."[6]

"My wealth has come from a combination of living in America, some lucky genes, and compound interest," said Buffett. "My luck was accentuated by my living in a market system that sometimes produces distorted results, though overall it serves our country well." To keep it all in perspective, Buffett humbly reminds us that he happens to work "in an economy that rewards someone who saves lives of others on a battlefield with a medal, rewards a great teacher with thank-you notes from parents, but rewards those who can detect the mispricing of securities with sums reaching into the billions." He called it fate's capricious distribution of "long straws."[7]

That may be true. But in my mind, Buffett carved his own destiny, which determined his own fate—not the other way around. This is the story of how Warren Buffett made his own long straw.

Personal History and Investment Beginnings

Warren Edward Buffett was born August 30, 1930, in Omaha, Nebraska. He was the seventh generation of Buffetts to call Omaha home. The first Nebraskan Buffett opened a grocery store in 1869.

Buffett's grandfather also ran a grocery store and once employed a young Charlie Munger, the future vice chairman of Berkshire Hathaway. Buffett's father, Howard, was a local stockbroker and banker who later became a Republican Congressman.

It was said that as soon as Warren Buffett was born he was fascinated by numbers. That may be a stretch, but it is well documented that before he entered kindergarten he was already a calculating machine. As young boys, he and his best friend Bob Russell would sit on the Russell family porch recording license-plate numbers of the cars that passed by. When darkness fell, he and Bob would go inside, spread the *Omaha World-Herald* on the floor, and count the number of times each letter appeared in the paper. They then tallied their calculations in a scrapbook, as if it was top-secret information.

One of young Buffett's most prized toys came from his Aunt Alice, who was quite fond of her peculiar but immensely likable nephew and made him an irresistible offer: If he would agree to eat his asparagus, she would give him a stopwatch. Buffett was mesmerized by this precise counting machine and used it in endless little-boy ventures, like marble races. He would summon his two sisters into the bathroom, fill the tub with water, and then direct them to drop their marble into one end. The one whose marble reached the drain stopper first was the winner (utilizing the tub's sloped shape). Buffett, stopwatch at the ready, timed and recorded each race.

But it was the second gift from Aunt Alice that sent six-year-old Buffett into a new direction—a fascination not with just numbers, but with money. On Christmas day, Buffett ripped open his present and strapped onto his belt what would become his most treasured possession—a nickel-coated money changer. He quickly found many ways to put it to good use. He set up a table outside his house and sold Chiclets to anyone who passed by. He went door-to-door selling packs of gum and soda pop. He would by a six-pack of Coke at his grandfather's grocery store for 25 cents and sell the individual bottles for a nickel: 20 percent return on investment. He also sold, door-to-door, copies of the *Saturday Evening Post* and *Liberty* magazines. Each weekend he sold popcorn and peanuts at local football games. With him through all these enterprises was his money changer, taking in dollars and making change.[8]

What now sounds like an idyllic childhood took an abrupt turn when Buffett's father returned home one night to inform the family the bank where he worked had closed. His job was gone and their savings were lost. The Great Depression had finally made its way to Omaha. Buffett's grandfather, the grocery store owner, gave Howard money to help support his family.

Fortunately, the sense of hopelessness did not last long. Howard Buffett soon pulled himself up and got back on his feet, announcing that Buffett, Sklenicka & Company had opened for business at the Union State building on Farnam Street, the same street where Buffett would someday buy a house and start his investment partnership.

The effect of the Great Depression, albeit brief, was hard on Buffett's family. It also made a deep and profound impression on young Warren. "He emerged from those first hard years with an absolute drive to become very, very, very rich," wrote Roger Lowenstein, author of *Buffett: The Making of an American Capitalist.* "He thought about it before he was five years old. And from that time on, he scarcely stopped thinking about it."[9]

When Buffett turned 10, his father took him to New York. It was a birthday gift Howard gave to each of his children. "I told my Dad I wanted to see three things," said Buffett. "I wanted to see the Scott Stamp and Coin Company. I wanted to see the Lionel Train Company. I wanted to see the New York Stock Exchange."[10] After an overnight ride on the train, Buffett and his dad made their way to Wall Street, where they met with At Mol, a member of the exchange. "After lunch, a guy came along with a tray that had all these different kinds of tobacco leaves on it," recalled Buffett. "He made up a cigar for Mr. Mol, who picked out the leaves he wanted. And I thought, this is it. It doesn't get any better than this. A custom-made cigar."[11]

Later, Howard Buffett introduced his son to Sidney Weinberg, a senior partner at Goldman Sachs, then considered the most famous man on Wall Street. Standing in Weinberg's office, Buffett was mesmerized by the photographs and documents on the wall. He took note of the framed original letters, knowing full well they were written by famous people. While Howard and Sidney talked about financial issues of the day, Buffett was oblivious, walking around and around Weinberg's office staring at the artifacts. When it was time to go, Sidney Weinberg put his arm around Buffett and jokingly asked him what stock he liked. "He'd forgotten it all the next day," Buffett recalled, "but I remembered it forever."[12]

Even before Buffett traveled to New York, he was already intrigued with stocks and the stock market. He was a frequent visitor to his dad's brokerage office, where he would stare at stock and bond certificates that hung on the wall, just like in Sidney Weinberg's office. Often he would bounce down the two flights of stairs right into the Harris Upham brokerage firm. Many of the brokers became fond of the pesky kid who never seemed to stop asking questions. From time to time they would allow young Warren to chalk the prices of stocks on the blackboard.

On Saturday mornings, when the stock exchange was open for two hours, Buffett would hang out with his paternal great-uncle Frank Buffett and his maternal great-uncle John Barber at the brokerage office. According to Buffett, Uncle Frank was a perpetual bear and Uncle John was the ever-optimistic bull. Each competed for Buffett's attention with stories of how they thought the world would unfold. All the while, Buffett stared straight ahead at the Trans-Lux stock ticker, trying to make sense of the continually changing stock prices. Each weekend he read the "Trader" column in *Barron's*. Once he finished reading all the books on his father's bookshelf, he consumed all the investment books at the local library. Soon he began charting stock prices himself, trying to understand the numerical patterns that were flashing by his eyes.

No one was surprised when 11-year-old Buffett announced he was ready to buy his first shares of stock. However, they were shocked when he informed his family he wanted to invest $120, money he had saved from selling soda pop, peanuts, and magazines. He decided on Cities Service Preferred, one of his father's favorite stocks, and enticed his sister Doris to join him. They each bought three shares, for an investment of $114.75 each. Buffett had studied the price chart; he was confident.

That summer the stock market declined, hitting its yearly low in June. The two junior Buffetts saw their stocks decline 30 percent. Not a day went by when Doris did not pester Warren about their loss, so when Cities Service Preferred recovered to $40 per share, he sold their holdings, for a $5 profit.

To Buffett's chagrin, Cities Service Preferred soon soared to $202 a share. After commissions, Buffett calculated he had forgone a profit of over $492. Since it had taken him five years to save $120, he figured he had just given up 20 years of work. It was a painful lesson, but ultimately a valuable one. Buffett swore that, first, he would never again be sidetracked by what he paid for the stock, and, second, he would not settle for small profits. At the wise age of 11, Buffett had already learned one of the most important lessons in investing—patience. (More about this crucial quality in Chapter 7.)

In 1942, when Buffett was 12, his father was elected to the U.S. Congress and moved the family to Washington. The change was hard on the young boy. Miserable and hopelessly homesick, he was allowed to return to Omaha for a year, to live with his grandfather and Aunt Alice. The following year, 1943, Warren gave Washington another chance.

With no friendly brokerage firms to hang out in, gradually Buffett's interest moved away from the stock market and toward entrepreneurial ventures. At age 13, he was working two paper routes, delivering the *Washington Post* and the *Washington Times-Herald*. At Woodrow Wilson High School, he made friends with Don Danly, who quickly became infected with Buffett's enthusiasm for making money. The two pooled their savings and bought reconditioned pinball machines for $25. Buffett convinced a local barber to let them put a machine in his shop for half the profits. After the first day of operation, they returned to find $4 in nickels in their very first machine. The Wilson Coin-Operated Machine Company expanded to seven machines, and soon Buffett was taking home $50 per week.

By the time Buffett graduated from high school, his savings from various endeavors totaled $9,000. He promptly announced that he saw no reason to go to college, as it would interfere with his business ventures. His father overruled him, and by the fall

Buffett found himself enrolled at the University of Pennsylvania's Wharton School of Business and Finance. Despite Wharton's emphasis on business and finance, Buffett was unimpressed with the university. "Not exactly turned on by it," he confessed; "it didn't seem like I was learning a lot."[13] The Wharton curriculum stressed the theoretical aspects of business; what interested Buffett were the practical aspects of a business—how to make money. After two years at Wharton (1947–1949), he transferred to the University of Nebraska. He took 14 courses in one year and graduated in 1950. He was not yet 20 years old.

Back in Omaha, Buffett reconnected with the stock market. He started collecting hot tips from brokers and subscribed to publishing services. He resurrected his price charts and studied books on technical analysis. He applied the McGee point-and-figure system and every other system he could think of, trying to figure out what would work. Then one day, browsing in the local library, he came across a recently published book titled *The Intelligent Investor* by Benjamin Graham. "That," he said, "was like seeing the light."[14]

Graham's treatises on investing, including *Security Analysis* (1934), cowritten with David Dodd, so influenced Buffett that he left Omaha and traveled to New York to study with Graham at the Columbia University Graduate School of Business. Graham preached the importance of understanding a company's intrinsic value. He believed investors who accurately calculated this value and bought shares below it in price could be profitable in the market. This mathematical approach appealed to Buffett's love of numbers.

In Graham's class were 20 students. Many were older than Buffett and several were working on Wall Street. In the evening, these Wall Street professionals sat in Graham's class discussing which stocks were massively undervalued, and the next day they would be back at work buying the stocks analyzed the night before and making money.

It was soon clear to everyone that Buffett was the brightest student. He often raised his hand to answer Graham's question before Graham had finished asking it. Bill Ruane, who later cofounded the Sequoia Fund with Rick Cuniff, was in the same class. He recalls that there was an instantaneous chemistry between Graham and Buffett, and the rest of the class was primarily an audience.[15] Buffett's grade for the class was an A+—the first A+ Graham had awarded in 22 years of teaching.

After graduating from Columbia, Buffett asked Graham for a job but was turned down. At first he was stung by the rejection but later was told that the firm preferred to fill the slots at Graham-Newman with Jewish analysts who, it was perceived, were being treated unfairly on Wall Street. Undeterred, Buffett returned to Omaha, where he joined Buffett-Falk Company, his father's brokerage. He hit the ground running, eagerly recommending stocks that met Graham's value criteria. All the while Buffett stayed in touch with Graham, sending him stock ideas after stock ideas. Then, in 1954, Graham called with news: The religious barrier had been lifted and there was a seat at Graham-Newman if he was still interested. Buffett was on the next plane to New York.

During his tenure at Graham-Newman, Buffett became fully immersed in his mentor's investment approach. In addition to Buffett, Graham also hired Walter Schloss, Tom Knapp, and Bill Ruane. Schloss went on to manage money at WJS Ltd. Partners for 28 years. Knapp, a Princeton chemistry major, was a founding partner in Tweedy, Browne Partners. Ruane cofounded the Sequoia Fund.

For Buffett, Graham was much more than a tutor. "It was Graham who provided the first reliable map to that wondrous and often forbidding city, the stock market," wrote Roger Lowenstein. "He laid out a methodological basis for picking stocks, previously a pseudoscience similar to gambling."[16] Since the days when 11-year-old Buffett first purchased Cities Service Preferred, he had spent half of his life studying the mysteries of the stock market. Now he had answers. Alice Schroeder, author of *The Snowball: Warren Buffett and the Business of Life*, wrote, "Warren's reaction was that of a man emerging from the cave in which he had been living all his life, blinking in the sunlight as he perceived reality for the first time." According to Schroeder, Buffett's original "concept of a stock was derived from the patterns formed by the prices at which pieces of paper were traded. Now he saw that those pieces of paper were simply symbols of an underlying truth."[17]

In 1956, two years after Buffett arrived, Graham-Newman disbanded and Graham, then 61, decided to retire. Once again Buffett returned to Omaha. Armed with the knowledge he had acquired from Graham, and with the financial backing of family and friends, he began a limited investment partnership. He was 25 years old.

The Buffett Partnership Ltd.

The Buffett Partnership began with seven limited partners who together contributed $105,000. Buffett, the general partner, started with $100. The limited partners received 6 percent annually on their investments and 75 percent of the profits above this bogey; Buffett earned the other 25 percent. But the goal of partnership was relative, not absolute. Buffett's intention, he told his partners, was to beat the Dow Jones Industrial Average by 10 percentage points.

Buffett promised his partners that "our investments will be chosen on the basis of value not popularity" and that the partnership "will attempt to reduce permanently capital loss (not short-term quotational loss) to a minimum."[18] Initially, the partnership bought undervalued common stocks based on Graham's strict criteria. In addition, Buffett also engaged in merger arbitrage—a strategy in which the stocks of two merging companies are simultaneously bought and sold to create a riskless profit.

Out of the gate, the Buffett partnership posted incredible numbers. In its first five years (1957–1961), a period in which the Dow was up 75 percent, the partnership gained 251 percent (181 percent for limited partners). Buffett was beating the Dow not by the promised 10 percentage points but by an average of 35.

As Buffett's reputation became more widely known, more people asked him to manage their money. As more investors came in, more partnerships were formed, until Buffett decided in 1962 to reorganize everything into a single partnership. That year Buffett moved the partnership office from his home to Kiewit Plaza in

Omaha, where his office remains today. The following year, Buffett made one of his most famous investments, one that served to boost his already growing reputation.

One of the worst corporate scandals in the 1960s occurred when the Allied Crude Vegetable Oil Company, led by Tino De Angelis, discovered it could obtain loans based on the inventory of its salad oil. Using one simple fact—that oil floats on top of water—De Angelis rigged the game. He built a refinery in New Jersey, put in 139 five-story storage tanks to hold soybean oil, then filled the tanks with water topped with just a few feet of salad oil. When inspectors arrived to confirm inventory, Allied employees would clamber up to the top of the tanks, dip in a measuring stick, and call out a false number to the inspectors on the ground. When the scandal broke, it was learned that Bank of America, Bank Leumi, American Express, and other international trading companies had backed over $150 million in fraudulent loans.

American Express was one of the biggest casualties of what became known as the salad oil scandal. The company lost $58 million and its share price dropped by over 50 percent. If Buffett had learned anything from Ben Graham, it was this: When a stock of a strong company sells below its intrinsic value, act decisively.

Buffett was aware of the $58 million loss, but what he did not know was how customers viewed the scandal. So he hung out at the cash registers of Omaha restaurants and discovered there was no drop-off in the use of the famous American Express Green Card. He also visited several banks in the area and learned that the financial scandal was having no impact on the sale of American Express Travelers Cheques.

Returning to his office, Buffett promptly invested $13 million—a whopping 25 percent of the partnership assets—in shares of American Express. Over the next two years, the shares tripled and the partners netted a cool $20 million in profit. It was pure Graham, and pure Buffett.

In the beginning, Buffett confined the partnership to buying undervalued securities and certain merger arbitrage announcements. But in the fifth year, he purchased his first controlling interest in a business—the Dempster Mill Manufacturing Company, a maker of farm equipment. Next he began buying shares in an ailing New England textile company called Berkshire Hathaway, and by 1965 he had control of the business.

■ ■ ■

In differential calculus, an inflection point is a point on a curve at which the curvature changes from being plus to minus or minus to plus. Inflection points can also occur in companies, industries, economies, geopolitical situations, and individuals as well. I believe the 1960s proved to be Buffett's inflection point—where Buffett the investor evolved into Buffett the businessperson. It was also a period when the market itself reached an inflection point. Since 1956, the valuation strategy outlined by Graham and used by Buffett had dominated the stock market. But by the mid-1960s a new era was unfolding. It was called the "Go-Go" years—the "Go-Go" referred to growth stocks. It was a time when greed begin driving the market and where fast money was made and lost in the pursuit of high-flying performance stocks.[19]

Despite the underlying shift in market psychology, the Buffett Partnership continued to post outstanding results. By the end of 1966, the partnership had gained 1,156 percent (704 percent for limited partners), blitzing the Dow, which was up 123 percent over the same period. Even so, Buffett was becoming increasingly uneasy. Whereas the market had been dancing to the principles outlined by Graham, the new music being played in the stock market made little sense to Buffett.

In 1969, Buffett decided to end the investment partnership. He found the market highly speculative and worthwhile values increasingly scarce. By the late 1960s, the stock market was dominated by highly priced growth stocks. The Nifty Fifty were on the tip of every investor's tongue. Stocks like Avon, Polaroid, and Xerox were trading at fifty to one hundred times earnings. Buffett mailed a letter to his partners confessing that he was out of step with the current market environment. "On one point, however, I am clear," he said.

"I will not abandon a previous approach whose logic I understand, although I find it difficult to apply, even though it may mean forgoing large and apparently easy profits, to embrace an approach which I don't fully understand, have not practiced successfully and which possibly could lead to substantial permanent loss of capital."[20]

At the beginning of the partnership, Buffett had set a goal of outperforming the Dow by an average of 10 percentage points each year. Between 1957 and 1969, he did beat the Dow—not by 10 percentage points a year but by 22! When the partnership disbanded, investors received their portions. Some were given an education in municipal bonds and others were directed to a money manager. The only individual whom Buffett recommended was Bill Ruane, his old classmate at Columbia. Ruane agreed to manage some of the partners' money, and thus was born the Sequoia Fund. Other members of the partnership, including Buffett, took their portions in Berkshire Hathaway stock. Buffett's share of the partnership had grown to $25 million, and that was enough to give him control of Berkshire Hathaway.

When Buffett disbanded the partnership, many thought the "money changer's" best days were behind him. In reality, he was just getting started.

Berkshire Hathaway

The original company, Berkshire Cotton Manufacturing, was incorporated in 1889. Forty years later, Berkshire combined operations with several other textile mills, resulting in one of New England's largest industrial companies. During this period, Berkshire produced approximately 25 percent of the country's cotton needs and absorbed 1 percent of New England's electrical capacity. In 1955, Berkshire merged with Hathaway Manufacturing, and the name was subsequently changed to Berkshire Hathaway.

Unfortunately, the years following the merger were dismal. In less than 10 years, stockholders' equity dropped by half and losses from operations exceeded $10 million. During the next 20 years, Buffett, along with Ken Chace, who managed the textile group, labored intensely to turn around the New England textile mills. Results were disappointing. Returns on equity struggled to reach double digits.

By the 1970s, shareholders of Berkshire Hathaway began to question the wisdom of retaining an investment in textiles. Buffett made no attempt to hide the difficulties and on several occasions explained his thinking: The textile mills were the largest employer in the area; the workforce was an older age group that possessed relatively nontransferable skills; management had shown a high degree of enthusiasm; the unions were being reasonable; and, very importantly, Buffett believed that some profits could be realized from the textile business.

However, he made it clear that he expected the textile group to earn positive returns on modest capital expenditures. "I won't close down a business of subnormal profitability merely to add a fraction of a point to our corporate returns," said Buffett. "I also feel it is inappropriate for even an exceptionally profitable company to fund an operation once it appears to have unending losses in prospect. Adam Smith would disagree with my first proposition and Karl Marx would disagree with my second; the middle ground," he explained, "is the only position that leaves me comfortable."[21]

As Berkshire Hathaway entered the 1980s, Buffett was coming to grips with certain realities. First, the very nature of the textile business made high returns on equity improbable. Textiles are commodities, and commodities by definition have a difficult time distinguishing their products from those of competitors. Foreign competition, employing a cheap labor force, was squeezing profit margins. Second, in order to stay competitive the textile mills would require significant capital improvements, a prospect that is frightening in an inflationary environment and disastrous if the business returns are anemic.

Buffett was faced with a difficult choice. If he made large capital contributions to the textile division in order to remain competitive, Berkshire would be left with poor returns on what was becoming an expanding capital base. If he did not reinvest, Berkshire's textile mills would become less competitive with other domestic textile manufacturers. Whether Berkshire reinvested or not, foreign competition continued to have an advantage by employing a cheaper labor force.

By 1980, the annual report revealed ominous clues for the future of the textile group. That year, the group lost its prestigious lead-off position in the Chairman's Letter. By the next year, the textile group was not discussed in the letter at all. Then, the inevitable: In July 1985, Buffett closed the books on the textile group, thus ending a business that had begun some 100 years earlier.

Despite the misfortunes of the textile group, the experience was not a complete failure. First, Buffett learned a valuable lesson about corporate turnarounds: They seldom succeed. Second, the textile group did generate enough capital in the early years to buy an insurance company, and that is a much brighter story.

Insurance Operations

In March 1967, Berkshire Hathaway purchased, for $8.6 million, the outstanding stock of two insurance companies headquartered in Omaha: National Indemnity Company and National Fire & Marine Insurance Company. It was the beginning of Berkshire Hathaway's phenomenal success story.

To appreciate the phenomenon, it is important to recognize the true value of owning an insurance company. Insurance companies are sometimes good investments, sometimes not. They are, however, always terrific investment *vehicles*. Policyholders, in paying premiums, provide a constant stream of cash; insurance companies invest this cash until claims are filed. Because of the uncertainty of when claims will occur, insurance companies opt to invest in liquid securities—primarily short-term fixed income securities, longer-dated bonds, and stocks. Thus Warren Buffett acquired not only two modestly healthy companies, but also a cast-iron vehicle for managing investments.

In 1967, the two insurance companies had a bond portfolio worth more than $24.7 million and a stock portfolio worth $7.2 million. In two years, the combined portfolio approached $42 million. This was a handsome portfolio for a seasoned stock picker like Buffett. He had already experienced some limited success managing the textile company's securities portfolio. When Buffett took control of Berkshire in 1965, the company had $2.9 million in marketable securities. By the end of the first year Buffett had enlarged the securities account to $5.4 million. In 1967, the dollar return from investing was three times the return of the entire textile division, which had 10 times the equity base of the common stock portfolio.

It has been argued that when Buffett entered the insurance business and exited the textile business, he merely exchanged one commodity for another. Insurance companies, like textiles, are selling a product that is indistinguishable. Insurance policies are standardized and can be copied by anyone. There are no trademarks, patents, advantages in location, or raw materials that distinguish one from another. It is easy to get licensed, and insurance rates are an open book. Often the most distinguishable attribute of an insurance company is its personnel. The efforts of individual managers have enormous impact on an insurance company's performance. Over the years, Buffett has added several insurance companies to the Berkshire insurance group. One prominent addition, now well known thanks to a clever advertising campaign, is GEICO. By 1991, Berkshire Hathaway owned nearly half of GEICO's outstanding common shares. For the next three years, the company's impressive performance continued to climb; so did Buffett's interest. In 1994, Berkshire announced it owned 51 percent of the company, and serious discussion began on GEICO joining the Berkshire family. Two years later, Buffett wrote a check for $2.3 billion and GEICO became a wholly owned business.

Buffett was not done. In 1998, he paid seven times the amount he had spent to buy the remaining outstanding shares of GEICO—about $16 billion in Berkshire Hathaway stock—to acquire a reinsurance company called General Re. It was his biggest acquisition up to that date.

Over the years, Buffett has continued to buy insurance companies, but without question his smartest acquisition was a person—Ajit Jain, whom he hired to run the Berkshire Hathaway Reinsurance

Group. Ajit, born in 1951, earned an engineering degree at the prestigious Indian Institutes of Technology. He worked for IBM for three years, then enrolled at Harvard to gain a business degree.

Although Ajit had no insurance background, Buffett quickly recognized his brilliance. From a starting point in 1985, Ajit built the Reinsurance Group's float (premiums earned but losses not paid) to $34 billion in a little over 20 years. According to Buffett, Ajit "insures risks that no one else has the desire or the capital to take on. His operation combines capacity, speed, decisiveness, and most importantly, brains in a manner that is unique in the insurance business."[22] Not a day goes by without Buffett and Ajit having a conversation. To give you an idea of Ajit's value, in the 2009 Berkshire annual report, Buffett wrote, "If Charlie, I and Ajit are ever in a sinking boat—and you can only save one of us—swim to Ajit."

The Man and His Company

Warren Buffett is not easy to describe. Physically he is unremarkable, with looks that are more grandfatherly than corporate titan. Intellectually he is considered a genius, yet his down-to-earth relationship with people is truly uncomplicated. He is simple, straightforward, forthright, and honest. He displays an engaging combination of sophisticated dry wit and cornball humor. He has a profound reverence for those things logical and a foul distaste for imbecility. He embraces the simple and avoids the complicated.

Reading his annual reports, one is struck by how comfortable Buffett is quoting the Bible, John Maynard Keynes, or Mae West. Of course the operable word is *reading*. Each report is 60 to 70 pages of dense information: no pictures, no color graphics, no charts. Those disciplined enough to start on page 1 and to continue uninterrupted are rewarded with a healthy dose of financial acumen, folksy humor, and unabashed honesty. Buffett is very candid in his reporting. He emphasizes both the pluses and the minuses of Berkshire's businesses. He believes that people who own stock in Berkshire Hathaway are owners of the company, and he tells them as much as he would like to be told if he were in their shoes.

The company that Buffett directs is the embodiment of his personality, his business philosophy (which is identically tied to his investment philosophy), and his own unique style. Berkshire Hathaway, Inc. is complex but not complicated. There are just two major parts; the operating businesses and the stock portfolio, made possible by the earnings of the noninsurance businesses and the insurance companies' float. Running through it all is Warren Buffett's down-to-earth way of looking at businesses he's considering buying outright, a business he's evaluating for common stock purchase, or the management of his own company.

Today, Berkshire Hathaway is divided into three major groups: its Insurance Operations; its Regulated Capital-Intensive Businesses, which includes MidAmerican Energy and the railroad Burlington Northern Santa Fe; and Manufacturing, Services and Retailing Operations, with products ranging from lollipops to jet airplanes. Collectively, these businesses generated, in 2012, $10.8 billion in earnings for Berkshire Hathaway compared to the $399 million Buffett the businessperson earned in 1988. At year-end 2012, Berkshire Hathaway's portfolio of investments had a market value of $87.6 billion against a cost basis of $49.8 billion. Twenty-five years ago, in 1988, Buffett the investor had a portfolio valued at $3 billion against a cost basis of $1.3 billion.

Over the past 48 years, starting in 1965, the year Buffett took control of Berkshire Hathaway, the book value of the company has grown from $19 to $114,214 per share, a compounded annual gain of 19.7 percent; during that period, the Standard & Poor's (S&P) 500 index gained 9.4 percent, dividends included. That is a 10.3 percent relative outperformance earned for almost five decades. As I said earlier, when the "money changer" shut down the Buffett Partnership, he was just getting started.

Five-Sigma Event

For years academicians and investment professionals have debated the validity of what has come to be known as the efficient market theory. This controversial theory suggests that analyzing stocks is a waste of time because all available information is already reflected in current prices. Those who adhere to this theory claim, only partly in jest, that investment professionals could throw darts at a page of stock quotes and pick winners just as successfully as a seasoned financial analyst who spends hours poring over the latest annual report or quarterly statement.

Yet the success of some individuals who continually beat the indexes—most notably Warren Buffett—suggests that the efficient market theory is flawed. Efficient market theoreticians counter that it is not the theory that is flawed. Rather, they say, individuals like Buffett are a five-sigma event, a statistical phenomenon so rare it practically never occurs.[23] It would be easy to side with those who claim Buffett is a statistical rarity. No one has ever come close to repeating his investment performance, whether it was the 13-year results from the Buffett Partnership or the almost five-decade performance record at Berkshire Hathaway. When we tabulate the results of almost every investment professional, noting their inability to beat the major indexes over time, it prompts the question: Is the stock market indeed unassailable, or is it a question of the methods used by most investors?

Last, we have Buffett's own words to consider. "What we do is not beyond anyone else's competence. I feel the same way about managing that I do about investing: it is just not necessary to do extraordinary things to get extraordinary results."[24] Most would dismiss Buffett's explanation as nothing more than his special brand of Midwestern humility. But I have taken his word on the matter, and it is the subject of this book.

CHAPTER 2

The Education of Warren Buffett

Even a five-sigma phenomenon with a stunningly powerful intellect must rely on the teachings of those who came before him, for not even he can skip the process of learning his trade. Warren Buffett's education is, as we shall see, a synthesis of three distinct investment philosophies from the minds of three powerful figures: Benjamin Graham, Philip Fisher, and Charlie Munger.

The Graham influence on Buffett is well known; in fact, some consider it all-encompassing. This is not altogether surprising, considering the entwined histories of the two men. Buffett was first an interested reader of Graham, then a student, an employee, a collaborator, and, finally, Graham's peer. Graham molded Buffett's untrained mind. However, those who consider Buffett to be the singular product of Graham's teachings are ignoring the influence of two other towering financial thinkers: Philip Fisher and Charlie Munger. We will study both of them in this chapter.

Benjamin Graham

Graham is considered the dean of financial analysis. As Adam Smith notes, "Before him there was no [financial analysis] profession and after him they call it that."[1] Today he is best known for two celebrated works: *Security Analysis*, coauthored with David Dodd and originally published in 1934, and *The Intelligent Investor*, originally published in 1949. Part of the enduring significance of *Security*

Analysis is its timing: This seminal book appeared just a few years after the 1929 stock market crash, a world-changing event that had a major impact on the author and profoundly influenced his ideas. While other academicians sought to explain this economic phenomenon, Graham helped people regain their financial footing and proceed with a profitable course of action.

Ben Graham earned a bachelor of science degree from Columbia University in 1914, at the age of 20. He was fluent in Greek and Latin and had a scholarly interest in mathematics and philosophy. However, despite his no-business education, he began a career on Wall Street. His first job was as a messenger at the brokerage firm of Newburger, Henderson & Loeb, posting bond and stock prices on a blackboard for $12 a week. From messenger, he rose to writing research reports and soon was awarded a partnership in the firm. By 1919, at age 25, he was earning an annual salary of $600,000—almost $8 million in 2012 dollars.

In 1926, Graham formed an investment partnership with Jerome Newman. It was this partnership that hired Buffett some 30 years later. Graham-Newman survived the 1929 crash, the Great Depression, World War II, and the Korean War, before it was dissolved in 1956.

Few people know that Graham was financially ruined by the 1929 crash. For the second time in his life (the first being when his father died, leaving the family financially unprotected), Graham set about to rebuild his fortune. He found inspiration at his alma mater, where he had just started teaching night courses in finance. The haven of academia allowed Graham the opportunity for reflection and reevaluation. With the counsel of David Dodd, also a professor at Columbia, Graham produced what became the classic treatise on conservative investing.

Between them, Graham and Dodd had over 15 years of investment experience. It took them four years to complete *Security Analysis*. When the book first appeared, in 1934, Louis Rich wrote in the *New York Times*: "It is a full-bodied, mature, meticulous and wholly meritorious outgrowth of scholarly probing and practical sagacity. If this influence should ever exert itself, it will come by causing the mind of the investor to dwell upon securities rather than upon the market."[2]

In the first edition, Graham and Dodd dedicated significant attention to corporate abuses. They had plenty of material. Before the Securities Act of 1933 and the Securities Exchange Act of 1934, corporate information was totally inadequate and often misleading. Most companies refused to divulge sales information, and the valuation of assets was frequently suspect. Corporate misinformation was used to manipulate the prices of securities, both in initial public offerings and in the aftermarkets. After the Securities Acts, corporate reforms were slow but deliberate. By the time the third edition of the book appeared in 1951, references to corporate abuses were eliminated and, in their place, Graham and Dodd addressed the problems of stockholder-management relations, principally management's competence and the policy of dividends.

The essence of *Security Analysis* is that a well-chosen diversified portfolio of common stocks, based on reasonable prices, can be a sound investment. Step by careful step, Graham helps investors to see the logic of his approach.

The first problem that Graham had to contend with was the lack of a single universal definition for *investment*. Quoting Justice Louis Brandeis, Graham pointed out that "investment is a word of many meanings." The issue, Graham noted, does not turn on whether the item is a stock (and therefore speculative by definition) or a bond (and therefore an investment). A poorly secured bond cannot be considered an investment just because it is a bond. Neither can a stock with a per-share price that is less than its net current assets be considered a speculation just because it is a stock. Intention is what counts, Graham said. Buying a security with borrowed money, in hopes of making a quick profit, is speculation, regardless of whether the security is a bond or a stock. Considering the complexities of the issue, Graham proposed his own definition: "An investment operation is one which, upon thorough analysis, promises safety of principal and a satisfactory return. Operations not meeting these requirements are speculative."[3] That simple sentence is densely packed with ideas, and they deserve our careful attention.

First, what did he mean by "thorough analysis"? He started with a succinct definition: "the careful study of available facts with the attempt to draw conclusions therefrom based on established principles and sound logic."[4] And then he went further, describing analysis as a three-step process: (1) descriptive, (2) critical, and (3) selective. The first phase involves gathering all the facts and presenting them in an intelligent manner. The second involves examining the merits of the standards used to communicate information: Have the facts been represented fairly? The final phase requires the analyst to pass judgment on the attractiveness of the security in question.

Next, Graham insists that for a security to be considered an investment, two conditions must be present: some degree of safety of principal *and* a satisfactory rate of return. As to the first, he cautioned that safety is not absolute; a highly unusual or improbable occurrence can put even a safe bond into default. Rather, he said, the investment should be considered safe from loss under reasonable conditions.

Satisfactory return—the second necessity—also earned a caution, because *satisfactory*, as Graham correctly noted, is a subjective term. He did say that the return can be any amount, however low, as long as the investor acts with a degree of intelligence and adheres to the full definition of investment. Someone who conducts a thorough financial analysis based on sound logic and makes a choice for a reasonable rate of return without compromising safety of principal would be, by Graham's definition, an investor, not a speculator.

Throughout his career Graham continued to be disturbed by the issues of investment and speculation. Toward the end of his life, he watched with dismay as institutional investors embraced actions that were clearly speculative. Shortly after the 1973–1974 bear market, Graham was invited to attend a conference of money managers hosted by Donaldson, Lufkin, and Jenrette, and was deeply shocked by what he heard. "I could not comprehend," he said, "how the management of money by institutions had degenerated from sound investment to this rat race of trying to get the highest possible return in the shortest period."[5]

Graham's second contribution—after establishing a clear and lasting distinction between investment and speculation—was a methodology for buying common stocks that would qualify them as an investment rather than speculation. His methodology turned on a concept he called margin of safety, and here too his thinking was driven by the 1929 crash.

The danger of 1929 was not that speculation tried to masquerade as investing, but rather that investing fashioned itself into speculation. Graham noted that optimism based on history was rampant—and dangerous. Encouraged by the past, investors projected forward an era of continued growth and prosperity, and began to lose their sense of proportion about price. Graham said people were paying prices for stocks without any sense of mathematical expectation; stocks were worth any price that the optimistic market quoted. At the height of this insanity, the line between investment and speculation blurred.

As an antidote to such risky behavior, Graham proposed a way of selecting stocks that relied on what he called the "margin of safety." In this approach, investors who are optimistic about a company's future growth have two techniques for adding the stock to their portfolios: (1) purchase shares when the overall market is trading at low prices (generally, this occurs during a bear market or a similar type of correction), or (2) purchase the stock when it trades below its intrinsic value even though the overall market is not substantially cheap. In either technique, said Graham, a margin of safety is present in the purchase price.

The first technique—buying only at market lows—has some built-in difficulties. It entices the investor to develop some formula that indicates when the market is expensive and when it is cheap. The investor then becomes a hostage to predicting market turns, a process that is far from certain. Also, when the market is fairly valued, investors are unable to profitably purchase common stocks. However, waiting for a market correction before purchasing stocks may become tiring and, in the end, self-defeating.

Graham suggested that an investor's energies would be better applied to the second technique: identifying undervalued securities regardless of the overall market price level. For this strategy to work systematically, Graham said, investors need a way to identify stocks that are selling below their calculated value. It was his goal to outline such a strategy, and to do so he developed a quantitative approach that was unknown before *Security Analysis.*

Graham reduced the concept of sound investing to the concept he called the margin of safety. With it, he sought to unite all securities—stocks and bonds—in a singular approach to investing.

Establishing a margin of safety concept for bonds was not too difficult. If, for example, an analyst reviewed the operating history of a company and discovered that, on average, for the past five years, a company was able to earn annually five times its fixed charges, then the company's bonds possessed a margin of safety. Graham did not expect investors to accurately determine the company's future income. Instead, he figured that if the margin between earnings and fixed charges was large enough, investors would be protected from an unexpected decline in the company's income.

The real test was Graham's ability to adapt the concept for common stocks. He reasoned that a margin of safety existed for a common stock if its price was below its intrinsic value. And the obvious next question is: How does one determine intrinsic value? Again Graham starts his answer with a succinct definition: intrinsic value is "that value which is determined by the facts." These facts include a company's assets, its earnings and dividends, and any future definite prospects.

Of those, Graham believed the single most important factor is future earnings power. That led him to a simple formula: A company's intrinsic value can be determined by estimating the future earnings of the company and multiplying those earnings by an appropriate capitalization factor. This capitalization factor, or multiplier, is influenced by the company's stability of earnings, assets, dividend policy, and financial health.

He added a strong caution: The success of this approach is limited by our ability to calculate a company's economic future, a calculation that is unavoidably imprecise. Future factors such as sales volume, pricing, and expenses are difficult to forecast, which makes applying a multiplier that more complex.

In spite of that, Graham believed that the margin of safety could work successfully in three areas: (1) in stable securities such as bonds and preferred stocks; (2) in comparative analysis; and (3) in selecting stocks, *provided* the spread between price and intrinsic value is large enough. Graham asked us to accept that intrinsic value is an elusive concept. It is distinct from the market's quotation price. Originally, intrinsic value was thought to be the same as a company's book value, or the sum of its real assets minus its obligations. This notion led to the early belief that intrinsic value was definite. However, analysts came to know that the value of a company was not only its net real assets but also the value of earnings that these assets produce. Graham proposed that it was not essential to determine a company's exact intrinsic value; even an approximate value, compared against the selling price, would be sufficient to gauge the margin of safety.

Financial analysis is not an exact science, Graham reminded us. To be sure, certain quantitative factors lend themselves to thorough analysis: balance sheets, income statements, assets and liabilities, earnings, and dividends. We must not, however, overlook certain qualitative factors that are not easily analyzed but are nonetheless essential ingredients in determining a company's intrinsic value. Two of these are management capability and the nature of the business. The issue for Graham was: How much attention should be paid to them?

He had misgivings about the emphasis placed on qualitative factors. Opinions about management and the nature of a business are not easily measured, and that which is difficult to measure can be badly measured. Optimism over qualitative factors often found its way to a higher multiplier. Graham's experience led him to believe that, to the extent investors moved away from hard assets and toward intangibles, they invited a potentially risky way of thinking. If, on the other hand, a greater amount of a company's intrinsic value is the sum of measurable, quantitative factors, Graham figured that the investor's downside was more limited. Fixed assets are measurable. Dividends are measurable. Current and historical earnings are measurable. Each of these factors can be demonstrated by figures and becomes a source of logic referenced by actual experience.

Make sure of your ground, said Graham. Start with net asset values as the fundamental departure point. If you bought assets, your downside was limited to the liquidation value of those assets. Nobody, he reasoned, can bail you out of optimistic growth projections if those projections are unfilled. If a company was perceived to be an attractive business and its superb management was predicting high future earnings, it would no doubt attract a growing number of stock buyers. "So they [investors] will buy it," said Graham, "and in doing so they will bid up the price and hence the price to earnings ratio. As more and more investors become enamored with the promised return, the price lifts free from underlying value and floats freely upward, creating a bubble that expands beautifully until it must finally burst."[6]

Graham said that having a good memory was his one burden. The memory of being financially ruined twice in a lifetime led him to embrace an investment approach that stressed downside protection versus upside potential.

There are two rules to investing, said Graham. The first rule is: Don't lose. The second rule is: Don't forget the first rule. Graham solidified this "don't lose" philosophy into two specific, tangible guidelines that cemented his margin of safety: (1) buy a company for less than two-thirds of its net asset value, and (2) focus on stocks with low price-to-earnings ratios.

The first approach, buying a stock for a price that is less than two-thirds of its net assets, fit neatly into Graham's sense of the present and satisfied his desire for some mathematical expectation. Graham gave no weight to a company's plant, property, and equipment. Furthermore, he deducted all of the company's short- and long-term liabilities. What remained were the current assets. If the stock price was below this per-share value, Graham considered this to be a foolproof method of investing. He did clarify that the results were based on the probable outcome of a group of stocks (diversification), not on the basis of individual results.

There's just one problem with this approach: Stocks that fit the criteria can be hard to find, especially during bull markets. Acknowledging that waiting for a market correction might be unreasonable, Graham turned to his second idea: to buy stocks that were down in price and sold at a low price-to-earnings ratio. He hastened to add that the company must have *some* net asset value; in other words, the company must owe less than its worth.

Throughout his career, Graham worked with several variations of this approach. Shortly before his death in 1976, he was revising the fifth edition of *Security Analysis* with Sidney Cottle. At that time, Graham was analyzing the financial results of stocks that were purchased based on these criteria: a 10-year low price-to-earnings multiple, a stock price that was equal to half its previous market high, and of course, a net asset value. Graham tested stocks back to 1961 and found the results very promising.

Over the years, many other investors have searched for similar shortcuts for determining intrinsic value. And while Graham's low price-to-earnings ratio approach is still generally favored, we have learned that making decisions based solely on accounting ratios is not enough to ensure profitable returns. Today, most investors rely on John Burr Williams's classic definition of value, as described in his book *The Theory of Investment Value* (Harvard University Press, 1938): The value of any investment is the discounted present value of its future cash flow. We will learn more about the dividend discount model in Chapter 3.

For now, we should note that both Graham's methods—buying a stock for less than two-thirds of net asset value, and buying stocks with low price-to-earnings multiples—had a common characteristic. The stocks that he selected based on those methods were deeply out of favor with the market and, for whatever reason, were priced below their value. Graham felt strongly that these stocks, priced "unjustifiably low," were attractive purchases.

Graham's conviction rested on certain assumptions. First, he believed that the market frequently mispriced stocks, usually because of the human emotions of fear and greed. At the height of optimism, greed moves stocks beyond their intrinsic value, creating an overpriced market. At other times, fear moves prices below intrinsic value, creating an undervalued market. His second assumption was based on the statistical phenomenon known as *reversion to the mean*, although he did not use that term. More eloquently, he quoted the poet Horace: "Many shall be restored that now have fallen, and many shall fall that now are in honor." However stated, by statistician or poet, Graham believed that an investor could profit from the corrective forces of an inefficient market.

Philip Fisher

While Graham was writing *Security Analysis*, Philip Fisher was beginning his career as an investment counselor. After graduating from Stanford's Graduate School of Business Administration, Fisher began work as an analyst at the Anglo London & Paris National Bank in San Francisco. In less than two years, he was made head of the bank's statistical department. From this perch, he witnessed the 1929 stock market crash. Then, after a brief and unproductive career with a local brokerage house, Fisher decided to start his own counseling firm. On March 31, 1931, Fisher & Company began soliciting clients.

Starting an investment counseling firm in the early 1930s might have appeared foolhardy, but Fisher figured he had two advantages. First, any investor who had any money left after the crash was probably very unhappy with his or her existing broker. Second, in the midst of the Depression, businesspeople had plenty of time to sit and talk with Fisher.

At Stanford, one of Fisher's business classes required him to accompany his professor on periodic visits to companies in the San Francisco area. The professor would get the business managers to talk about their operations, and often helped them solve an immediate problem. Driving back to Stanford, Fisher and his professor would recap what they observed about the companies and managers they had visited. "That hour each week," Fisher later said, "was the most useful training I ever received."[7]

From these experiences, Fisher came to believe that superior profits could be made by (1) investing in companies with above-average potential and (2) aligning oneself with the most capable management. To isolate these exceptional companies, Fisher developed a point system that qualified a company according to the characteristics of its business and management.

The characteristic of a company that most impressed Fisher was its ability to grow sales and profits over the years, at rates greater than the industry average.[8] To do that, Fisher believed that a company needed to possess "products or services with sufficient market potential to make possible a sizable increase in sales for several years."[9] Fisher was not so much concerned with consistent annual increases in sales. Rather, he judged a company's success over a period of several years. He was aware that changes in the business cycle would have a material effect on sales and earnings. However, he believed that two types of companies would, decade by decade, show promise of above-average growth: (1) those that were "fortunate and able" and (2) those that were "fortunate because they are able."

Aluminum Company of America (Alcoa) was an example, he said, of the first type. The company was "able" because the founders of the company were people of great ability. Alcoa's management foresaw the commercial uses of its product and worked aggressively to capitalize the aluminum market to increase sales. The company was also "fortunate," said Fisher, because events outside of management's immediate control were having a positive impact on the company and its market. The swift development of airborne transportation was rapidly increasing the sales of aluminum. Because of the aviation industry, Alcoa was benefiting far more than management had originally envisioned.

DuPont was a good example of a company that was "fortunate because it was able," according to Fisher. If DuPont had stayed with its original product, blasting powder, the company would have fared as well as most typical mining companies. But because management capitalized on the knowledge it had gained by manufacturing gunpowder, DuPont was able to launch new products—including nylon, cellophane, and Lucite—that created their own markets, ultimately producing billions of dollars in sales for DuPont.

A company's research and development efforts, noted Fisher, contribute mightily to the sustainability of its above-average growth in sales. Obviously, he explained, neither DuPont nor Alcoa would have succeeded over the long term without a significant commitment to research and development. Even nontechnical businesses need a dedicated research effort to produce better products and more efficient services.

In addition to research and development, Fisher examined a company's sales organization. According to him, a company could develop outstanding products and services but, unless they were "expertly merchandised," the research and development effort would never translate into revenues. It is the responsibility of the sales organization, Fisher explained, to help customers understand the benefits of a company's products and services. A sales organization, he added, should also monitor its customers' buying habits and be able to spot changes in customers' needs. The sales organization, according to Fisher, becomes the invaluable link between the marketplace and the research and development unit.

However, market potential alone is insufficient. Fisher believed that a company, even one capable of producing above-average sales growth, was an inappropriate investment if it was unable to generate a profit for shareholders. "All the sales growth in the world won't produce the right type of investment vehicle if, over the years, profits do not grow correspondingly," he said.[10] Accordingly, Fisher sought companies that not only were the lowest-cost producers of products or services but were dedicated to remaining so. A company with a low break-even point, or a correspondingly high profit margin, is better able to withstand depressed economic environments. Ultimately, it can drive out weaker competitors, thereby strengthening its own market position.

No company, said Fisher, will be able to sustain its profitability unless it is able to break down the costs of doing business while simultaneously understanding the cost of each step in the manufacturing process. To do so, he explained, a company must install adequate accounting controls and cost analysis. This cost information, Fisher noted, enables a company to direct its resources to those products or services with the highest economic potential. Furthermore, accounting controls will help identify snags in a company's operations. These snags, or inefficiencies, act as an early-warning device aimed at protecting the company's overall profitability. Fisher's sensitivity about a company's profitability was linked with another concern: a company's ability to grow in the future without requiring equity financing. If the only way a company can grow is to sell shares, he said, the larger number of shares outstanding will cancel out any benefit that stockholders might realize from the company's growth. A company with high profit margins, explained Fisher, is better able to generate funds internally, and these funds can be used to sustain its growth without diluting shareholders' ownership. In addition, a company that is able to maintain adequate cost controls over its fixed assets and working capital needs is better able to manage its cash needs and avoid equity financing.

Fisher was aware that superior companies not only possess above-average business characteristics but, equally important, are directed by people with above-average management capabilities. These managers are determined to develop new products and services that will continue to spur sales growth long after current products or services are largely exploited. Many companies, Fisher noted, have adequate growth prospects because their lines of products and services will sustain them for several years, but few companies have policies in place to ensure consistent gains for 10 to 20 years. "Management," he said, "must have a viable policy for attaining these ends with all the willingness to subordinate immediate profits for the greater long-range gains that this concept requires."[11] Subordinating immediate profits, he explained, should not be confused with sacrificing immediate profits. An above-average manager has the ability to implement the company's long-range plans while simultaneously focusing on daily operations.

Fisher considered another trait critical: Does the business have a management of unquestionable integrity and honesty? Do the managers behave as if they are trustees for the stockholders, or does it appear they are only concerned with their own well-being?

One way to determine their intention, Fisher suggested, is to observe how managers communicate with shareholders. All businesses, good and bad, will experience a period of unexpected difficulties. Commonly, when business is good, management talks freely, but when business declines, some managers clam up rather than talking openly about the company's difficulties. How management responds to business difficulties, Fisher noted, tells a lot about the people in charge of the company's future.

For a business to be successful, he argued, management must also develop good working relations with all its employees. Employees should genuinely feel that their company is a good place at which to work. Blue-collar employees should feel that they are treated with respect and decency. Executive employees should feel that promotion is based on ability, not favoritism.

Fisher also considered the depth of management. Does the chief executive officer have a talented team, he asked, and is the CEO able to delegate authority to run parts of the business?

Finally, Fisher examined the specific characteristics of a company: its business and management aspects, and how it compares to other businesses in the same industry. In this search, Fisher tried to uncover clues that might lead him to understand the superiority of a company in relation to its competitors. He argued that reading only the financial reports of a company is not enough to justify an investment. The essential step in prudent investing, he explained, is to uncover as much about the company as possible, from people who are familiar with the company. Fisher admitted that this was a catchall inquiry that would yield what he called "scuttlebutt." Today, we might call it the business grapevine. If handled properly, Fisher claimed, scuttlebutt will provide substantial clues that will enable the investor to identify outstanding investments.

Fisher's scuttlebutt investigation led him to interview as many sources as possible. He talked with customers and vendors. He sought out former employees as well as consultants who had worked for the company. He contacted research scientists in universities, government employees, and trade association executives. He also interviewed competitors. Although executives may sometimes hesitate to disclose too much about their own company, Fisher found that they never lacked an opinion about their competitors. "It is amazing," he said, "what an accurate picture of the relative points of strength and weakness of each company in an industry can be obtained from one representative cross-section of the opinions of those who in one way or another are concerned with any particular company."[12]

Most investors are unwilling to commit the time and energy Fisher felt was necessary for understanding a company. Developing a scuttlebutt network and arranging interviews are time-consuming activities; replicating the scuttlebutt process for each company under consideration can be overwhelming. Fisher found a simple way to reduce his workload—he reduced the number of companies whose stock he owned. He always said he would rather own shares in a few outstanding companies than in a larger number of average businesses. Generally, his portfolios included fewer than 10 companies, and three or four companies represented 75 percent of his entire equity portfolio.

Fisher believed that, to be successful, investors needed to do only a few things well. One was investing in companies that were within the circle of competence. Fisher said his earlier mistakes were "to project my skill beyond the limits of my experience. I began investing outside the industries which I believed I thoroughly understood, in completely different spheres of activity; situations where I did not have comparable background knowledge."[13]

Charlie Munger

When Warren Buffett began his investment partnership in 1956, he had just over $100,000 in capital. One early task, therefore, was to persuade additional investors to sign on. Buffett was making his usual and carefully detailed pitch to his neighbors, Dr. and Mrs. Edwin Davis, when suddenly Dr. Davis interrupted him and abruptly announced they'd give him $100,000. When Buffett asked why, Davis replied, "Because you remind me of Charlie Munger."[14]

Even though both men grew up in Omaha and had many acquaintances in common, Buffett and Charlie did not actually meet until 1959. By that time, Charlie had moved to southern California. When he returned to Omaha for a visit when his father died, Dr. Davis decided it was time the two young men met, and brought them together for dinner at a local restaurant. It was the beginning of an extraordinary partnership.

Charlie, the son of a lawyer and grandson of a federal judge, had established a successful law practice in Los Angeles, but his interest in the stock market was already strong. At the first dinner, the two young men found much to talk about, including stocks. From then on, they communicated often, with Buffett frequently urging Charlie to quit law and concentrate on investing. For a while, Charlie did both. In 1962, he formed an investment partnership, much like Buffett's, while maintaining his law practice. Three very successful years later, he left the law altogether, although to this day he has an office in the firm that bears his name.

We will briefly examine the performance history of Charlie's investment partnership in Chapter 5. For now, it's revealing to note that his partnership in Los Angeles and Buffett's in Omaha were similar in approach; both sought to purchase at some discount to underlying value and both had outstanding investment results. It is not surprising, then, that they bought some of the same stocks. Charlie, like Buffett, began buying shares of Blue Chip Stamps in the late 1960s, and eventually became chairman of its board. When Berkshire and Blue Chip Stamps merged in 1978, Charlie became Berkshire Hathaway's vice chairman.

The working relationship between Charlie and Buffett was not formalized in an official partnership agreement, but it has evolved over the years into something perhaps even closer and more symbiotic. Even before Charlie joined the Berkshire board, the two made many investment decisions together, often conferring daily; gradually their business affairs became more interlinked.

Today, Charlie continues as vice chairman of Berkshire Hathaway. In every way, he functions as Buffett's acknowledged co-managing partner and alter ego. To get a sense of how closely the two are aligned, you only have to count the number of times Buffett has reported that "Charlie and I" did this, or decided that, or believe this, or looked into that, or think this—almost as if "Charlie and I" were the name of one person.

To their working relationship, Charlie brought not only financial acumen, but also the foundation of business law. He also brought an intellectual perspective that is quite different from Buffett's. Charlie is passionately interested in many areas of knowledge—science, history, philosophy, psychology, mathematics—and believes each of those fields holds important concepts that thoughtful people can, and should, apply to all their endeavors, including investment decisions. To achieve "worldly wisdom," said Charlie, you must build a latticework of mental models that unites all the big ideas in the world.[15] Those who want to fully appreciate the depth and breadth of Charlie's knowledge should read his wonderful book *Poor Charlie's Almanack: The Wit and Wisdom of Charles T. Munger* (Donning Co. Publishers, 2005).

Together, all these threads—financial knowledge, background in law, and appreciation of lessons from other disciplines—produced in Charlie an investment philosophy somewhat different from Buffett's. Whereas Buffett, unwaveringly dedicated to Ben Graham, continued to search for stocks selling at bargain prices, Charlie was moving toward the principles outlined by Phil Fisher. In his mind, it was far better to pay a fair price for a great company than a great price for a fair company.

How Charlie helped Buffett cross over the Rubicon of deep-value investing and begin to consider purchasing higher-quality companie is found in the story of Berkshire's acquisition of See's Candies.

In 1921, a 71-year-old grandmother named Mary See opened a small neighborhood candy shop in Los Angeles, selling chocolates made from her own recipes. With the help of her son and his partner, the business slowly grew into a small chain in southern and northern California. It survived the Depression, survived sugar rationing during World War II, and survived intense competition, through one unchanging strategy: Never compromise the quality of the product.

Some 50 years later, See's had become the premier chain of candy shops on the West Coast, and Mary See's heirs were ready to move on to the next phase of their lives. Chuck Huggins, who had joined the company 30 years earlier, was given the job of finding the best buyer and coordinating the sale. Several suitors came calling, but no engagement was announced.

Late in 1971, an investment adviser to Blue Chip Stamps, of which Berkshire Hathaway was then the majority shareholder, proposed that Blue Chip should buy See's. The asking price was $40 million, but because See's had $10 million in cash, the net price was actually $30 million. Still Buffett was skeptical. See's was valued at three times book value, a very steep price according to Graham's value-based precepts.

Charlie convinced Buffett that paying what he thought was a steep price was actually a good deal. Buffett offered $25 million and the sellers accepted. For Buffett, it was the first major move away from Graham's philosophy of buying a company only when it was underpriced in relation to its hard book value. It was the beginning of a plate-tectonic shift in Buffett's thinking, and he acknowledges that it was Charlie who pushed in a new direction. "It was," Charlie later remarked, "the first time we paid for quality."[16] Ten years later, Buffett was offered $125 million to sell See's—five times the 1972 purchase price. He decided to pass.

One reason Buffett and Charlie's partnership has lasted so long is that both men possess an uncompromising attitude toward commonsense business principles. Both exhibit managerial qualities necessary to run high-quality businesses. Berkshire Hathaway's shareholders are blessed in having managing partners who look after their interests and help them make money in all economic environments. With Buffett's policy on mandatory retirement—he doesn't believe in it—Berkshire's shareholders have benefited not from one mind, but two, for over 35 years.

A Blending of Intellectual Influences

Shortly after Graham's death in 1976, Buffett became the designated steward of Graham's value approach to investing. Indeed, Buffett's name became synonymous with value investing.[17] It is easy to see why. He was the most famous of Graham's dedicated students, and Buffett himself never misses an opportunity to acknowledge the intellectual debt he owes Graham. Even today, Buffett considers Graham to be the one individual, after his father, who had the most influence on his investment life.[18] He even named his firstborn son after his mentor: Howard Graham Buffett.

How, then, does Buffett reconcile his intellectual indebtedness to Graham with stock purchases like the Washington Post Company (1973), Capital Cities/ABC (1986), the Coca-Cola Company (1988), and IBM (2011)? None of these companies passed Graham's strict financial test, yet Buffett made significant investments in all of them.

As early as 1965, Buffett was becoming aware that Graham's strategy of buying cheap stocks had limitations.[19] Graham, he said, would buy a stock so low in price that some "hiccup" in the company's business would allow investors to sell their shares at higher prices. Buffett called this strategy the "cigar butt" approach to investing. Walking down the street, an investor eyes a cigar butt lying on the ground and picks it up for one last puff. Although it's a lousy smoke, its bargain price makes the puff all the more worthwhile. For Graham's strategy to work consistently, Buffett argued, someone must play the role of liquidator. If not liquidator, then some other investor must be willing to purchase shares of your company, forcing the price of the stock upward.

Buffett explains: If you paid $8 million for a company whose assets are $10 million, you will profit handsomely if the assets are sold on a timely basis. However, if the underlying economics of the business are poor and it takes 10 years to sell the business, your total return is likely to be below average. "Time is the friend of the wonderful business," Buffett noted, "the enemy of the mediocre."[20] Unless he could facilitate the liquidation of his poorly performing companies and profit from the difference between his purchase price and the market value of the company's assets, his performance would, over time, replicate the poor economics of the underlying business.

From his earliest investment mistakes, Buffett began moving away from Graham's teachings. "I evolved," he once confessed, but "I didn't go from ape to human or human to ape in a nice even manner."[21] He was beginning to appreciate the qualitative nature of certain companies, compared to the quantitative aspects of others, but he still found himself searching for bargains. "My punishment," he said, "was an education in the economics of short-line farm implementation manufacturers (Dempster Mill

Manufacturing), third-place department stores (Hochschild-Kohn), and New England textile manufacturers (Berkshire Hathaway)."[22] Attempting to explain his dilemma, Buffett quoted Keynes: "The difficulty lies not in the new ideas but in escaping from the old ones." Buffett's evolution was delayed, he admitted, because what Graham taught him was so valuable.

In 1984, speaking before students at Columbia University to mark the fiftieth anniversary celebration of *Security Analysis*, Buffett explained that there is a group of successful investors who acknowledge Ben Graham as their common intellectual patriarch.[23] Graham provided the theory of margin of safety, but each student has developed different ways to apply his theory to determine a company's business value. However, the common theme is that they are all searching for some discrepancy between the value of a business and the price of its securities. People who are confused by Buffett's purchases of Coca-Cola and IBM fail to separate theory from methodology. Buffett clearly embraces Graham's margin of safety theory, but he has steadfastly moved away from Graham's methodology. According to Buffett, the last time it was easy to profit from Graham's methodology was the 1973–1974 bear market bottom.

Remember that, when evaluating stocks, Graham did not think about the specifics of the business or the capabilities of management. He limited his research to corporate filings and annual reports. If there was a mathematical probability of making money because the share price was less than the assets of the company, Graham purchased the company. To increase the probability of success, he purchased as many of these statistical equations as possible.

If Graham's teaching were limited to these precepts, Buffett would have little regard for him today. But the margin of safety theory was so profound and so important to Buffett that all other current weaknesses of Graham's methodology can be overlooked. Even today, Buffett continues to embrace Graham's primary idea, the margin of safety. It has been almost 65 years since he first read Ben Graham. Nonetheless, Buffett never hesitates to remind everyone, "I still think those are the three right words."[24] The key lesson that Buffett took from Graham was: Successful investing involves purchasing stocks when their market price is at a significant discount to their underlying business value.

In addition to the margin of safety, which became the intellectual framework of Buffett's thinking, Graham helped Buffett appreciate the folly of following stock market fluctuations. Stocks have an investment characteristic and a speculative characteristic, Graham believed, and the speculative characteristics are a consequence of human fear and greed. Those emotions, present in most investors, cause stock prices to gyrate far above and, more important, far below a company's intrinsic value. Graham taught Buffett that if he could insulate himself from the emotional whirlwinds of the stock market, he had an opportunity to exploit the irrational behavior of other investors, who purchased stocks based on emotion, not logic.

From Graham, Buffett learned how to think independently. If you reach a logical conclusion based on sound judgment, Graham counseled Buffett, do not be dissuaded just because others disagree. "You are neither right or wrong because the crowd disagrees with you," Graham wrote. "You are right because your data and reasoning are right."[25]

Phil Fisher was in many ways the exact opposite of Ben Graham. Fisher believed that, to make sound decisions, investors needed to become fully informed about a business. That meant investigating all aspects of the company. They had to look beyond the numbers and learn about the business itself, for the type of business it was mattered a great deal. They also needed to study the attributes of the company's management, for management's abilities could affect the value of the underlying business. They were urged to learn as much as they could about the industry in which the company operated, and about its competitors. Every source of information should be exploited. From Fisher, Buffett learned the value of scuttlebutt. Throughout the years, Buffett developed an extensive network of contacts who have been helpful in assisting him in evaluating different businesses.

Finally, Fisher taught Buffett not to overstress diversification. He believed that it was a mistake to teach investors that putting their eggs in several different baskets reduces risk. The danger in purchasing too many stocks, he felt, is that it becomes impossible to watch all the eggs in all the baskets. Investors run the risk of putting too much in a company they are unfamiliar with. In his view, buying shares in a company without taking time to develop a thorough understanding of the business is far riskier than having a limited diversification.

The differences between Graham and Fisher are apparent. Graham, the quantitative analyst, emphasized those factors that could be measured: fixed assets, current earnings, and dividends. His investigative research was limited to corporate filings and annual reports. He spent no time interviewing customers, competitors, or managers.

Fisher's approach was the antithesis of Graham's. Fisher, the qualitative analyst, emphasized factors that he believed increased the value of a company: principally, future prospects and management capability. Whereas Graham was interested in purchasing only cheap stocks, Fisher was interested in purchasing companies that had the potential to increase their intrinsic value over the long term. He would go to great lengths—and even conduct extensive interviews—to uncover bits of information that might improve his selection process.

After Buffett read Phil Fisher's book *Common Stocks and Uncommon Profits*, he sought out the writer. "When I met him, I was as impressed by the man as his ideas." Buffett said. "Much like Ben Graham, Fisher was unassuming, generous in spirit and an extraordinary teacher." Graham and Fisher's investment approaches differ, notes Buffett, but they are "parallel in the investment world."[26] Taking the liberty of rephrasing, I would say that instead of paralleling, in Warren Buffett they dovetail: his investment approach is a combination of a qualitative understanding of the business and its management (as taught by Fisher) and a quantitative understanding of price and value (as taught by Graham).

Warren Buffett once said, "I am 15 percent Fisher and 85 percent Benjamin Graham."[27] This remark has been widely quoted, but it is very important to remember that it was made in 1969. In the intervening years, Buffett has made a gradual but definite shift toward Fisher's philosophy of buying a select few businesses and owning those businesses for several years. My hunch is that if he were to make a similar statement today, the balance would come pretty close to 50/50.

In a very real sense, Charlie is the active embodiment of Fisher's qualitative theories. From the start, Charlie had a keen appreciation of the value of a better business and the wisdom of paying a reasonable price for it. However, in one important aspect, Charlie is also the present-day echo of Ben Graham. Years earlier, Graham taught Buffett the twofold significance of emotion in investing: the mistakes it triggers for those who make irrational decisions based on it, and the opportunities it thus creates for those who can avoid falling into the same traps. Charlie, through his readings in psychology, has continued to develop that theme. He calls it "the psychology of misjudgment," a notion we look at more fully in Chapter 6, and through persistent emphasis he keeps it an integral part of Berkshire's decision making. It is one of Charlie's most important contributions.

Buffett's dedication to Ben Graham, Phil Fisher, and Charlie Munger is understandable. Graham gave Buffett the intellectual basis for investing—the margin of safety—and helped him learn to master his emotions in order to take advantage of market fluctuations. Fisher gave Buffett an updated, workable methodology that enabled him to identify good long-term investments and manage a focused portfolio over time. Charlie helped Buffett appreciate the economic returns that come from buying and owning great businesses. To this, Charlie helped educate Buffett on the psychological missteps that often occur when individuals make financial decisions. The frequent confusion surrounding Buffett's investment actions is easily understood when we acknowledge that Buffett is the synthesis of all three men.

"It is not enough to have good intelligence," wrote Descartes; "the principal thing is to apply it well." Application is what separates Buffett from other investment managers. A number of his peers are highly intelligent, disciplined, and dedicated. Buffett stands above them all because of his formidable ability to integrate the strategies of these three wise men into one cohesive approach.

CHAPTER 3

Buying a Business

THE TWELVE IMMUTABLE TENETS

There is no fundamental difference, according to Warren Buffett, between buying a business outright and buying a piece of that business, in the form of shares of stock. Of the two, he has always preferred to directly own a company, for it permits him to influence the business's most critical issue: capital allocation. Buying its common stock instead has one big disadvantage: You can't control the business. But this is offset, Buffett explains, by two distinct advantages: First, the arena for selecting noncontrolled businesses—the stock market—is significantly larger. Second, the stock market provides more opportunities for finding bargains. In either case, Buffett invariably follows the same strategy. He looks for companies he understands, with favorable long-term prospects, that are operated by honest and competent people, and, importantly, are available at attractive prices.

"When investing," he says, "we view ourselves as business analysts, not as market analysts, not as macroeconomic analysts, and not even as security analysts."[1] This means that Buffett works first and foremost from the perspective of a businessperson. He looks at the business holistically, examining all quantitative and qualitative aspects of its management, its financial position, and its purchase price.

If we go back through time and review all of Buffett's purchases, looking for commonalities, it is possible to discern a set of basic principles, or tenets, that guide his decisions. If we extract these tenets and spread them out for a closer look, we see that they naturally group themselves into four categories:

1. *Business tenets*—three basic characteristics of the business itself.
2. *Management tenets*—three important qualities that senior managers must display.
3. *Financial tenets*—four critical financial decisions that the company must maintain.
4. *Market tenets*—two interrelated cost guidelines.

Not all of Buffett's acquisitions will display all the 12 tenets, but taken as a group, these tenets constitute the core of his equity investment approach.

These 12 tenets also serve as the principles by which Buffett runs Berkshire Hathaway. The same qualities he looks for in the businesses he buys, he expects to see when he walks through the front door of his office each day.

Business Tenets

For Buffett, stocks are an abstraction.[2] He doesn't think in terms of market theories, macroeconomic concepts, or sector trends. He makes investment decisions based only on how a business operates. He believes that if people are drawn to an investment because of superficial notions rather than business fundamentals, they are more likely to be scared away at the first sign of trouble and, in all likelihood, will lose money in the process. Instead, Buffett concentrates on learning all he can about the business under consideration. He focuses on three main areas:

1. A business must be simple and understandable.
2. A business must have a consistent operating history.

Tenets of the Warren Buffett Way

Business Tenets

Is the business simple and understandable?

Does the business have a consistent operating history?

Does the business have favorable long-term prospects?

Management Tenets

Is management rational?

Is management candid with its shareholders?

Does management resist the institutional imperative?

Financial Tenets

Focus on return on equity, not earnings per share.

Calculate "owner earnings."

Look for companies with high profit margins.

For every dollar retained, make sure the company has created at least one dollar of market value.

Market Tenets

What is the value of the business?

Can the business be purchased at a significant discount to its value?

Simple and Understandable

In Buffett's view, investors' financial success is correlated to how well they understand their investment. This is a distinguishing trait that separates investors with a business orientation from most hit-and-run types—people who are constantly buying and selling.

Over the years, Buffett has owned a vast array of businesses in many different industries. Some of these companies he controlled; in others, he was or is a minority shareholder. But he is acutely aware of how all these businesses operate. He understands the revenues, expenses, cash flows, labor relations, pricing flexibility, and capital allocation needs of every single one of Berkshire's holdings.

Buffett is able to maintain this high level of knowledge about Berkshire's businesses because he purposely limits his selection to companies that are within his area of financial and intellectual understanding. His logic is compelling. If you own a company (either outright or as a shareholder) in an industry you do not fully understand, you cannot possibly interpret developments accurately or make wise decisions.

Investment success is not a matter of how much you know but how realistically you define what you *don't* know. "Invest in your circle of competence," Buffett counsels. "It's not how big the circle is that counts; it's how well you define the parameters."[3]

Consistent Operating History

Buffett not only avoids the complex, but he also avoids purchasing companies that are either solving difficult business problems or fundamentally changing direction because their previous plans were unsuccessful. It has been his experience that the best returns are achieved by companies that have been producing the same product or service for several years. Undergoing major business changes increases the likelihood of committing major business errors.

"Severe change and exceptional returns usually don't mix," Buffett observes.[4] Most people, unfortunately, invest as if the opposite were true. Investors tend to be attracted to fast-changing industries or companies that are in the midst of a corporate reorganization. For some unexplained reason, says Buffett, investors are so infatuated with what tomorrow may bring that they ignore today's business reality.

Buffett cares very little for stocks that are hot at any given moment. He is far more interested in buying into companies that he believes will be successful and profitable for the long term. And while predicting the future success is certainly not foolproof, a steady track record is a relatively reliable track record. When a company has demonstrated consistent results with the same type of products year after year, it is not unreasonable to assume that those results will continue.

Buffett also tends to avoid businesses that are solving difficult problems. Experience has taught him that turnarounds seldom turn. It can be more profitable to look for good businesses at reasonable prices than difficult businesses at cheaper prices. "Charlie and I have not learned how to solve difficult business problems," Buffett admits. "What we have learned to do is to avoid them. To the extent that we have been successful, it is because we concentrated on identifying one-foot hurdles that we could step over rather than because we acquired any ability to clear seven-footers."[5]

Favorable Long-Term Prospects

Buffett divides the economic world into two unequal parts: a small group of great businesses, which he terms franchises, and a much larger group of bad businesses, of which most are not worth purchasing. He defines a franchise as a company providing a product or service that is (1) needed or desired, (2) has no close substitute, and (3) is not regulated. These traits allow the company to hold its prices, and occasionally raise them, without the fear of losing market share or unit volume. This pricing flexibility is one of the defining characteristics of a great business; it allows the company to earn above-average returns on capital.

"We like stocks that generate high returns on invested capital," says Buffett, "where there is a strong likelihood that [they] will continue to do so."[6] He added, "I look at the long-term competitive advantage, and [whether] that's something that is enduring."[7]

Individually and collectively, these great businesses create what Buffett calls a *moat*—something that gives the company a clear advantage over others and protects it against incursion from competition. The bigger the moat, and the more sustainable, the better he likes it. "The key to investing," he explains, "is determining the competitive advantage of any given company and, above all, the durability of the advantage. The products or services that have wide, sustainable moats around them are the ones that deliver rewards to investors. The most important thing for me is figuring out how big a moat there is around the business. What I love, of course, is a big castle and a big moat with piranhas and crocodiles."[8]

Last, Buffett tells us, in one of his many succinct bits of wisdom, "the definition of a great company is one that will be great for 25 to 30 years."[9]

Conversely, a bad business offers a product that is virtually indistinguishable from the products of its competitors—a commodity. Years ago, basic commodities included oil, gas, chemicals, copper, lumber, wheat, and orange juice. Today, computers, automobiles, airline service, banking, and insurance have become commodity-type products. Despite mammoth advertising budgets, they are unable to achieve meaningful product differentiation.

Commodity businesses, generally, are low-returning businesses and "prime candidates for profit trouble."[10] Their product is basically no different from anyone else's, so they can compete only on the basis of price—which, of course, cuts into profit margins. The most dependable way to make a commodity business profitable is to become the low-cost provider. The only other time commodity businesses turn a healthy profit is during periods of tight supply—a factor that can be extremely difficult to predict. A key to determining the long-term profit of a commodity business, Buffett notes, is the ratio of "supply-tight to supply-ample years." However, this ratio is often fractional. "What I like," he confides, "is economic strength in an area where I understand it and where I think it will last."[11]

Management Tenets

When considering a new investment or a business acquisition, Buffett looks very hard at the quality of management. He tells us that the companies or stocks Berkshire purchases must be operated by honest and competent managers whom he can admire and trust. "We do not wish to join with managers who lack admirable qualities," he says, "no matter how attractive the prospects of their business. We've never succeeded in making good deals with a bad person."[12]

When he finds managers he admires, Buffett is generous with his praise. Year after year, readers of the Chairman's Letter in

Berkshire's annual reports find Buffett's warm words about those who manage the various Berkshire companies.

He is just as thorough when it comes to the management of companies whose stock he has under consideration. In particular, he looks for three traits:

1. Is management rational?
2. Is management candid with shareholders?
3. Does management resist the institutional imperative?

The highest compliment Buffett can pay a manager is that he or she unfailingly behaves and thinks like an owner of the company. Managers who behave like owners tend not to lose sight of the company's prime objective—increasing shareholder value—and they tend to make rational decisions that further that goal. Buffett also greatly admires managers who take seriously their responsibility to report candidly and fully to shareholders and who have the courage to resist what he has termed the institutional imperative—blindly following industry peers.

Rationality

The most important management act is the allocation of the company's capital. It is the most important because allocation of capital, over time, determines shareholder value. Deciding what to do with the company's earnings—reinvest in the business or return money to shareholders—is, in Buffett's mind, an exercise in logic and rationality. "Rationality is the quality that Buffett thinks distinguishes the style with which he runs Berkshire—and the quality he often finds lacking in other corporations," wrote Carol Loomis of *Fortune* magazine.[13]

The question of where to allocate earnings is linked to where that company is in its life cycle. As a company moves through its economic life cycle, its growth rates, sales, earnings, and cash flows change dramatically. In the development stage, a company loses money as it develops products and establishes markets. During the next stage, rapid growth, the company is profitable but growing so fast that it cannot support the growth; often it must not only retain all of its earnings but also borrow money or issue equity to finance growth. In the third stage, maturity, the growth rate slows and the company begins to generate more cash than it needs for development and operating costs. In the last stage, decline, the company suffers declining sales and earnings but continues to generate excess cash. It is in phases three and four, but particularly phase three, that the question arises: How should those earnings be allocated?

If the extra cash, reinvested internally, can produce an above-average return on equity, a return that is higher than the cost of capital, then the company should retain all of its earnings and reinvest them. That is the only logical course. Retaining earnings in order to reinvest in the company at *less* than the average cost of capital is completely irrational. It is also quite common.

A company that provides average or below-average investment returns but generates cash in excess of its needs has three options: (1) It can ignore the problem and continue to reinvest at below-average rates, (2) it can buy growth, or (3) it can return the money to shareholders. It is at this crossroads that Buffett keenly focuses on management's decisions, for it is here that management will behave rationally or irrationally.

Generally, managers who continue to reinvest despite below-average returns do so in the belief that the situation is temporary. They are convinced that with managerial prowess, they can improve their company's profitability. Shareholders become mesmerized with management's forecast of improvements. If a company continually ignores this problem, cash will become an increasingly idle resource and the stock price will decline.

A company with poor economic returns, excess cash, and a low stock price will attract corporate raiders, which is the beginning of the end of current management tenure. To protect themselves, executives frequently choose the second option instead: purchasing growth by acquiring another company.

Announcing acquisition plans has the effect of exciting shareholders and dissuading corporate raiders. However, Buffett is skeptical of companies that need to buy growth. For one thing, growth often comes at an overvalued price. For another, a company that must integrate and manage a new business is apt to make mistakes that could be costly to shareholders.

In Buffett's mind, the only reasonable and responsible course for companies that have a growing pile of cash that cannot be reinvested at above-average rates is to return that money to the shareholders. For that, two methods are available: (1) initiating or raising a dividend and (2) buying back shares.

With cash in hand from their dividends, shareholders have the opportunity to look elsewhere for higher returns. On the surface, this seems like a good deal, and therefore many people view increased dividends as a sign of companies that are doing well. Buffett believes this is true only if investors can get more for their cash than the company could generate if it retained the earnings and reinvested in the company.

If the real value of dividends is sometimes misunderstood, the second mechanism for returning earnings to the shareholders—stock repurchases—is even more so. That's because the benefit to the owners is, in many respects, less direct, less tangible, and less immediate.

When management repurchases stock, Buffett feels that the reward is twofold. If the stock is selling below its intrinsic value, then purchasing shares makes good business sense. If a company's stock price is $50 and its intrinsic value is $100, then each time management buys its stock, it is acquiring $2 of intrinsic value for every $1 spent. Transactions of this nature can be very profitable for the remaining shareholders.

Furthermore, Buffett says, when executives actively buy the company's stock in the market, they are demonstrating that they have the best interests of their owners at heart, rather than a careless need to expand the corporate structure. That kind of stance sends signals to the market, attracting other investors looking for a well-managed company that increases shareholder wealth. Frequently, shareholders are rewarded twice—once from the initial open market purchase and then subsequently as investor interest has a positive effect on price.

Candor

Buffett holds in high regard managers who report their company's financial performance fully and genuinely, who admit mistakes as well as share successes, and are in all ways candid with shareholders. In particular, he respects managers who are able to communicate the performance of their company without hiding behind generally accepted accounting principles (GAAP).

"What needs to be reported," argues Buffett, "is data—whether GAAP, non-GAAP, or extra-GAAP—that helps the financially literate readers answer three key questions: (1) Approximately how much is the company worth? (2) What is the likelihood that it can meet its future obligations? (3) How good a job are its managers doing, given the hand they have been dealt?"[14]

Buffett also admires managers who have the courage to discuss failure openly. Over time, every company makes mistakes, both large and inconsequential. Too many managers, he believes, report with excess optimism rather than honest explanation, serving perhaps their own interests in the short term but no one's interests in the long run.

Most annual reports, he says bluntly, are a sham. That's why in his own annual reports to Berkshire Hathaway shareholders, Buffett is very open about Berkshire's economic and management performance, both good and bad. Throughout the years, he has admitted the difficulties that Berkshire encountered in both the textile and insurance businesses, and his own management failures in regard to these businesses. In the 1989 Berkshire Hathaway annual report, he started a practice of listing his mistakes formally, called "Mistakes of the First Twenty-Five Years (A Condensed Version)." Two years later, the title was changed to "Mistake Du Jour." Here, Buffett confessed not only mistakes made but opportunities lost because he failed to act appropriately.

Critics have noted that it's a bit disingenuous for Buffett to publicly admit his mistakes; because of his large personal ownership of Berkshire's common stock, he never has to worry about being fired. This is true. But by modeling candor, Buffett is quietly creating a new approach to management reporting. It is Buffett's belief that candor benefits the manager at least as much as the shareholder. "The CEO who misleads others in public," he says, "may eventually mislead himself in private."[15] Buffett credits Charlie Munger with helping him understand the value of studying one's mistakes, rather than concentrating only on successes.

The Institutional Imperative

If management stands to gain wisdom and credibility by facing mistakes, why do so many annual reports trumpet only success? If allocation of capital is so simple and logical, why is capital so poorly allocated? The answer, Buffett has learned, is an unseen force he calls "the institutional imperative"—the lemming-like tendency of corporate managers to imitate the behavior of others, no matter how silly or irrational it may be.

It was the most surprising discovery of his business career. At school he was taught that experienced managers were honest and intelligent, and automatically made rational business decisions. Once out in the business world, he learned instead that "rationality frequently wilts when the institutional imperative comes into play."[16]

Buffett believes that the institutional imperative is responsible for several serious, but distressingly common, conditions: "(1) [The organization] resists any change in its current direction; (2) just as work expands to fill available time, corporate projects or acquisitions will materialize to soak up available funds; (3) any business craving of the leader, however foolish, will quickly be supported by detailed rate-of-return and strategic studies prepared by his troops; and (4) the behavior of peer companies, whether they are expanding, acquiring, setting executive compensation or whatever, will be mindlessly imitated."[17]

Buffett learned this lesson early. Jack Ringwalt, head of National Indemnity, which Berkshire acquired in 1967, made what seemed a stubborn move. While most insurance companies were writing policies on terms guaranteed to produce inadequate returns—or worse, a loss—Ringwalt stepped away from the market and refused to write new policies. Buffett recognized the wisdom of Ringwalt's decision and followed suit. Today, all of Berkshire's insurance companies still operate on this principle: Just because everyone else is doing something, that doesn't make it right.

What is behind the institutional imperative that drives so many businesses? Human nature. Most managers are unwilling to look foolish with, for example, an embarrassing quarterly loss when others in their industry are still producing quarterly gains, even though they assuredly are heading, like lemmings, into the sea.

It is never easy to make unconventional decisions or to shift direction. Still, a manager with strong communication skills should be able to persuade owners to accept a short-term loss in earnings and a change in the company's direction if that strategy will yield superior results over time. Inability to resist the institutional imperative, Buffett has learned, often has less to do with the owners of the company than with the willingness of its managers to accept fundamental change. And even when managers accept the need for radical change, carrying out this plan is often too difficult for most managers to accomplish. Instead, many succumb to the temptation to buy a new company rather than face the financial facts of the current problem.

Why would they do this? Buffett isolates three factors as being most influential in management's behavior.

1. Most managers cannot control their lust for activity. Such hyperactivity often finds its outlet in business takeovers.
2. Most managers are constantly comparing their business's sales, earnings, and executive compensation to other companies within and beyond their industry. These comparisons invariably invite corporate hyperactivity.
3. Most managers have an exaggerated sense of their own capabilities.

Another common problem, we have learned, is poor allocation skills. CEOs often rise to their position by excelling in other areas of the company, including administrative, engineering, marketing, or production. With little experience in allocating capital, they turn instead to staff members, consultants, or investment bankers, and inevitably the institutional imperative enters the decision-making process. If the CEO craves a potential acquisition that requires a 15 percent return on investment to justify purchase, it's amazing, Buffett points out, how smoothly the troops report back that the business can actually achieve 15.1 percent.

The final justification for the institutional imperative is mindless imitation. The CEO of Company D says to himself, "If Companies A, B, and C are all doing the same thing, it must be all right for us to behave the same way."

They are positioned to fail—not, Buffett believes, because of venality or stupidity, but because the institutional dynamics of the imperative make it difficult to resist doomed behavior. Speaking before a group of Notre Dame students, Buffett displayed a list of 37 investment banking firms. Every single one, he explained, had failed, even though the odds for success were in their favor. He ticked off the positives: The volume of the New York Stock Exchange had multiplied 15-fold, and the firms were headed by hardworking people with very high IQs, all of whom had an intense desire to succeed. Yet all failed. Buffett paused. "You think about that," he said sternly, his eyes scanning the room. "How could they get a result like that? I'll tell you how—mindless imitation of their peers."[18]

Taking the Measure of Management

Buffett would be the first to admit that evaluating managers along these dimensions—rationality, candor, and independent thinking—is more difficult than measuring financial performance, for the simple reason that human beings are more complex than numbers.

Indeed, many analysts believe that because measuring human activity is vague and imprecise, we simply cannot value management with any degree of confidence, and therefore the exercise is futile. Without a decimal point, they seem to suggest, there is nothing to measure. Others hold the view that the value of management is fully reflected in the company's performance statistics—including sales, profit margins, and return on equity—and no other measuring stick is necessary.

Both of these opinions have some validity, but neither is, in m view, strong enough to outweigh the original premise. The reason for taking the time to evaluate management is that it yield early warning signs of eventual financial performance. If you look closely at the words and actions of the management team, you will find clues that will help you measure the value of the team's work long before it shows up in the company's financial reports or in the stock pages of a daily newspaper. Doing so will take some digging and that may be enough to discourage the weak of heart or lazy That is their loss and your gain.

For gathering the necessary information, Buffett offers a few tips Review annual reports from a few years back, paying special attention to what management said then about the strategies for the future. Then compare those plans to today's results; how fully were the plans realized? Also compare the strategies of a few years ago to this year's strategies and ideas; how has the thinking changed? Buffett also suggests it can be very valuable to compare annual reports of the company in which you are interested with reports of similar companies in the same industry. It is not always easy to find exact duplicates, but even relative performance comparisons can yield insights.

It's worth pointing out that quality of management by itself is not sufficient to attract Buffett's interest. No matter how impressive management is, he will not invest in people alone, because he knows there is a point where even the brightest and most capable managers cannot rescue a difficult business. Buffett has been fortunate to work with some of the brightest managers in corporate America, including Tom Murphy and Dan Burke at Capital Cities/ABC, Roberto Goizueta and Donald Keough at Coca-Cola, and Carl Reichardt at Wells Fargo. However, he's quick to point out, "If you put these same guys to work in a buggy whip company, it wouldn't have made much difference."[19] He adds, "When a management with a reputation for brilliance tackles a business with a reputation for poor fundamental economics, it is the reputation of the business that stays intact."[20]

Financial Tenets

The financial tenets by which Buffett values both managerial excellence and economic performance are all grounded in some typically Buffett-like principles. For one thing, he does not take yearly results too seriously. Instead, he focuses on five-year averages. Profitable returns, he wryly notes, don't always coincide with the time it takes the planet to circle the sun. He also has little patience with accounting sleight-of-hand that produces impressive year-end numbers but little real value. Instead, he is guided by these four principles:

1. Focus on return on equity, not earnings per share.
2. Calculate "owner earnings" to get a true reflection of value.
3. Look for companies with high profit margins.
4. For every dollar retained, make sure the company has created at least one dollar of market value.

Return on Equity

Customarily, analysts measure annual company performance by looking at earnings per share (EPS). Did EPS increase over the prior year? Did the company beat expectations? Are the earnings high enough to brag about?

Buffett considers earnings per share a smoke screen. Since most companies retain a portion of their previous year's earnings as a way to increase their equity base, he sees no reason to get excited about record EPS. There is nothing spectacular about a company that increases EPS by 10 percent if, at the same time, it is growing its earning base by 10 percent. That's no different, he explains, from putting money in a savings account and letting the interest accumulate and compound. To measure a company's annual performance, Buffett prefers return on equity—the ratio of operating earnings to shareholders' equity.

To use this ratio, we need to make several adjustments. First, all marketable securities should be valued at cost and not at market value, because values in the stock market as a whole can greatly influence the returns on shareholders' equity in a particular company. For example, if the stock market rose dramatically in one year, thereby increasing the net worth of a company, a truly outstanding operating performance would be diminished when compared to a larger denominator. Conversely, falling prices reduce shareholders' equity, which means that mediocre operating results appear much better than they really are.

Second, we must also control the effects that unusual items may have on the numerator of this ratio. Buffett excludes all capital gains and losses, as well as any extraordinary items that may increase or decrease operating earnings. He is seeking to isolate the specific annual performance of a business. He wants to know how well management accomplishes its task of generating a return on operations of the business given the capital employed. That, he says, is the single best judge of management's economic performance.

Furthermore, Buffett believes that a business should achieve good returns on equity while employing little or no debt. Buffett knows that companies can increase their return on equity by increasing their debt-to-equity ratio, but he is not impressed. "Good business or investment decisions," he says, "will produce quite satisfactory results with no aid from leverage."[21] Furthermore, highly leveraged companies are vulnerable during economic slowdowns. Buffett would rather err on the side of financial quality than risk the welfare of Berkshire's owners by increasing the risk that is associated with high debt levels.

Despite his conservative stance, Buffett does not have a phobia about debt. In fact, he prefers to borrow money in anticipation of using it farther down the road, rather than after a need is announced. It would be ideal, he notes, if the timing of business acquisitions profitably coincided with the availability of funds, but experience has shown that just the opposite occurs. Cheap money has a tendency to force asset prices higher. Tight money and higher interest rates raise liability costs and often force the prices of assets downward. Just when the best prices are available for purchasing businesses, the cost of money (higher interest rates) is likely to diminish the attractiveness of the opportunity. For this reason,

Buffett says, companies should manage their assets and liabilities independently of each other.

This philosophy of borrowing now in the hope of finding a good business opportunity later will penalize near-term earnings. However, Buffett acts only when he is reasonably confident the return of the future business will more than offset the expense of the debt. And there's another consideration: Because the availability of attractive business opportunities is limited, Buffett wants Berkshire to be prepared. "If you want to shoot rare, fast-moving elephants," he advises, "you should always carry a gun."[22]

Buffett does not give any suggestions as to what debt levels are appropriate or inappropriate for a business. This is wholly understandable: Different companies, depending on their cash flows, can manage different levels of debt. What Buffett does say is that a good business should be able to earn a good return on equity without the aid of leverage. Companies that depend on debt for good returns on equity should be viewed suspiciously.

Owner Earnings

"The first point to understand," Buffett says, "is that not all earnings are created equal."[23] Companies with high assets compared to profits, he points out, tend to report ersatz earnings. Because inflation exacts a toll on asset-heavy businesses, the earnings of these companies take on a mirage-like quality. Hence, accounting earnings are useful to the analyst only if they approximate the company's expected cash flow.

But even cash flow, Buffett warns, is not a perfect tool for measuring value; in fact, it often misleads investors. Cash flow is an appropriate way to measure businesses that have large investments in the beginning and smaller outlays later on, such as real estate development, gas fields, and cable companies. Manufacturing companies, on the other hand, which require ongoing capital expenditures, are not accurately valued using only cash flow.

A company's cash flow is customarily defined as net income after taxes plus depreciation, depletion, amortization, and other noncash charges. The problem with this definition, explains Buffett, is that it leaves out a critical economic fact: capital expenditures. How much of this year's earnings must the company use for new equipment, plant upgrades, and other improvements needed to maintain its economic position and unit volume? According to Buffett, an overwhelming majority of U.S. businesses require capital expenditures that are roughly equal to their depreciation rates. You can defer capital expenditures for a year or so, he says, but if over the long period you don't make the necessary capital expenditures, your business will surely decline. These capital expenditures are as much an expense as are labor and utility costs.

Popularity of cash flow numbers heightened during the leveraged buyout period because the exorbitant prices paid for businesses were justified by a company's cash flow. Buffett believes that cash flow numbers "are frequently used by marketers of businesses and securities in attempts to justify the unjustifiable and thereby sell what should be unsalable. When earnings look inadequate to service debt of a junk bond or justify a foolish stock price, how convenient it becomes to focus on cash flow."[24] But you cannot focus on cash flow, Buffett warns, unless you are willing to subtract the necessary capital expenditures.

Instead of cash flow, Buffett prefers to use what he calls "owner earnings"—a company's net income plus depreciation, depletion, and amortization, less the amount of capital expenditures and any additional working capital that might be needed. But he admits that owner earnings do not provide the precise calculation that many analysts demand. Calculating future capital expenditures often requires estimates. Still, he says, quoting Keynes, "I would rather be vaguely right than precisely wrong."

Profit Margins

Like Philip Fisher, Buffett is aware that great businesses make lousy investments if management cannot convert sales into profits. There's no big secret to profitability: It all comes down to controlling costs. In his experience, managers of high-cost operations tend to find ways to continually add to overhead, whereas managers of low-cost operations are always finding ways to cut expenses.

Buffett has little patience with managers who allow costs to escalate. Frequently, these same managers have to initiate a restructuring program to bring costs in line with sales. Each time a company announces a cost-cutting program, he knows its management has not figured out what expenses can do to a company's owners. "The really good manager," Buffett says, "does not wake up in the morning and say, 'This is the day I'm going to cut costs,' any more than he wakes up and decides to practice breathing."[25]

Buffett singles out the accomplishments of some of the best management teams he has worked with, including Carl Reichardt and Paul Hazen at Wells Fargo and Tom Murphy and Dan Burke at Cap Cities/ABC, for their relentless attacks on unnecessary expenses. These managers, he says, "abhor having a bigger head count than is needed," and both managerial teams "attack costs as vigorously when profits are at record levels as when they are under pressure."[26]

Buffett himself can be tough when it comes to costs and unnecessary expenses. He understands the right size staff for any business operation and believes that for every dollar of sales, there is an appropriate level of expenses. He is very sensitive about Berkshire's profit margins.

Berkshire Hathaway is a unique corporation. It does not have a legal department, or a public relations or investor relations department. There are no strategic planning departments staffed with MBA-trained workers plotting mergers and acquisitions. Berkshire's after-tax corporate expenses run less than 1 percent of operating earnings. Most companies of Berkshire's size have corporate expenses 10 times higher.

The One-Dollar Premise

Speaking broadly, the stock market answers the fundamental question: What is this particular company worth? Buffett proceeds in the belief that if he has selected a company with favorable long-term economic prospects, run by able and shareholder-oriented managers, the proof will be reflected in the increased market value of the company. The same, Buffett explains, holds for retained earnings. If a company employs retained earnings nonproductively over an extended period, eventually the market (justifiably) will price the shares of the company lower. Conversely, if a company has been able to achieve above-average returns on augmented capital, that success will be reflected in an increased stock price.

However, we also know that while the stock market will track business values reasonably well over long periods, in any one year prices can gyrate widely for reasons other than value. So Buffett has created a quick test to judge not only the economic attractiveness of a business but how well management has accomplished its goal of creating shareholder value: the one-dollar rule. The increase in value should, at the very least, match the amount of retained earnings dollar for dollar. If the value goes up more than the retained earnings, so much the better. All in all, Buffett explains, "Within this gigantic auction arena, it is our job to select a business with economic characteristics allowing each dollar of retained earnings to be translated eventually into at least a dollar of market value."[27]

Market Tenets

All the principles embodied in the tenets described thus far lead to one decision point: buying or not buying shares in a company. Anyone at that point must weigh two factors: Is this company a good value, and is this a good time to buy it—that is, is the price favorable?

Price is established by the stock market. Value is determined by the analyst, after weighing all the known information about a company's business, management, and financial traits. Price and value are not necessarily equal. If the stock market were always efficient, prices would instantaneously adjust to all available information. Of course we know this does not occur—at least not all the time. The prices of securities move above and below company values for numerous reasons, not all of them logical.

Theoretically, the actions of an investor are determined by the differences between price and value. If the price of a business is below its per-share value, a rational investor will purchase shares of the business. Conversely, if the price is higher than value, that investor will pass. As the company moves through its economic value life cycle, the analyst will periodically reassess the company's value in relation to market price, and buy, sell, or hold shares accordingly.

In sum, then, rational investing has two components.

1. What is the value of the business?
2. Can the business be purchased at a significant discount to its value?

Determine the Value

Through the years, financial analysts have used many formulas for calculating the intrinsic value of a company. Some are fond of various shorthand methods: low price-to-earnings ratios, low price-to-book values, and high dividend yields. But the best system, according to Warren Buffett, was determined more than 70 years ago by John Burr Williams in his book *The Theory of Investment Value*. Paraphrasing Williams, Buffett tells us that the value of a business is determined by the net cash flow expected to occur over the life of the business discounted at an appropriate interest rate. "So valued," he says, "all businesses, from manufacturers of buggy whips to operators of cellular telephones, become economic equals."[28]

The mathematical exercise, Buffett tells us, is very similar to valuing a bond. A bond has both a coupon and a maturity date that determines its future cash flows. If you add up all the bond's coupons and divide the sum by the appropriate discount rate (the interest rate of the bond's maturity), the price of the bond will be revealed. To determine the value of a business, the analyst estimates the coupons (owner earnings' cash flow) that the business will generate for a period of time into the future, and then discounts all of these coupons back to the present.

For Buffett, determining a company's value is easy as long as you plug in the right variables: the stream of cash flow and the proper discount rate. In his mind, the predictability of a company's future cash flow should take on a "coupon-like" certainty like that found in bonds. If the business is simple and understandable, and if it has operated with consistent earnings power, Buffett is able to determine the future cash flows with a high degree of certainty. If he cannot, he will not attempt to value a company. This is the distinction of his approach.

After he has determined the future cash flows of a business, Buffett applies what he considers the appropriate discount rate. Many people will be surprised to learn that the discount rate he uses is simply the rate of the long-term U.S. government bond, nothing else. That is as close as anyone can come to a risk-free rate.

Academics argue that a more appropriate discount rate would be the risk-free rate (the long-term bond rate) *plus* an equity risk premium, added to reflect the uncertainty of the company's future cash flows. But as we will learn later, Buffett dismisses the concept of an equity risk premium because it is an artifact of the capital asset pricing model that, in turn, uses price volatility as a measure of risk. In simple terms, the higher the price volatility, the higher the equity risk premium.

But Buffett thinks the whole idea that price volatility is a measure of risk is nonsense. In his mind, business risk is reduced, if not eliminated, by focusing on companies with consistent and predictable earnings. "I put a heavy weight on certainty," he says. "If you do that, the whole idea of a risk factor doesn't make sense to me. Risk comes from not knowing what you're doing."[29] Of course, a company's future cash flow cannot be predicted with the same certainty as a bond's contractual coupon payment. Nevertheless, Buffett is more comfortable using the risk-free rate alone than adding several percentage points in risk premium just because a company's stock price bounces up and down more than the bounciness of the overall market. Still, if you are uncomfortable with ignoring equity risk, you can compensate by demanding a bigger margin of safety in the purchase price.

Last, there are times when long-term interest rates are abnormally low. During these periods, we know that Buffett is more cautious and likely adds a couple of percentage points to the risk-free rate to reflect a more normalized interest rate environment.

Despite Buffett's claims, critics argue that estimating future cash flow is tricky, and selecting the proper discount rate can leave room for substantial errors in valuation. Instead, these critics have employed various shorthand methods to identify value. Some—those we call "value investors"—use low price-to-earnings ratios, low price-to-book values, and high dividend yields. They have vigorously back-tested these ratios and concluded that success can be had by isolating and purchasing companies with exactly these accounting ratios. Others claim to have identified value by selecting companies with above-average growth in earnings; they are customarily called "growth investors." Typically, growth companies possess high price-to-earnings ratios and low dividend yields—the exact opposite of what value investors look for.

Investors who seek to purchase value must often choose between the "value" and "growth" approaches. Buffett admits that years ago he participated in this intellectual tug-of-war. Today, he thinks the debate between these two schools of thought is nonsense. Growth and value investing are joined at the hip, he says. Value is the discounted present value of an investment's future cash flow; growth is simply a calculation to determine value.

Growth in sales, earnings, and assets can either add to or detract from an investment's value. Growth can add to the value when the return on invested capital is above average, thereby assuming that when a dollar is being invested in the company, at least one dollar of market value is being created. However, growth for a business earning low returns on capital can be detrimental to shareholders. For example, the airline business had been a story of incredible growth, but its inability to earn decent returns on capital has left most owners of these companies in a poor position.

All the shorthand methods—high or low price-to-earnings ratios, price-to-book ratios, and dividend yields, in any number of combinations—fall short. Buffett sums it up for us: Whether "an investor is indeed buying something for what it is worth and is therefore truly operating on the principle of obtaining value for his investment . . . irrespective of whether a business grows or doesn't, displays volatility or smoothness in earnings, or carries a high price or low in relation to its current earnings and book value, the investment shown by the discounted-flows-of-cash calculation to be the cheapest is the one that the investor should purchase."[30]

Buy at Attractive Prices

Focusing on good businesses—those that are understandable, with enduring economics, run by shareholder-oriented managers—by itself is not enough to guarantee success, Buffett notes. First, he has to buy at sensible prices and then the company has to perform to his business expectations. If we make mistakes, he points out, it is either because of (1) the price we paid, (2) the management we joined, or (3) the future economics of the business. Miscalculations in the third instance are, he notes, the most common.

It is Buffett's intention not only to identify businesses that earn above-average returns, but to purchase them at prices far below their indicated value. Graham taught the importance of buying a stock only when the difference between its price and its value represented a margin of safety.

The margin-of-safety principle assists Buffett in two ways. First, it protects him from downside price risk. If he calculates the value of a business to be only slightly higher than its per-share price, he will not buy the stock; he reasons that if the company's intrinsic value were to dip even slightly because he misappraised future cash flow, eventually the stock price would drop, too, perhaps below what he paid for it. But if the margin between purchase price and intrinsic value is large enough, the risk of declining intrinsic value is less. If Buffett purchases a company at a 25 percent discount to intrinsic value and the value subsequently declines by 10 percent, his original purchase price will still yield an adequate return.

The margin of safety also provides opportunities for extraordinary stock returns. If Buffett correctly identifies a company with above-average economic returns, the value of the stock over the long term will steadily march upward as the share price mimics the return of the business. If a company consistently earns 15 percent on equity, its share price will advance more each year than that of a company that earns 10 percent on equity. Additionally, if Buffett, by using the margin of safety, is able to buy this outstanding business at a significant discount to its intrinsic value, Berkshire will earn an extra bonus when the market corrects the price of the business. "The market, like the Lord, helps those who help themselves," Buffett says. "But unlike the Lord, the market does not forgive those who know not what they do."[31]

Anatomy of a Long-Term Stock Price

For readers who more readily process information visually, I created the graphic in Figure 3.1. It shows, in concentrated form, most of the key ingredients of Buffett's approach.

A great business (center column), over time (the x-axis), will produce rising shareholder value (the y-axis) as long as it is bought at a good price (left-hand column), and managerial decisions (right-hand column) avoid extinction in the market, do better than simply matching market rate, and instead lead to increased value in the company.

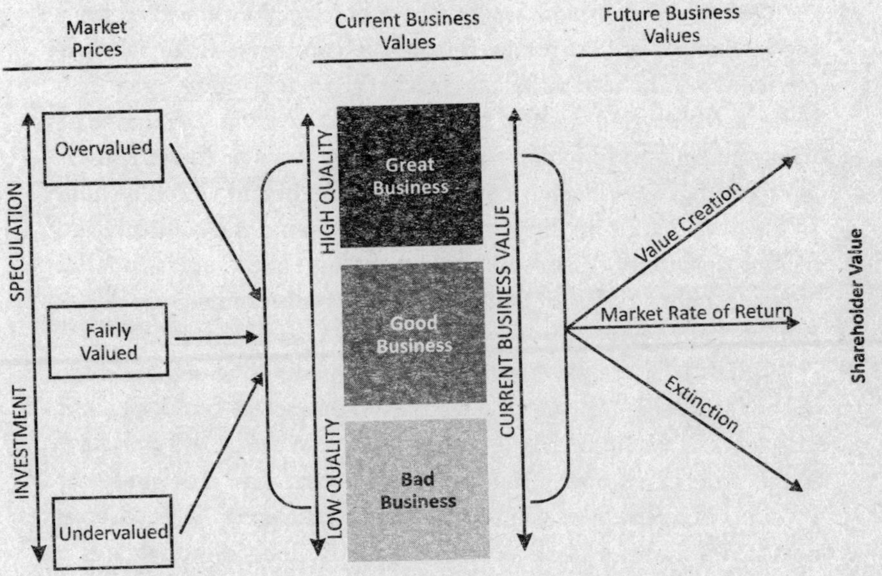

To witness these tenets in action, refer to the case studies in Chapter 4.

The Intelligent Investor

The most distinguishing trait of Buffett's investment philosophy is the clear understanding that, by owning shares of stock, he owns businesses, not pieces of paper. The idea of buying stock without understanding the company's operating functions—including its products and services, inventories, working capital needs, capital reinvestment needs (e.g., plant and equipment), raw material expenses, and labor relations—is unconscionable, says Buffett. In the summation of *The Intelligent Investor*, Benjamin Graham wrote, "Investing is most intelligent when it is most businesslike." These words are, Buffett often says, "the nine most important words ever written about investing."

Investors have a choice: They can decide to conduct themselves like the owner of a business, with all that implies, or spend their time trading securities just for the sake of being in the game—or indeed for any reason other than business fundamentals.

Owners of common stocks who perceive they merely own a piece of paper are far removed from the company's financial statements. They behave as if the market's ever-changing price is a more accurate reflection of their stock's value than the business's balance sheet and income statement. They draw or discard stocks like playing cards. Buffett considers this the height of foolishness. In his view, there's no difference between owning the company and owning a share of it, and the same mentality should apply to both. "I am a better investor because I am a businessman," confesses Buffett, "and a better businessman because I am an investor."[32]

Buffett is often asked what types of companies he will purchase in the future. First, he says, he will avoid commodity businesses and managers in whom he has little confidence. What he will purchase is the type of company that he understands, one that possesses good economics and is run by trustworthy managers. "A good business is not always a good purchase," says Buffett, "although it is a good place to look for one."[33]

CHAPTER 4

Common Stock Purchases

NINE CASE STUDIES

Over the years, Buffett's common stock purchases have become a part of Berkshire's folklore. Behind each investment is a unique story. The purchase of the Washington Post Company in 1973 was far different from the 1980 purchase of GEICO. Certainly Buffett's $500 million investment in Capital Cities, which in turn helped Tom Murphy buy the American Broadcasting Company, was unlike his billion-dollar investment in the Coca-Cola Company. And every one of these stock purchases differed from the investments he made years later in Wells Fargo, General Dynamics, American Express, IBM, and Heinz. But for those of us hoping to understand fully Buffett's thinking, all these common stock purchases share one very important trait: They allow us to observe his business, management, financial, and market tenets in action.

With the exception of Cap Cities, all of these companies have remained in the Berkshire fold and continue to prosper. Only the Washington Post Company and General Dynamics do not make the list as Berkshire's top common stock holdings.

In this chapter we examine each purchase in its historical context. This allows us to better analyze Buffett's thinking at the time of the investment as it relates to the company, the industry, and the stock market.

The Washington Post Company

In 1931, the *Washington Post* was one of five dailies competing for readers in the nation's capital. Two years later, the *Post*, unable to pay for its newsprint, was placed in receivership. That summer, the company was sold at auction to satisfy creditors. Eugene Meyer, a millionaire financier, bought the *Washington Post* for $825,000. For the next two decades, he supported the paper until it turned a profit. Management of the paper passed to Philip Graham, a brilliant Harvard-educated lawyer, who had married Meyer's daughter Katharine. In 1954, Philip Graham convinced Eugene Meyer to purchase a rival newspaper, the *Times-Herald*. Later, Graham purchased *Newsweek* magazine and two television stations before his tragic suicide in 1963. It is Phil Graham who is credited with transforming the *Washington Post* from a single newspaper into a media and communications company.

After Graham's death, control of the *Washington Post* passed to Katharine Graham. Although she had no experience in managing a major corporation, she quickly distinguished herself by confronting difficult business issues. Much of Katharine Graham's success can be attributed to her genuine affection for the *Post*. She had observed how her father and husband had struggled to keep the company viable, and she realized that to be successful, the company would need a decision maker, not a caretaker. "I quickly learned that things don't stand still," she said. "You have to make decisions."[1] And she made two doozies, decisions that had a pronounced impact on the newspaper: hiring Ben Bradlee as managing editor and then inviting Warren Buffett to become a director of the company. Bradlee encouraged Katharine Graham to publish the Pentagon Papers and to pursue the Watergate investigation, which earned the *Washington Post* a reputation for prize-winning journalism. For his part, Buffett taught Katharine Graham how to run a successful business.

Buffett had first met Katharine Graham in 1971. At the time, he owned stock in the *New Yorker*. Hearing that the magazine might be for sale, he asked Katharine Graham whether the *Washington Post* would be interested in purchasing it. Although the sale never materialized, Buffett came away very much impressed with the publisher of the *Post*.

About that time, the *Washington Post*'s financial structure was headed for profound changes. Under the terms of a trust established by Eugene and Agnes Meyer, Katharine and Philip Graham owned all of the *Post*'s voting stock. After Phil Graham's death, Katharine Graham inherited control of the company. Over the years, Eugene Meyer had gifted thousands of shares of private *Post* stock to several hundred employees in gratitude for their loyalty and service. He also funded the company's profit-sharing plan with private stock. As the company prospered, the value of the *Washington Post* skyrocketed from $50 per share in the 1950s to $1,154 in 1971. The profit-sharing plan and the personal holdings of employees required the company to maintain a market for the stock, an arrangement that proved to be an unproductive use of the company's cash. In addition, the Graham and Meyer family was facing stiff inheritance taxes.

In 1971, Katharine Graham decided to take the *Washington Post* public, thus erasing the burden of maintaining a market in its own stock, and enabling the family heirs to more profitably plan for their estates. The Washington Post Company was divided into two classes of stock. Class A common stock elected a majority of the board of directors, and class B elected a minority. Katharine Graham held 50 percent of the class A stock, thus effectively controlling the company. In June 1971 the Washington Post Company issued 1,354,000 shares of class B stock. Remarkably, two days later, despite government threats, Katharine Graham gave Ben Bradlee permission to publish the Pentagon Papers. In 1972, the price of both class A and B shares climbed steadily, from $24.75 in January to $38 in December.

But the mood on Wall Street was turning gloomy. In early 1973, the Dow Jones Industrial Average began to slide; by spring, it was down more than 100 points to 921. The Washington Post Company share price was slipping as well; by May it was down to $23. Wall Street brokers were buzzing about IBM—the stock had declined more than 69 points, breaking through its 200-day average; they warned that the technical breakdown was a bad omen for the rest of the market. That same month, gold broke through $100 per ounce, the Federal Reserve boosted the discount rate to 6 percent, and the Dow fell 18 points, its biggest loss in three years. By June, the discount rate was raised again, and the Dow headed down even further, passing through the 900 level.

And all the while, Buffett was quietly buying shares in the *Washington Post*. By June, he had purchased 467,150 shares at an average price of $22.75, a purchase worth $10,628,000.

At first Katharine Graham was unnerved. The idea of a nonfamily member owning so much *Post* stock, even though it was noncontrolling, was unsettling. Buffett assured Mrs. Graham that Berkshire's purchase was for investment purposes only. To reassure her, he suggested that Don Graham, Katharine's son, be given a proxy to vote Berkshire's shares. That clinched it. Katharine Graham responded by inviting Buffett to join the board of directors in 1974, and soon made him chairman of the finance committee.

Buffett's role at the *Washington Post* is widely known. He helped Katharine Graham persevere during the pressman strikes of the 1970s, and he also tutored Don Graham in business, helping him understand the role of management and its responsibility to its owners. Don, in turn, was an eager student who listened to everything Buffett said. Writing years later, Don Graham promised to "continue to manage the company for the benefit of shareholders, especially long-term shareholders whose perspective extends well beyond quarterly or even yearly results. We will not measure our success by the size of our revenues or the number of companies we control." Graham vowed always to "manage costs rigorously" and "to be disciplined about the uses we make of our cash.[2]

Tenet: *Simple and Understandable*

Buffett's grandfather once owned and edited the *Cuming County Democrat*, a weekly newspaper in West Point, Nebraska. His grandmother helped out at the paper and also set the type at the family's printing shop. His father, while attending the University of Nebraska, edited the *Daily Nebraskan.* Buffett himself was once the circulation manager for the *Lincoln Journal.* It has often been said that if Buffett had not embarked on a business investing career, he most surely would have pursued journalism.

In 1969, Buffett bought his first major newspaper, the *Omaha Sun,* along with a group of weekly papers. Although he respected high-quality journalism, Buffett thought of newspapers first and always as businesses. He expected profits, not influence, to be the rewards for a paper's owners. Owning the *Omaha Sun* taught him the business dynamics of a newspaper. He had four years of hands-on experience owning a newspaper before he bought his first share of the Washington Post Company.

Tenet: Consistent Operating History

Buffett tells Berkshire's shareholders that his first financial connection with the Washington Post Company was at age 13. He delivered both the *Washington Post* and the *Times-Herald* on his paper route while his father served in Congress. Buffett likes to remind others that with his dual delivery route, he merged the two papers long before Phil Graham bought the *Times-Herald.*

Obviously Buffett was aware of the newspaper's rich history, and he considered *Newsweek* magazine a predictable business. The Washington Post Company had for years been reporting the stellar performance of its broadcast division, and Buffett quickly learned the value of the company's television stations. Buffett's personal experience with the company and its own successful history led him to believe that the company was a consistent and dependable business performer.

Tenet: Favorable Long-Term Prospects

"The economics of a dominant newspaper," Buffett wrote in 1984, "are excellent, among the very best in the world."[3] Take note that Buffett said this almost 30 years ago, a full decade before the Internet's potential was first being realized.

In the early 1980s, there were 1,700 newspapers in the United States and approximately 1,600 operated without any direct competition. The owners of newspapers, Buffett noted, like to believe that the exceptional profits they earn each year are a result of their paper's journalistic quality. The truth is that even a third-rate newspaper can generate adequate profits if it is the only paper in town. Now it's true that a high-quality paper will achieve a higher penetration rate, but even a mediocre paper, he explains, is essential to a community for its bulletin-board appeal. Every business in town, every home seller, and every individual who wants to get a message out to a community needs the circulation of a newspaper to do so. Like Canadian media entrepreneur Lord Thomson, Buffett believed that owning a newspaper was like receiving a royalty on every business in town that wanted to advertise.

In addition to their franchise quality, newspapers possess valuable economic goodwill. As Buffett points out, newspapers have low capital needs, so they can easily translate sales into profits. Even when a newspaper installs expensive computer-assisted printing presses and electronic newsroom systems, they are quickly paid for by lower fixed-wage costs. During the 1970s and 1980s, newspapers were also able to increase prices relatively easily, thereby generating above-average returns on invested capital and reducing the harmful effects of inflation.

Tenet: Determine the Value

In 1973, the total market value for the Washington Post Company was $80 million. Yet Buffett claims that "most security analysts, media brokers, and media executives would have estimated WPC's intrinsic value at $400 to $500 million."[4] How did Buffett arrive at that estimate? Let us walk through the numbers, using Buffett's reasoning.

We'll start by calculating owner earnings for the year: net income ($13.3 million) plus depreciation and amortization ($3.7 million) minus capital expenditures ($6.6 million) yields 1973 owner earnings of $10.4 million. If we divide these earnings by the long-term U.S. government bond yield (6.81 percent), the value of the

Washington Post Company reaches $150 million, almost twice the market value of the company but well short of Buffett's estimate.

Buffett tells us that, over time, the capital expenditures of a newspaper will equal depreciation and amortization charges, and therefore net income should approximate owner earnings. Knowing this, we can simply divide net income by the risk-free rate and now reach a valuation of $196 million.

If we stop here, the assumption is that the increase in owner earnings will equal the rise in inflation. But we know that newspapers have unusual pricing power; because most are monopolies in their community, they can raise their prices at rates higher than inflation. If we make one last assumption—the *Washington Post* has the ability to raise real prices by 3 percent—the value of the company is closer to $350 million. Buffett also knew that the company's 10 percent pretax margins were below its 15 percent historical average margins, and he knew that Katharine Graham was determined that the *Post* would once again achieve these margins. If pretax margins improved to 15 percent, the present value of the company would increase by $135 million, bringing the total intrinsic value to $485 million.

Tenet: Buy at Attractive Prices

Even the most conservative calculation of the company's value indicates that Buffett bought the Washington Post Company for at least half its intrinsic value. He maintains that he bought the company at less than one-quarter of its value. Either way, he clearly bought the company at a significant discount to its present value. Buffett satisfied Ben Graham's premise that buying at a discount creates a margin of safety.

Tenet: Return on Equity

When Buffett purchased the stock in the *Washington Post,* its return on equity was 15.7 percent. That was an average return for most newspapers and only slightly better than that of the Standard & Poor's (S&P) 500 Industrials index. But within five years, the *Post*'s return on equity doubled. By then it was twice as high as the S&P Industrials and 50 percent higher than the average newspaper. Over the next 10 years, the *Post* maintained its supremacy, reaching a high of 36 percent return on equity in 1988.

These above-average returns are more impressive when we observe that the company has, over time, purposely reduced its debt. In 1973, the ratio of long-term debt to shareholders' equity stood at 37 percent, the second-highest ratio in the newspaper group. Astonishingly, by 1978 Katharine Graham had reduced the company's debt by 70 percent. In 1983, long-term debt to equity was 2.7 percent—one-tenth the newspaper group average—yet the *Post* generated a return on equity 10 percent higher than these companies. In 1986, after investing in the cellular telephone systems and purchasing Capital Cities' 53 cable systems, debt in the company was an uncharacteristic high of $336 million. Within a year, it was reduced to $155 million. By 1992, long-term debt was $51 million and the company's long-term debt to equity was 5.5 percent compared to the industry average of 42.7 percent.

Tenet: Profit Margins

Six months after the Washington Post Company went public, Katharine Graham met with Wall Street security analysts. The first order of business, she told them, was to maximize profit for the company's existing operations. Profits continued to rise at the television stations and *Newsweek*, but profitability at the newspaper was leveling off. Much of the reason, said Mrs. Graham, was high production costs, namely wages. After the *Post* purchased the *Times-Herald*, profits had surged. Each time the unions struck the paper (1949, 1958, 1966, 1968, 1969), management had opted to pay their demands rather than risk a shutdown of the paper. During this time, Washington, DC, was still a three-newspaper town. Throughout the 1950s and 1960s, increasing wage costs dampened profits. This problem, Mrs. Graham told the analysts, was going to be solved.

As union contracts began to expire in the 1970s, Mrs. Graham enlisted labor negotiators who took a hard line with the unions. In

1974, the company defeated a strike by the Newspaper Guild and, after lengthy negotiations, the printers settled on a new contract. Mrs. Graham's firm stance came to a head during the pressmen's strike in 1975. The strike was violent and bitter. The pressmen lost sympathy when they vandalized the pressroom before striking. Management worked the presses; members of the Guild and the printers' union crossed the picket lines. After four months, Mrs. Graham announced that the paper was hiring nonunion pressmen. The company had won.

In the early 1970s, the financial press wrote that "the best that could be said about The Washington Post Company's performance was it rated a gentleman's C in profitability."[5] Pretax margins in 1973 were 10.8 percent—well below the company's historical 15 percent margins earned in the 1960s. After successfully renegotiating the union contracts, the *Post*'s fortunes improved. By 1988, pretax margin reached a high of 31.8 percent, which compared favorably to its newspapers group average of 16.9 percent and the S&P Industrials average of 8.6 percent.

Tenet: Rationality

The *Washington Post* generated substantial cash flow for its owners. Because it generated more cash than it could reinvest in its primary businesses, management was confronted with two choices: return the money to shareholders and/or profitably invest the cash into new opportunities. It is Buffett's preference to have companies return excess earnings to shareholders. The Washington Post Company, while Katharine Graham was president, was the first newspaper in its industry to repurchase shares in large quantities. Between 1975 and 1991, the company bought an unbelievable 43 percent of its shares at an average price of $60 per share.

A company can also choose to return money to shareholders by increasing the dividend. In 1990, confronted with substantial cash reserves, the Washington Post Company voted to increase the annual dividend to shareholders from $1.84 to $4.00, a 117 percent increase.

In the early 1990s, Buffett concluded that newspapers would remain above-average businesses when compared to American industry in general, but they were destined to become less valuable than he or any other media analyst had predicted years earlier, principally because newspapers had lost their pricing flexibility. In previous years, when the economy slowed and advertisers cut spending, newspapers could maintain profitability by raising linage rates. Today, newspapers are no longer monopolies. Advertisers have found cheaper ways to reach their customers; cable television, direct mail, newspaper inserts, and—most of all—the wide use of the Internet have all taken advertising dollars away from newspapers.

By 1991, Buffett was convinced that the change in profitability represented a long-term secular change as well as a temporary cyclical change. "The fact is," he confessed, "newspaper, television, and magazine properties have begun to resemble businesses more than franchises in their economic behavior."[6] Cyclical changes hurt short-term earnings but do not reduce a company's intrinsic value. Secular changes reduce earnings and also reduce intrinsic value. However, the change in intrinsic value of the Washington Post Company, Buffett said, was moderate compared to other media companies. The reasons were twofold. First, the *Post*'s $50 million long-term debt was more than offset by its $400 million in cash holdings. The *Washington Post* is the only public newspaper that is essentially free of debt. "As a result," Buffett said, "the shrinkage in the value of their assets has not been accentuated by the effects of leverage."[7]

Tenet: The One-Dollar Premise

Buffett's goal is to select companies in which each dollar of retained earnings is translated into a least one dollar of market value. This test can quickly identify companies whose managers, over time, have been able to optimally invest their company's capital. If retained earnings are invested in the company and produce above-average returns, the proof will be a proportionally greater rise in the company's market value.

From 1973 to 1992, the Washington Post Company earned $1.755 billion for its owners. From these earnings, the company paid shareholders $299 million and retained $1.456 billion to reinvest in the company. In 1973, the total market value of the Washington Post Company was $80 million. By 1992, the market value had grown to $2.630 billion. Over those 20 years, for every $1.00 the company retained, it created $1.81 in market value for shareholders.

Still, there is one more way to judge the success of the Washington Post Company under Katharine Graham's leadership. In his very insightful book *The Outsiders: Eight Unconventional CEOs and Their Radically Rational Blueprint for Success*, William Thorndike helps us best appreciate how well both company and its CEO actually performed. "From the time of the company's IPO in 1971 until [Katharine Graham] stepped down as chairman in 1993, the compounded annual return for shareholders was a remarkable 22.3 percent, dwarfing both the S&P (7.4 percent) and her peers (12.4 percent). A dollar invested at the IPO was worth $89 by the time she retired, versus $5 for the S&P and $14 for her peer group. Katharine Graham outperformed the S&P by *eighteenfold* and her peers by over *sixfold*. She was simply the best newspaper executive in the country during her twenty-two-year period by a wide margin."[8]

GEICO Corporation

The Government Employees Insurance Company (GEICO) was founded in 1936 by Leo Goodwin, an insurance accountant.[9] He envisioned a company that insured only preferred-risk drivers and sold this insurance directly by mail. He had discovered that government employees, as a group, had fewer accidents than the general public. He also knew that by selling directly to the driver, the company would eliminate the overhead associated with agents, typically 10 to 25 percent of every premium dollar. Goodwin figured that if he isolated careful drivers and passed along the savings from issuing insurance policies directly, he would have a recipe for success.

Goodwin invited a Fort Worth, Texas, banker named Cleaves Rhea to be his partner. Goodwin invested $25,000 and owned

25 percent of the stock; Rhea invested $75,000 for 75 percent. In 1948, the company moved from Texas to Washington, D.C. That year, the Rhea family decided to sell its interest in the company, and Rhea enlisted Lorimer Davidson, a Baltimore bond salesperson, to help with the sale. In turn, Davidson asked David Kreeger, a Washington, D.C., lawyer, to help him find buyers, and Kreeger approached the Graham-Newman Corporation. Ben Graham decided to buy half of Rhea's stock for $720,000; Kreeger and Davidson's Baltimore associates bought the other half. The Securities and Exchange Commission forced Graham-Newman, because it was an investment fund, to limit its holdings of GEICO to 10 percent of the company, so Graham had to distribute GEICO's stock to the fund's partners. Years later, when GEICO became a billion-dollar company, Graham's personal shares were worth millions.

Lorimer Davidson, at Goodwin's invitation, joined GEICO's management team. In 1958, he became chairman and led the company until 1970. During this period, the board extended the eligibility for GEICO's car insurance to include professional, managerial, technical, and administrative workers. GEICO's insurance market now included 50 percent of all car owners, up from 15 percent. The new strategy was a success. Underwriting profits soared because the new group of drivers turned out to be just as careful as government employees.

These were the company's golden years. Between 1960 and 1970, insurance regulators were mesmerized by GEICO's success, and shareholders saw their share price soar. The company's premium-to-surplus ratio rose above 5:1. This ratio measures the risk that a company takes (premiums written) compared to its policyholders' surplus (capital that is used to pay claims). Because insurance regulators were so impressed with GEICO, the company was allowed to exceed the industry average ratio.

By the late 1960s, GEICO's fortunes were beginning to dim. In 1969, the company reported that it had underestimated its reserves for that year by $10 million. Instead of earning $2.5 million, the company actually posted a loss. The adjustment to income was made the next year, but again the company underestimated reserves—this time by $25 million—so 1970's underwriting profit instead showed a disastrous loss.

The revenues an insurance company receives from policyholders are called earned premiums. From these premiums, the company promises to provide coverage to the automobile driver during the year. Costs to an insurance company include insured losses, which are claims brought by drivers, and loss expenses, the administrative costs of settling the claims. These total costs must reflect not only payments made during the year, but estimates of claims yet to be paid. Estimates, in turn, are divided into two categories: claim costs and expenses, which the company expects to pay during the year, and adjustment reserves, set aside to cover underestimated reserves from earlier years. Because of litigation, some insurance claims are not settled for several years and often involve substantial payments for legal and medical expenses. The problem confronting GEICO was that not only had it written insurance policies that were poised to create an underwriting loss, but its estimates for earlier reserves were inadequate as well.

In 1970, Davidson retired and was replaced by David Kreeger, the Washington lawyer. Running the company fell to Norman Gidden, who had served as president and chief executive officer. What happened next suggests that GEICO was attempting to grow out of its reserve mess created in 1969 and 1970. Between 1970 and 1974, the number of new auto policies grew at an 11 percent annual rate compared to a 7 percent average from 1965 to 1970. In addition, in 1972 the company embarked on an expensive and ambitious decentralization program that required significant investments in real estate, computer equipment, and personnel.

By 1973, the company, facing fierce competition, lowered its eligibility standards to expand its market share. Now GEICO's automobile drivers, for the first time, included blue-collar workers and drivers under age 21, two groups with checkered histories. Both of these strategic changes, the corporate expansion plan and the plan to insure a greater number of motorists, occurred simultaneously with the lifting of the country's 1973 price controls. Soon, auto repair and medical care costs exploded.

Underwriting losses at GEICO began to appear in the fourth quarter of 1974. For the year, the company reported a $6 million underwriting loss, its first in 28 years. Amazingly, the premium-to-surplus ratio that year was 5:1. Nonetheless, the company continued to pursue growth, and by the second quarter of 1975, GEICO reported more losses and announced it was eliminating the company's $0.80 dividend.

Gidden employed the consulting firm of Milliman & Robertson to make recommendations on how GEICO could reverse its slide. The results of the study were not encouraging. The company, the consultants said, was underreserved by $35 million to $70 million and would need a capital infusion to stay viable. The board accepted the consultants' study and made the announcement to its shareholders. In addition, the board projected that 1975's underwriting loss would approach a staggering $140 million (the actual result was $126 million). Shareholders and insurance regulators were dumbfounded.

In 1972, GEICO's share price had reached a high of $61. By 1973, the share price was cut in half, and in 1974, it fell further to $10. In 1975, when the board announced the projected losses, the stock dropped to $7. Several stockholders, charging fraud, filed class-action suits against the company. Executives at GEICO blamed inflation and outrageous legal and medical costs for the company's woes. But these problems confronted all insurers. GEICO's problem was that it had moved away from its successful tradition of insuring only careful drivers. Furthermore, it was no longer checking corporate expenses. As the company expanded the list of insured drivers, its earlier loss assumptions were woefully inadequate to cover new and more frequent claims. At a time when a company was underestimating its insured losses, it simultaneously was increasing fixed expenses.

At the March 1976 GEICO annual meeting, Gidden confessed that another president might have handled the company's problems better. He announced that the company's board of directors had appointed a committee to seek new management. GEICO's share price was still weakening—it was now $5 and heading lower.[10]

After the 1976 annual meeting, GEICO announced that John J. Byrne, a 43-year-old marketing executive from Travelers Corporation, would become the new president. Soon after Byrne's appointment, the company announced a $76 million preferred stock offering to shore up its capital. But shareholders had lost hope, and the stock drifted down to $2 per share.

During this period, Warren Buffett was quietly and doggedly buying stock in GEICO. As the company teetered on the edge of bankruptcy, he invested $4.1 million, gathering 1,294,308 shares at an average price of $3.18.

Tenet: Simple and Understandable

When Buffett attended Columbia University in 1950, his teacher, Ben Graham, was a director of GEICO. His curiosity stimulated, Buffett went to Washington, D.C., one weekend to visit the company. On Saturday, he knocked on the company's door and was let in by a janitor, who led him to the only executive in the office that day, Lorimer Davidson. Buffett peppered him with questions, and Davidson spent the next five hours schooling his young visitor on GEICO's distinctions. Philip Fisher would have been impressed.

Later, when Buffett returned to Omaha and his father's brokerage firm, he recommended that the firm's clients buy GEICO. He himself invested $10,000, approximately two-thirds of his net worth, in its stock. Many investors resisted his recommendation. Even Omaha's insurance agents complained to Howard Buffett that his son was promoting an "agentless" insurance company. Frustrated, Warren Buffett sold his GEICO shares a year later, at a 50 percent profit, and did not again purchase shares in the company until 1976.

Undaunted, Buffett continued to recommend insurance stocks to his clients. He bought Kansas City Life at three times its earnings. He owned Massachusetts Indemnity & Life Insurance Company in Berkshire Hathaway's security portfolio, and in 1967 he purchased the controlling interest in National Indemnity. For the next 10 years, Jack Ringwalt, the CEO of National Indemnity, educated Buffett on the mechanics of running an insurance company. That experience, more than any other, helped Buffett understand how an insurance company makes money. It also, despite GEICO's shaky financial situation, gave him confidence to purchase the company.

In addition to Berkshire's $4.1 million investment in GEICO's common stock, Buffett also invested $19.4 million in its convertible preferred stock issue, which raised additional capital for the company. Two years later, Berkshire converted these preferred shares into common, and in 1980, Buffett invested another $19 million of Berkshire's money in the company. Between 1976 and 1980, Berkshire invested a total of $47 million, purchasing 7.2 million shares of GEICO at an average price of $6.67 per share. By 1980, that investment had appreciated 123 percent. It was now worth $105 million and had become Buffett's largest holding.

Tenet: Consistent Operating History

On first reaction, we might assume that Buffett violated his consistency tenet. Clearly, GEICO's operations in 1975 and 1976 were anything but consistent. When Byrne became president of GEICO, his job was to turn around the company, and turnarounds, Buffett has often said, seldom turn. So how do we explain Berkshire's purchase of GEICO?

For one thing, it appears to be a turnaround exception. Byrne successfully turned the company and positioned it to compete again for insurance. But more important, Buffett said, GEICO was not terminal, only wounded. Its franchise of providing low-cost agentless insurance was still intact. Furthermore, in the marketplace, there still existed safe drivers who could be insured at rates that would provide a profit for the company. On a price basis, GEICO would always beat its competitors. For decades, GEICO generated substantial profits for its owners by capitalizing on its competitive strengths. These strengths, said Buffett, were still in place. GEICO's troubles in the 1970s had nothing to do with a diminution of its franchise. Rather, the company, because of operating and financial troubles, became sidetracked. Even with no net worth, GEICO was still worth a lot of money because its franchises were still in one piece.

Tenet: Favorable Long-Term Prospects

Although automobile insurance is a commodity product, Buffett says a commodity business can make money if it has a cost advantage that is both sustainable and wide. This description aptly fits GEICO. We also know that management in a commodity business is a crucial variable. GEICO's leadership, since Berkshire's purchase, has demonstrated that it, too, has a competitive advantage.

Tenet: Candor

When John (Jack) Byrne took over GEICO in 1976, he convinced both insurance regulators and competitors that if GEICO went bankrupt, it would be bad for the entire industry. His plan for rescuing the company included raising capital, obtaining a reinsurance treaty with other companies to reinsure a portion of GEICO's business, and cutting costs aggressively. "Operation Bootstrap," as Byrne called it, was the battle plan aimed at returning the company to profitability.

In his first year, Byrne closed 100 offices, reduced employment from 7,000 to 4,000, and turned in GEICO's license to sell insurance in both New Jersey and Massachusetts. Byrne told New Jersey regulators he would not renew the 250,000 policies that were costing the company $30 million a year. Next, he did away with the computerized systems that allowed policyholders to renew their insurance without providing updated information. When Byrne required the new information, he found the company was underpricing 9 percent of its renewal policies. When GEICO repriced them, 400,000 policyholders decided to discontinue their insurance. Altogether, Byrne's actions reduced the number of policyholders from 2.7 million to 1.5 million, and the company went from being the nation's 18th largest insurer in 1975 to 31st a year later. Despite this reduction, GEICO, after losing $126 million in 1976, earned an impressive $58.6 million on $463 million in revenues in 1977, Byrne's first full year of responsibility.

Clearly, GEICO's dramatic recovery was Byrne's doing, and his steadfast discipline on corporate expenses sustained GEICO's recovery for years. Byrne told shareholders that the company must return to its first principle of being the low-cost provider of insurance. His reports detailed how the company continually reduced costs. Even in 1981, when GEICO was the country's seventh-largest writer of automobile insurance, Byrne shared his secretary with two other executives. He boasted how the company serviced 378 policies per GEICO employee, up from 250 years earlier. During his turnaround years, he was always a great motivator. "Byrne," said Buffett, "is like the chicken farmer who rolls an ostrich egg into the henhouse and says, 'Ladies, this is what the competition is doing.'"[11]

Over the years, Byrne happily reported the successful progress of GEICO; he was equally candid with his shareholders when the news turned bad. In 1985, the company temporarily stumbled when it had underwriting losses. Writing in the company's first-quarter report to shareholders, Byrne "likened the company's plight to that of the pilot who told his passengers, 'the bad news is that we are lost, but the good news is that we are making great time.'"[12] The company quickly regained its footing and the following year posted profitable underwriting results. But, just as important, the company gained the reputation for being candid with its shareholders.

Tenet: Rationality

Over the years, Jack Byrne demonstrated rational behavior managing GEICO's assets. After he took charge, he positioned the company for controlled growth. It was more profitable, Byrne figured, to grow at a slower rate that allowed the company to carefully monitor its losses and expenses than to grow twice as fast if it meant losing financial control. Even so, this controlled growth continued to generate excess returns for GEICO, and the mark of rationality is what the company did with the cash.

Starting in 1983, the company was unable to invest its cash profitably so it decided to return the money to its shareholders. Between 1983 and 1992, GEICO repurchased, on a postsplit basis, 30 million shares, reducing the company's total common shares outstanding by 30 percent. In addition to buying back stock, GEICO also began to increase the dividend it paid to its shareholders.

In 1980, the company's split-adjusted dividend was $0.09 per share; in 1992, it was $0.60 per share, a 21 percent annual increase.

Tenet: Return on Equity

In 1980, the return on equity at GEICO was 30.8 percent—almost twice as high as the peer group average. By the late 1980s, the company's return on equity began to decline, not because the business was floundering but because its equity grew faster than its earnings. Hence, part of the logic of paying out increasing dividends and buying back stock was to reduce capital and maintain an acceptable return on equity.

Tenet: Profit Margins

Investors can compare profitability of insurance companies in several ways. Pretax margins are one of the best measures. Over the 10-year period 1983 to 1992, GEICO's average pretax margins were the most consistent, with the lowest standard deviation, of any peer group company.

GEICO, as we now understand, paid meticulous attention to all its expenses and closely tracked the expenses associated with settling insurance claims. During this period, corporate expenses as a percentage of premiums written averaged 15 percent—half the industry average. This low ratio partly reflects the cost of insurance agents that GEICO does not have to pay.

GEICO's combined ratio of corporate expenses and underwriting losses was demonstrably superior to the industry average. From 1977 through 1992, the industry average beat GEICO's combined ratio only once, in 1977. Since then, GEICO's combined ratio has averaged 97.1 percent, more than 10 percentage points better than the industry average. GEICO posted an underwriting loss only twice—once in 1985 and again in 1992. The underwriting loss in 1992 was accentuated by the unusual number of natural disasters that struck the country that year. Without Hurricane Andrew and other major storms, GEICO's combined ratio would have been a low 93.8 percent.

Tenet: Determine the Value

When Buffett first started to buy GEICO for Berkshire Hathaway, the company was close to bankruptcy. But he says GEICO was worth a substantial sum, even with a negative net worth, because of the company's insurance franchise. Still, in 1976, the company, since it had no earnings, defied a mathematical determination of value as put forth by John Burr Williams, who defined present value as future cash flows discounted at an appropriate rate. Still, despite the uncertainty over GEICO's future cash flows, Buffett was sure that the company would survive and earn money in the future. How much and when were open to debate.

In 1980, Berkshire owned one-third of GEICO, invested at a cost of $47 million. That year, GEICO's total market value was $296 million. Even then, Buffett estimated that the company possessed a significant margin of safety. In 1980, the company earned $60 million on $705 million in revenues. Berkshire's share of GEICO's earnings was $20 million. According to Buffett, "to buy a similar $20 million of earnings in a business with first-class economic characteristics and bright prospects would cost a minimum of $200 million"—more if the purchase was for a controlling interest in the company.[13]

Even so, Buffett's $200 million assumption is realistic, given the Williams valuation theory. Assuming that GEICO could sustain this $60 million in earnings without the aid of any additional capital, the present value of GEICO, discounted by the then-current 12 percent rate for a 30-year U.S. government bond, would have been $500 million—almost twice GEICO's 1980 market value. If the company could grow this earnings power at 2 percent real, or at 15 percent before current inflation, the present value would increase to $600 million, and Berkshire's share would equal $200 million. In other words, in 1980, the market value of GEICO's stock was less than half the discounted present value of its earnings power.

Tenet: The One-Dollar Premise

Between 1980 and 1992, the market value of GEICO grew from $296 million to $4.6 billion—an increase of $4.3 billion. During these 13 years, GEICO earned $1.7 billion. It paid shareholders, in common stock dividends, $280 million and retained $1.4 billion for reinvestment. Thus, for every dollar retained, GEICO created $3.12 in market value for its shareholders. This financial accomplishment demonstrates not only GEICO's superior management and niche marketing, but its ability to reinvest shareholder money at optimal rates.

Further proof of GEICO's superiority: a $1 investment in GEICO in 1980, excluding dividends, increased to $27.89 by 1992. This is an astonishing 29.2 percent compounded annual rate of return, far greater than the industry average and the S&P 500 index, which both gained 8.9 percent during the same period.

Capital Cities/ABC

Cap Cities had its beginning in the news business. In 1954, Lowell Thomas, the famous journalist; his business manager, Frank Smith; and a group of associates bought Hudson Valley Broadcasting Company, which included an Albany, New York, television and AM radio station. At that time, Thomas Murphy was a product manager at Lever Brothers. Frank Smith, who was a golfing partner of Murphy's father, hired the younger Murphy to manage the company's television station. In 1957, Hudson Valley purchased a Raleigh-Durham television station, and the company's name was changed to Capital Cities Broadcasting, reflecting that both Albany and Raleigh were capitals of their respective states.

In 1960, Murphy hired Dan Burke to manage the Albany station. Burke was the brother of one of Murphy's Harvard classmates, Jim Burke, who later became chairman of Johnson & Johnson. Dan Burke, an Albany native, was left in charge of the television station while Murphy returned to New York, where he was named president of Capital Cities in 1964. Thus began one of the most successful corporate partnerships in American business. During the next three decades, Murphy and Burke ran Capital Cities, and together they made more than 30 broadcasting and publishing acquisitions, the most notable being the purchase of ABC in 1985.

Buffett first met Tom Murphy in the late 1960s at a New York luncheon arranged by one of Murphy's classmates. The story goes that Murphy was so impressed with Buffett that he invited him to join the board of Capital Cities.[14] Buffett declined, but he and Murphy became close friends, keeping in touch over the years. Buffett first invested in Capital Cities in 1977; unexplainably, but profitably, he sold the position the following year.

In December 1984, Murphy approached Leonard Goldenson, chairman of American Broadcasting Companies, with the idea of merging the two companies. Although initially rebuffed, Murphy contacted Goldenson again in January 1985. The Federal Communications Commission (FCC) had increased the number of television and radio stations that a single company could own from seven to 12, effective in April that year. This time Goldenson agreed. Goldenson, then 79 years old, was concerned about his successor. Although ABC had several potential candidates, none was, in his opinion, ready for leadership. Murphy and Burke were considered the best managers in the media and communications industry. By agreeing to merge with Cap Cities, Goldenson was ensuring that ABC would remain in strong management hands. American Broadcasting Companies entered the negotiating room with high-priced investment bankers. Murphy, who always negotiated his own deals, brought his trusted friend Warren Buffett. Together they worked out the first-ever sale of a television network and the largest media merger in history up to that point.

Capital Cities offered American Broadcasting Companies a total package worth $121 per ABC share ($118 in cash per share and one-tenth warrant to purchase Capital Cities worth $3 per share). The offer was twice the value at which ABC's stock traded the day before the announcement. To finance the $3.5 billion deal, Capital Cities would borrow $2.1 billion from a banking consortium, sell overlapping television and radio stations worth approximately $900 million, and also sell restricted properties that a network was not allowed to own, including cable properties subsequently sold to the Washington Post Company. The last $500 million came from Buffett. He agreed that Berkshire Hathaway would purchase three million newly issued shares of Cap Cities at a price of $172.50 per share. Murphy again asked his friend to join the board, and this time Buffett agreed.

Tenet: Simple and Understandable

After serving on the board of the Washington Post Company for more than 10 years, Buffett understood the business of television broadcasting and newspaper and magazine publishing. Buffett's business understanding of television networks grew with Berkshire's own purchase of ABC once in 1978 and again in 1984.

Tenet: Consistent Operating History

Both Capital Cities and American Broadcasting Companies had profitable operating histories dating back more than 30 years. ABC averaged 17 percent return on equity and 21 percent debt to equity from 1975 through 1984. Capital Cities, during the 10 years before its offer to purchase ABC, averaged 19 percent return on equity and 20 percent debt to capital.

Tenet: Favorable Long-Term Prospects

Broadcasting companies and networks are blessed with above-average economics. Like newspapers, and for much the same reason, they generate a great deal of economic goodwill. Once a broadcasting tower is built, capital reinvestment and working capital needs are minor and inventory investment is nonexistent. Movies and programs can be bought on credit and settled later when advertising dollars roll in. Thus, as a general rule, broadcasting companies produce above-average returns on capital and generate substantial cash in excess of their operating needs.

The risks to networks and broadcasters include government regulation, changing technology, and shifting advertising dollars. Governments can deny the renewal of a company's broadcasting license, but this is rare. Cable programs, in 1985, were a minor threat to networks. Although some viewers tuned in cable shows, the overwhelming majority of television viewers still preferred network programming. Also during the 1980s, advertising dollars for free-spending consumers were growing substantially faster than the country's gross domestic product. To reach a mass audience, advertisers still counted on network broadcasting. The basic economics of networks, broadcasting companies, and publishers were, in Buffett's mind, above average, and in 1985, the long-term prospects for these businesses were highly favorable.

Tenet: Determine the Value

Berkshire's $517 million investment in Capital Cities at that time was the single-largest investment Buffett ever made. How Buffett determined the combined value of Capital Cities and ABC is open for debate. Murphy agreed to sell Buffett three million shares of Capital Cities/ABC for $172.50 per share. But we know that price and value are often two different figures. Buffett's practice, we have learned, is to acquire a company only when there is a significant margin of safety between the company's intrinsic value and its purchase price. However, with the purchase of Capital Cities/ABC, he admittedly compromised this principle.

If we discount Buffett's offer of $172.50 per share by 10 percent (the approximate yield of the 30-year U.S. government bond in 1985) and multiply this value by 16 million shares (Cap Cities had 13 million shares outstanding plus three million issued to Buffett), the present value of this business would need to have earnings power of $276 million. Capital Cities' 1984 earnings net after depreciation and capital expenditures were $122 million, and ABC's net income after depreciation and capital expenditures was $320 million, making the combined earnings power $442 million. But the combined company would have substantial debt: the approximately $2.1 billion that Murphy had to borrow would cost the company $220 million a year in interest. So the net earnings of the combined company were approximately $200 million.

There were additional considerations. Murphy's reputation for improving the cash flow of purchased businesses simply by reducing expenses was legendary. Capital Cities' operating margins were

28 percent, whereas ABC's were 11 percent. If Murphy could improve the operating margins of the ABC properties by one-third, to 15 percent, the company would throw off an additional $125 million each year, and the combined earnings power would equal $225 million annually. The per-share present value of a company earning $325 million with 16 million shares outstanding discounted at 10 percent was $203 per share—a 15 percent margin of safety over Buffett's $172.50 purchase price. "I doubt if Ben's up there applauding me on this one," Buffett quipped, in reference to Ben Graham.[15]

The margin of safety that Buffett accepted could be expanded if we make certain assumptions. Buffett says that conventional wisdom during this period argued that newspapers, magazines, or television stations would be able to increase earnings forever at 6 percent annually—without the need for additional capital.[16] The reasoning, he explains, was that capital expenditures would equal depreciation rates and the need for working capital would be minimal. Hence, income could be thought of as freely distributed earnings. This means that an owner of a media company possessed a perpetual annuity that would grow at 6 percent for the foreseeable future without the need of any additional capital. Compare that, Buffett suggests, to a company that is able to grow only if capital is reinvested. If you owned a media company that earned $1 million and expected to grow at 6 percent, it would be appropriate, says Buffett, to pay $25 million for this business ($1 million divided by a risk-free rate of 10 percent less the 6 percent growth rate). Another business that earned $1 million but could not grow earnings without reinvested capital might be worth $10 million ($1 million divided by 10 percent).

If we take this finance lesson and apply it to Cap Cities, the value of Cap Cities increased from $203 per share to $507, or a 66 percent margin of safety over the $172.50 price that Buffett agreed to pay. But there were a lot of "ifs" in these assumptions. Would Murphy be able to sell a portion of Capital Cities/ABC combined properties for $900 million? (He actually got $1.2 billion.) Would he be able to improve operating margins at American Broadcasting Companies? Would he be able to continually count on the growth of advertising dollars?

Buffett's ability to obtain a significant margin of safety in Capital Cities was complicated by several factors. First, the stock price of Cap Cities had been rising over the years. Murphy and Burke were doing an excellent job of managing the company, and the company's share price reflected this. So, unlike GEICO, Buffett did not have the opportunity to purchase Cap Cities cheaply because of a temporary business decline. The stock market, which had been steadily rising, didn't help, either. And, because this was a secondary stock offering, Buffett had to take a price for Cap Cities' shares that was close to its then-trading value.

If there was any disappointment over the issue of price, Buffett was comforted by the quick appreciation of those same shares. On Friday, March 15, 1985, Capital Cities' share price was $176. On Monday afternoon, March 18, Capital Cities announced it would purchase American Broadcasting Companies. The next day, by market close, Capital Cities' share price was $202.75. In four days, the price had risen 26 points, a 15 percent appreciation. Buffett's profit was $90 million and the deal was not due to close until January 1986.

The margin of safety that Buffett received buying Capital Cities was significantly less than with other purchases. So why did he proceed? The answer was Tom Murphy. Had it not been for Murphy, Buffett admits he would not have invested in the company. Murphy was Buffett's margin of safety. Capital Cities/ABC was an exceptional business, the kind of business that attracts Buffett. But there is also something special about Murphy. "Warren adores Tom Murphy," said John Byrne. "Just to be partners with him is attractive to [Buffett]."[17]

Cap Cities' management philosophy is decentralization. Murphy and Burke hire the best people possible and then leave them alone to do their job. All decisions are made at the local level. Burke found this out early in his relationship with Murphy. Burke, while managing the Albany TV station, mailed updated reports weekly to Murphy, who never responded. Burke finally got the message. Murphy promised Burke, "I won't come to Albany unless you invite me—or I have to fire you."[18] Murphy and Burke help set yearly budgets for their companies and review operating performance quarterly. With these two exceptions, managers were expected to operate their businesses as if they owned them. "We expect a great deal from our managers," wrote Murphy.[19]

And one thing Capital Cities' managers were expected to do was control costs. When they failed, Murphy was not shy about getting involved. When Capital Cities purchased ABC, Murphy's talent for cutting costs was badly needed. Networks tend to think in terms of ratings, not profits. Whatever was needed to increase ratings, the network thought, superseded cost evaluation. This mentality abruptly stopped when Murphy took over. With the help of carefully selected committees at ABC, Murphy pruned payrolls, perks, and expenses. Some 1,500 people, given generous severance packages, were let go. The executive dining rooms and private elevator at ABC were closed. The limousine at ABC Entertainment in Los Angeles that was used to drive Murphy during his first tour of the company's operation was discharged. On his next trip, he took a cab.

Such cost-consciousness was a way of life at Capital Cities. The company's Philadelphia television station, WPVI, the number-one station in the city, had a news staff of 100 compared with 150 at the CBS affiliate across town. Before Murphy arrived at ABC, the company employed 60 people to manage ABC's five television stations. Soon after the Cap Cities' acquisition, six people managed eight stations. WABC-TV in New York used to employ 600 people and generated 30 percent pretax margins. Once Murphy reconfigured the station, it employed 400 people with pretax margins north of 50 percent. Once a cost crisis was resolved, Murphy depended on Burke to manage operating decisions. He concentrated on acquisitions and shareholder assets.

Tenet: The Institutional Imperative

The basic economics of the broadcasting and network business assured Cap Cities it would generate ample cash flow. However, the industry's basic economics, coupled with Murphy's penchant for controlling costs, meant Cap Cities would have overwhelming cash flow. From 1988 through 1992, Cap Cities generated $2.3 billion in unencumbered cash. Given these resources, some managers might be unable to resist the temptation to spend the money, buying businesses and expanding the corporate domain. Murphy, too, bought a few businesses. In 1990, he spent $61 million acquiring small properties. At the time, the general market for most media properties was priced too high, he said.

Acquisitions had always been very important to Cap Cities in the development of its growth. Murphy was always on the lookout for media properties, but he remained steadfast in his discipline not to overpay for a company. Cap Cities, with its enormous cash flow, could easily gobble up other media properties, but as *BusinessWeek* reported, "Murphy would sometimes wait for years until he found the right property. He never made a deal just because he had the resources available to do it."[20] Murphy and Burke also realized that the media business was cyclical, and if a purchase was built on too much leverage, the risk to shareholders would be unacceptable. "Murphy never did a deal that either of us thought was capable of mortally wounding us," Burke said.[21]

A company that generates more cash than can be profitably reinvested in its business can buy growth, reduce leverage, or return the money to shareholders. Since Murphy was unwilling to pay the high asking prices for media companies, he chose instead to reduce leverage and buy back stock. In 1986, after the acquisition of ABC, total long-term debt at Cap Cities was $1.8 billion and the debt-to-capital ratio was 48.6 percent. Cash and cash equivalents at 1986 year-end amounted to $16 million. By 1992, long-term debt at the company was $964 million and the debt-to-capital ratio had dropped to 20 percent. Furthermore, cash and cash equivalents increased to $1.2 billion, making the company essentially debt free.

Murphy's strengthening of Cap Cities' balance sheet substantially reduced the company's risk. What he did next substantially increased its value.

Tenet: The One-Dollar Premise

From 1985 through 1992, the market value of Cap Cities/ABC grew from $2.9 billion to $8.3 billion. During this period, the company retained $2.7 billion in earnings, thereby creating $2.01 in market value for every $1 reinvested. This accomplishment was especially noteworthy considering that the company endured both a cyclical downturn in earnings, in 1990–1991, and a decline in its intrinsic value from secular changes in the network-broadcasting business. Even so, Berkshire's investment in Capital Cities/ABC grew from $517 million to $1.5 billion, a 14.5 percent compounded annual rate of return—better than both CBS and the Standard & Poor's 500 index.

Tenet: Rationality

In 1988, Cap Cities announced that it had authorized the repurchase of up to two million shares, 11 percent of the company's outstanding stock. In 1989, the company spent $233 million purchasing 523,000 shares of stock at an average price of $445—7.3 times the company's operating cash flow, compared to the asking prices of other media companies that were selling at 10 to 12 times cash flow. The following year, the company purchased 926,000 shares at an average price of $4,777, or 7.6 times operating cash flow. In 1992, the company continued to buy back its stock. That year it purchased 270,000 shares at an average cost of $434 per share, or 8.2 times cash flow. The price it paid for itself, Murphy reiterated, was still less than the price of other advertiser-supported media companies that he and Burke considered attractive. From 1988 through 1992, Cap Cities purchased a total of 1,953,000 shares of stock, investing $866 million.

In November 1993, the company announced a Dutch auction to purchase up to two million shares at prices between $590 and $630 per share. Berkshire participated in the auction, submitting one million of its three million shares. This act alone caused widespread speculation. Was the company unable to find an appropriate acquisition, putting itself up for sale? Was Buffett, by selling a third of his position, giving up on the company? Cap Cities denied the rumors. Opinions surfaced that Buffett would not have tendered stock that surely would have fetched a higher price if indeed the company was for sale. Cap Cities/ABC eventually purchased

1.1 million shares of stock—one million of them from Berkshire—at an average price of $630 per share. Buffett was able to redeploy $630 million without disrupting the marketplace for Cap Cities' shares while remaining the largest shareholder of the company, owning 13 percent of the shares outstanding.

Buffett has observed the operations and management of countless businesses over the years. But according to him, Cap Cities was the best-managed publicly owned company in the country. To prove his point, when Buffett invested in Cap Cities, he assigned all voting rights for the next 11 years to Murphy and Burke, as long as either one continued to manage the company. And if that was not enough to convince you of the high regard Buffett held for these men, consider this: "Tom Murphy and Dan Burke are not only great managers," Buffett said, "they are precisely the sort of fellows that you would want your daughter to marry."[22]

The Coca-Cola Company

In the fall of 1988, Donald Keough, president of Coca-Cola, could not help but notice that someone was buying shares of the company's stock in a big way. Just a year after the 1987 stock market crash, Coca-Cola's shares were still trading 25 percent below their precrash high. But the share price had finally found a floor because "some mysterious investor was gulping down shares by the caseload." When Keough discovered that the broker who was doing all the buying hailed from the Midwest, he immediately thought of his friend Warren Buffett, and decided to give him a call.

"Well, Warren, what's going on?" Keough began. "You don't happen to be buying any shares of Coca-Cola?" Buffett paused and then said, "It so happens that I am, but I would appreciate it if you would stay quiet about it until I disclose my ownership."[23] If word had ever gotten out that Buffett was buying Coca-Cola shares, it would have created a rush of buying, ultimately driving the share price higher, and he was not done adding to Berkshire's position.

By the spring of 1989, Berkshire Hathaway shareholders learned that Buffett had spent $1.02 billion buying Coca-Cola shares. He had bet a third of the Berkshire portfolio, and now owned 7 percent of the company. It was the single-largest Berkshire investment to date, and already Wall Street was scratching its head. Buffett had paid five times book value and over 15 times earnings, then a premium to the stock market, for a hundred-year-old company that sold soda pop. What did the Wizard of Omaha see that everyone else missed?

Coca-Cola is the world's largest beverage company. It sells more than 500 different sparkling and still refreshments in over 200 countries worldwide. Of those 500, 15 are billion-dollar brands, including Coca-Cola, Diet Coke, Fanta, Sprite, Vitaminwater, Powerade, Minute Maid, Simply, Georgia, and Dell Valle.

Buffett's relationship with Coca-Cola dates back to his childhood. He drank his first Coke when he was five years old, and soon afterward he started the entrepreneurial venture you may remember from Chapter 1, buying six Cokes for 25 cents and reselling them for five cents each. For the next 50 years, he observed the phenomenal growth of Coca-Cola but purchased instead textile mills, department stores, and farming equipment manufacturers. Even in 1986, when he formally announced that Cherry Coke would become the official soft drink of Berkshire Hathaway's annual meetings, Buffett had still not purchased one share of Coca-Cola. It wasn't until two years later, in the summer of 1988, that Buffett began to buy.

Tenet: Simple and Understandable

The business of Coca-Cola is relatively simple. The company purchases commodity inputs and mixes them to manufacture a concentrate that is sold to bottlers, who combine the concentrate with other ingredients. The bottlers then sell the finished product to retail outlets, including minimarts, supermarkets, and vending machines. The company also provides soft drink syrups to restaurants and fast-food retailers, who then sell soft drinks to consumers in cups and glasses.

Tenet: Consistent Operating History

No other company can match Coca-Cola's consistent operating history. The business was started in 1886, selling one beverage product. Today, almost 130 years later, Coca-Cola is selling the same beverage—plus a few others. The only significant difference is the company's size and geographic reach.

At the turn of the twentieth century, the company employed 10 traveling salesmen to cover the entire United States. At that point, the company was selling 116,492 gallons of syrup a year, for annual sales of $148,000. Fifty years after inception, the company was selling 207 million cases of soft drinks annually (having converted sales from gallons to cases). "It would be hard," Buffett has noted, "to name any company comparable to Coca-Cola and selling, as Coca-Cola does, an unchanged product that can point to a ten-year record anything like Coca-Cola's."[24] Today, with 1.7 billion servings daily, the Coca-Cola Company is the number-one global provider of beverages, ready-to-drink coffees, juices, and juice drinks.

Tenet: Favorable Long-Term Prospects

Shortly after Berkshire's 1989 public announcement that it owned 6.3 percent of the Coca-Cola Company, Buffett was interviewed by Melissa Turner, a business writer for the *Atlanta Constitution*. She asked Buffett a question he has been asked often: Why hadn't he purchased shares in the company sooner? By way of an answer, Buffett related what he was thinking at the time he finally made the decision.

"Let's say you are going away for ten years," he said, "and you wanted to make one investment and you know everything that you know now, but you couldn't change it while you were gone. What would you think about?" Of course the business would have to be simple and understandable. Of course the business would have to have demonstrated a great deal of business consistency over the years. And of course, the long-term prospects would have to be favorable. "If I came up with anything in terms of certainty, where I knew the market was going to grow, where I knew the leader was going to be the leader—I mean worldwide—and where I knew there would be big unit growth, I just don't know anything like Coke," Buffett explained. "I'd be relatively sure that when I came back they would be doing a hell of a lot more business than they do now."[25]

But why purchase at that particular time? Coca-Cola's business attributes, as described by Buffett, had existed for several decades. What caught his eye, he said, were the changes occurring at Coca-Cola during the 1980s under the leadership of Roberto Goizueta, chairman and CEO, and president Donald Keough.

Change was critical, and overdue. The 1970s were dismal years for Coca-Cola. The decade was marred by disputes with bottlers, accusations of mistreatment of migrant workers at the company's Minute Maid groves, environmentalists' claim that Coke's one-way containers contributed to the country's growing pollution problems, and the Federal Trade Commission's charges that the company's exclusive franchise system violated the Sherman Antitrust Act. Coca-Cola's international business was reeling as well. The Arab boycott of Coke, begun when the company issued an Israeli franchise, dismantled years of investment. Japan, where the company's earnings were growing the fastest, was a battlefield of corporate mistakes. Coke's 26-ounce take-home bottles were exploding—literally—on store shelves. In addition, Japanese consumers angrily objected to the company's use of artificial coal-tar coloring in Fanta Grape. When the company developed a new version using real grape skins, the contents fermented and the grape soda was tossed into Tokyo Bay.

Coca-Cola in the 1970s was a fragmented and reactive company rather than an innovator setting the pace within the beverage industry. Despite its problems, the company continued to generate millions of dollars in earnings. But instead of reinvesting in Coca-Cola's own beverage market, Paul Austin, appointed chairman in 1971 after serving as president since 1962, decided to diversify. He invested in water projects and shrimp farms, despite their slim profit margins. He also purchased a winery. Shareholders bitterly opposed this move, arguing that Coca-Cola should not be associated with alcohol. To deflect criticism, Austin directed unprecedented amounts of money for advertising campaigns.

Meanwhile Coca-Cola earned 20 percent on equity, but pretax margins were slipping. The market value of the company at the end of the bear market of 1974 was $3.1 billion. Six years later, that value had increased to $4.1 billion. In other words, from 1974 to 1980, the company's market value increased at an average annual rate of 5.6 percent, significantly underperforming the S&P 500 index. For every dollar the company retained in those six years, it created only $1.02 in market value.

Coca-Cola's corporate woes were exacerbated by Austin's intimidating and unapproachable behavior.[26] To make matters worse, his wife, Jeane, was a disruptive influence within the company. She redecorated corporate headquarters with modern art, shunning the company's classic Norman Rockwell paintings and even using a corporate jet for her art-buying trips. But it was her last order that contributed to her husband's downfall.

In May 1980, Mrs. Austin ordered the company's park closed to employee luncheons. Their food droppings, she complained, attracted pigeons on the well-manicured lawns. Employee morale hit an all-time low. Robert Woodruff, the company's 91-year-old patriarch, who had led Coca-Cola from 1923 until 1955 and was still chairman of the board's finance committee, had heard enough. He demanded Austin's resignation and replaced him with Roberto Goizueta.

Goizueta, raised in Cuba, was Coca-Cola's first foreign chief executive officer. He was as outgoing as Austin was reticent. One of his first acts was to bring together Coca-Cola's top 50 managers for a meeting in Palm Springs, California. "Tell me what we're doing wrong," he said. "I want to know it all and once it is settled, I want 100 percent loyalty. If anyone is not happy, we will make you a good settlement and say goodbye."[27] From this meeting evolved the company's "Strategy for the 1980s," a 900-word pamphlet outlining the corporate goals for Coca-Cola.

Goizueta encouraged his managers to take intelligent risks. He wanted Coca-Cola to initiate action rather than to be reactive. He began by cutting costs, and he demanded that any business that Coca-Cola owned must optimize its return on assets. These actions translated, immediately, into increasing profit margins.

Tenet: High Profit Margins

In 1980, Coca-Cola's pretax profit margins were a low 12.9 percent. Margins had been falling for five straight years and were substantially below the company's 1973 margins of 18 percent. In Goizueta's first year, pretax margins rose to 13.7 percent; by 1988, when Buffett bought his Coca-Cola shares, margins had climbed to a record 19 percent.

Tenet: Return on Equity

In "Strategy for the 1980s," Goizueta pointed out that the company would divest any business that no longer generated acceptable returns on equity. Any new business venture must have sufficient real growth potential to justify an investment. Coca-Cola was no longer interested in battling for share in a stagnant market. "Increasing earnings per share and effecting increased return on equity are still the name of the game," Goizueta announced.[28] His words were followed by actions: Coca-Cola's wine business was sold to Seagram's in 1983.

Although the company had earned a respectable 20 percent on equity during the 1970s, Goizueta was not impressed. He demanded better returns, and the company obliged. By 1988, Coca-Cola's return on equity had increased to 31 percent.

By any measurement, Goizueta's Coca-Cola was doubling and tripling the financial accomplishments of Austin's Coca-Cola. The results could be seen in the market value of the company. In 1980, that value was $4.1 billion. By the end of 1987, even after the stock market crash in October, market value had risen to $14.1 billion. In just seven years, Coca-Cola's market value increased at an average annual rate of 19.3 percent. For every dollar Coca-Cola retained during this period, it gained $4.66 in market value.

Tenet: Candor

Goizueta's strategy for the 1980s pointedly included shareholders. "We shall, during the next decade, remain totally committed to our shareholders and to the protection and enhancement of their investment," he wrote. "In order to give our shareholders an above-average total return on their investment," he explained, "we must choose businesses that generate returns in excess of inflation."[29]

Goizueta not only had to grow the business, which required capital investment; he also was obliged to increase shareholder value. To do so, Coca-Cola, by increasing profit margins and return on equity, was able to pay dividends while simultaneously reducing the dividend payout ratio. Dividends to shareholders in the 1980s were increasing 10 percent per year while the payout ratio was declining from 65 percent to 40 percent. This enabled Coca-Cola to reinvest a greater percentage of the company's earnings to help sustain its growth rate while not shortchanging shareholders.

Under Goizueta's leadership, Coca-Cola's mission statement became crystal clear; management's primary objective was to maximize shareholder value over time. To do so, the company focused on the high-return soft drink business. If successful, the evidence would be an increase in the growth of cash flow and increased return on equity, and ultimately an increased total return to shareholders.

Tenet: Rational Management

The growth in net cash flow not only allowed Coca-Cola to increase its dividend to shareholders, but also enabled the company to initiate its first ever buy-back program. In 1984, Goizueta announced that the company would repurchase six million shares of stock in the open market. Repurchasing stock is rational only if the intrinsic value of the company is higher than the market price. The strategic changes initiated by Goizueta, with emphasis on increasing the return on equity for shareholders, suggested to him that Coca-Cola had reached that tipping point.

Tenet: Owner Earnings

In 1973, owner earnings (net income plus depreciation minus capital expenditures) were $152 million. By 1980, owner earnings were $262 million, an 8 percent annual compounded growth rate. From 1981 through 1988, owner earnings grew from $262 million to $828 million, a 17.8 percent average annual compounded growth rate.

The growth in owner earnings was reflected in the share price of Coca-Cola. This is particularly obvious if we look at 10-year periods. From 1973 to 1982, the total return of Coca-Cola grew at an average annual rate of 6.3 percent. The following 10 years, from 1983 to 1992, when Goizueta's management approach was clearly visible, the average annual total return for the stock was 31.1 percent.

Tenet: The Institutional Imperative

When Goizueta took over Coca-Cola, one of his first moves was to jettison the unrelated businesses that Paul Austin had developed, and return the company to its core business: selling syrup. It was a clear demonstration of Coca-Cola's ability to resist the institutional imperative.

Reducing the company to a single-product business was undeniably a bold move. What made Goizueta's strategy even more remarkable was his willingness to take action at a time when others in the industry were doing the exact opposite. Several leading beverage companies were investing their profits in other unrelated businesses. Anheuser-Busch used the profits from its beer business to invest in theme parks. Brown Forman, a producer and distributor of wine and spirits, invested its profits in china, crystal, silver, and luggage businesses, all of which had much lower returns. Seagram Company, Ltd., a global spirits and wine business, bought Universal Studios. Pepsi, Coca-Cola's chief beverage rival, bought snack businesses (Frito-Lay) and restaurants, including Taco Bell, Kentucky Fried Chicken, and Pizza Hut.

It is important to note that not only did Goizueta's action focus the company's attention on its largest and most important product, but it worked to reallocate the company's resources into its most profitable business. Because the economic returns of selling syrup far outweighed the economic returns of the other businesses, the company was now reinvesting its profits in its highest-return business.

Tenet: Determine the Value

When Buffett first purchased Coca-Cola in 1988, people asked: "Where is the value of Coke?" The company's stock price was 15 times earnings and 12 times cash flow—a 30 percent and 50 percent premium to the market average. Buffett paid five times book value for a company with 6.6 percent earnings yield at a time when long-term bonds were yielding 9 percent. He was willing to do that because of Coke's extraordinary level of economic goodwill. The company was earning 31 percent on equity while employing relatively little in capital investment. Buffett has explained that price tells you nothing about value. The value of Coca-Cola, he said, like that of any other company, is determined by the total owner earnings expected to occur over the life of the business, discounted by the appropriate interest rate.

In 1988, owner earnings of Coca-Cola equaled $828 million. The 30-year U.S. Treasury bond (the risk-free rate) at that time traded near a 9 percent yield. Coca-Cola's 1988 owner earnings, discounted by 9 percent, would produce an intrinsic value of $9.2 billion. When Buffett purchased Coca-Cola, the market value was $14.8 billion. At first glance this seems to suggest that Buffett might have overpaid for the company. But remember that the $9.2 billion represents the discounted value of Coca-Cola's then-current owner earnings. If buyers were willing to pay a price for Coca-Cola that was 60 percent higher than $9.2 billion, it must have been because they perceived part of the value of Coca-Cola to be its future growth opportunities.

Analyzing Coca-Cola, we find that owner earnings from 1981 through 1988 grew at a 17.8 percent annual rate—faster than the risk-free rate of return. When this occurs, analysts use a two-stage discount model. It permits them to calculate future earnings when a company has extraordinary growth for a limited number of years, followed by a period of constant growth at a slower rate.

We can use this two-stage process to calculate the 1988 present value of the company's future cash flows. In 1988, Coca-Cola's owner earnings were $828 million. If we assume that Coca-Cola would be able to grow owner earnings at 15 percent per year for the next 10 years (a reasonable assumption, since that rate is lower than the company's previous seven-year average), by year 10 owner earnings would equal $3.349 billion. Let's further assume that, starting in year 11, that growth rate will slow to 5 percent per year. Using a discount rate of 9 percent (the long-term bond rate at the time), we can back-calculate the intrinsic value of Coca-Cola in 1988 to be $48.377 billion.

We can repeat this exercise using different growth rate assumptions. If we assume that Coca-Cola can grow owner earnings at 12 percent for 10 years, followed by 5 percent growth, the present value of the company, discounted at 9 percent, would be $38.163 billion. At 10 percent growth for 10 years and 5 percent thereafter, the value would be $32.497 billion. And even if we assume that Coca-Cola could only grow at a steady state of 5 percent throughout, the company would still be worth at least $20.7 billion.

Tenet: Buy at Attractive Prices

In June 1988, the price of Coca-Cola was approximately $10 per share (split adjusted). Over the next 10 months, Buffett acquired 93,400,000 shares, for a total investment of $1.023 billion. His average cost per share was $10.96. At the end of 1989, Coca-Cola represented 35 percent of Berkshire's common stock portfolio.

From the time Goizueta took control of Coca-Cola in 1980, the company's stock price had increased every year. In the five years before Buffett purchased his first shares, the average annual gain in share price was 18 percent. The company's fortunes were so good that Buffett was unable to purchase any shares at distressed prices. Still, he charged ahead. Price, he reminds us, has nothing to do with value.

The stock market's value of Coca-Cola in 1988 and 1989, during Buffett's purchase period, averaged $15.1 billion. But by Buffett's estimation, the intrinsic value of the company was anywhere from $20.7 billion (assuming a 5 percent growth in owner earnings) to $32.4 billion (assuming 10 percent growth), or $38.1 billion (assuming 12 percent growth), or $48.3 billion (assuming 15 percent growth). Buffett's margin of safety—the discount to intrinsic value—could be as low as a conservative 27 percent or as high as 70 percent.

The best business to own, says Buffett, is one that, over a long period of time, can employ ever-larger amounts of capital at sustainably high rates of return. In Buffett's mind, this was the perfect description of Coca-Cola. Ten years after Berkshire began investing in Coca-Cola, the market value of the company had grown from $25.8 billion to $143 billion. Over that time period, the company produced $26.9 billion in profits, paid out $10.5 billion in dividends to shareholders, and retained $16.4 billion for reinvestment. For every dollar the company retained, it created $7.20 in market value. At year-end 1999, Berkshire's original $1.023 billion investment in Coca-Cola was worth $11.6 billion. The same amount invested in the S&P 500 index would have been worth $3 billion.

General Dynamics

In 1990, General Dynamics was the country's second-largest defense contractor behind McDonnell Douglas Corporation. General Dynamics provided missile systems (Tomahawk, Sparrow, Stinger, and other advanced cruise missiles) in addition to air defense systems, space-launched vehicles, and fighter planes (F-16s) for the U.S. armed forces. In 1990, the company had combined sales of more than $10 billion. By 1993, sales had dropped to $3.5 billion. Despite that, shareholder value during this period increased sevenfold.

In 1990, the Berlin Wall crumbled, signaling the beginning of the end of the long and expensive Cold War. The following year, communism collapsed in the Soviet Union. With each hard-earned victory, from World War I to the Vietnam War, the United States had to reshape the massive concentration of its defense resources. Now that the Cold War was over, the U.S. military-industrial complex was in the midst of another reorganization.

In January 1991, General Dynamics appointed William Anders as chief executive. At the time, the share price was at a decade low of $19. Initially, Anders attempted to convince Wall Street that even with a shrinking defense budget, the company could earn higher valuations.

Hoping to remove any financial uncertainty that would prejudice analysts, he began to restructure the company. He cut capital expenditures and research development by $1 billion, cut employment by the thousands, and instituted an executive compensation program that was based on the performance of General Dynamics' share price.

It was not long before Anders began to realize that the defense industry had fundamentally changed and that to be successful, General Dynamics would have to take more dramatic steps than just pinching pennies. There simply was not enough defense business to go around. A smaller defense budget would ultimately require companies to downsize, diversify into nondefense businesses, or dominate what little defense business was available.

Tenet: The Institutional Imperative

In October 1991, Anders commissioned a consultant's study of the defense industry. The conclusions were sobering: When defense companies acquired nondefense businesses, failures occurred 80 percent of the time. As long as the defense industry was burdened with overcapacity, none of the defense companies would achieve efficiencies. Anders concluded that to be successful, General Dynamics would have to rationalize its business. He decided that General Dynamics would keep only those businesses that (1) demonstrated a market acceptance of its franchise-like product and (2) could achieve critical mass, the balance between research and development and production capacity that produces economies of scale and financial strength. Where critical mass could not be achieved, Anders said, the business would be sold.

Initially, Anders believed that General Dynamics would focus on its four core operations: submarines, tanks, aircraft, and space systems. These businesses were market leaders, and Anders figured they would remain viable even in a shrinking defense market. The rest of General Dynamics' businesses would be sold. So, in November 1991, General Dynamics sold its Data Systems to Computer Sciences for $200 million. The next year the company sold Cessna Aircraft to Textron for $600 million and its missile business to Hughes Aircraft for $450 million. In less than six months, the company raised $1.25 billion by selling noncore businesses.

Anders's actions woke up Wall Street. General Dynamics' share price in 1991 rose 112 percent. What Anders did next got Buffett's attention.

With the cash holdings, Anders declared that the company would first meet its liquidity needs and then bring down debt to ensure financial strength. After reducing debt, General Dynamics was still generating cash well in excess of its needs. Knowing that adding capacity to a shrinking defense budget did not make sense and that diversification into nondefense businesses invited failure, Anders decided to use the excess cash to benefit shareholders. In July 1992, under the terms of its Dutch auction, General Dynamics purchased 13.2 million shares at prices between $65.37 and $72.25, reducing its shares outstanding by 30 percent.

On the morning of July 22, 1992, Buffett called Anders to tell him that Berkshire had purchased 4.3 million shares of General Dynamics. Buffett told Anders that he was impressed with General Dynamics and that he bought the shares for investment purposes. In September, Buffett granted General Dynamics' board a proxy to vote Berkshire's shares so long as Anders remained chief executive.

Tenet: Rationality

Of all Berkshire's common stock purchases, none has caused as much confusion as General Dynamics. It had none of the traditional markings of Buffett's earlier purchases. It was not a company that was simple and understandable, it was not a consistent performer, and it did not have favorable long-term prospects. Not only was the company in an industry that was controlled by the government (90 percent of sales came from government contracts), but that industry was shrinking in size. General Dynamics had pitiful profit margins and below-average returns on equity. Furthermore, its future cash flows were unknown, so how could Buffett determine its value? The answer is that Buffett did not initially purchase

General Dynamics as a long-term common stock holding. He purchased it as an arbitrage opportunity, so the usual financial and business requirements did not apply.

"We were lucky in our General Dynamics purchase," Buffett wrote. "I had paid little attention to the company until last summer, when it announced it would repurchase about 30 percent of its shares by way of Dutch tender. Seeing an arbitrage opportunity, I began buying the stock for Berkshire, expecting to tender our holdings at a small profit."[30]

But he changed his mind. The original plan had been to tender Berkshire's shares at the Dutch auction "but then I began studying the company," said Buffett, "and the accomplishments of Bill Anders in the brief time he'd been CEO. And what I saw made my eyes pop. Bill had a clearly articulated and rational strategy; he had been focused and imbued with a sense of urgency in carrying it out; and the results were truly remarkable."[31] Buffett abandoned his thoughts of arbitraging General Dynamics and instead decided to become a long-term shareholder.

Clearly, Buffett's investment in General Dynamics was a testament to Bill Anders's ability to resist the institutional imperative. Although critics have argued that Anders liquidated a great company, Anders argues he simply monetized the unrealized value of the company. When he took charge in 1991, the stock of General Dynamics was trading at a 60 percent discount to book value. In the 10 previous years, General Dynamics had returned to shareholders a compounded annual return of 9 percent compared to the 17 percent for the 10 other defense companies and a 17.6 percent return for the Standard & Poor's 500 index. Buffett saw a company that was trading below book value, generating cash flow, and embarking on a divestiture program. Additionally, and most importantly, management was shareholder-oriented.

Although General Dynamics had earlier thought that the aircraft and space systems divisions would remain core holdings, Anders decided to sell these businesses. The aircraft business was sold to Lockheed. At the time, General Dynamics, Lockheed, and Boeing were one-third partners in the development of the next generation of tactical fighter, the F-22. By buying General Dynamics' aircraft division, Lockheed acquired the mature F-16 business and became a two-thirds partner with Boeing on the F-22 project. The space systems business was sold to Martin Marietta, maker of the Titan family of space launch vehicles. Together, selling the two businesses provided General Dynamics with $1.72 billion.

Flush with cash, the company again returned the money to its shareholders. In April 1993, the company issued a $20 per share special dividend to shareholders. In July the company issued an $18 special dividend, and in October gave $12 per share to its owners. In 1993, the company returned $50 in special dividends and raised the quarterly dividend from $0.40 to $0.60 per share. From July 1992 through the end of 1993, for its investment of $72 per share, Berkshire received $2.60 in common dividends, $50 in special dividends, and a share price that rose to $103. It amounted to a 116 percent return over 18 months. Not surprisingly, over this time period General Dynamics not only outperformed its peer group, but it also soundly beat the Standard & Poor's 500 index.

Wells Fargo & Company

If General Dynamics was the most confusing investment Buffett ever made, then the Wells Fargo & Company investment would certainly qualify as the most controversial. In October 1990, Buffett announced that Berkshire had purchased five million shares of Wells Fargo, investing $289 million in the company at an average $57.88 per share. Berkshire was now the largest shareholder of the bank, owning 10 percent of the shares outstanding.

Earlier in the year, Wells Fargo had traded as high as $86 per share, but then investors began abandoning California banks and thrifts. They feared the recession that was gripping the West Coast would soon cause wide loan losses in the commercial and residential real estate market. Since Wells Fargo had the most commercial real estate of any California bank, investors sold their stock and short sellers added to the downside pressure. The short interest in Wells

Fargo's stock jumped 77 percent in the month of October, about the same time that Buffett began purchasing shares in the company.

In the months following the announcement that Berkshire had become a major shareholder, the battle for Wells Fargo resembled a heavyweight fight. In one corner, Buffett was the bull, betting $289 million that Wells Fargo would increase in value. In the other corner, short sellers were the bears, betting that Wells Fargo, already down 49 percent for the year, was destined to fall further. The Feshbach brothers, the nation's biggest short sellers, were betting against Buffett. "Wells Fargo is a dead duck," said Tom Barton, a Dallas money manager for the Feshbachs. "I don't think it's right to call them a bankruptcy candidate but I think it's a teenager."[32] By that, Barton meant he thought that Wells Fargo would trade down into the teens. Buffett "is a famous bargain hunter and long-term investor," said George Salem, an analyst with Prudential Securities, but "California could become another Texas."[33] Salem was referring to the bank failures that had occurred in Texas during the decline in energy prices. Buffett "won't have to worry about who spends his fortune much longer," said John Liscio at *Barron's*, "not if he keeps trying to pick a bottom in bank stocks."[34]

Buffett was very familiar with the business of banking. In 1969, Berkshire Hathaway purchased 98 percent of the holdings of Illinois National Bank and Trust Company. Before the Bank Holding Act required Berkshire to divest its interest in the bank in 1979, Buffett reported the sales and earnings of the bank each year in Berkshire's annual reports. The bank took its place beside Berkshire's other controlled holdings.

Just as Jack Ringwalt helped Buffett understand the intricacy of the insurance business, Gene Abegg, who was chairman of Illinois National Bank, taught Buffett about the banking business. What he learned was banks were profitable businesses if they issued loans responsibly and curtailed costs. "Our experience has been that the manager of an already high-cost operation frequently is uncommonly resourceful in finding new ways to add to overhead," said Buffett, "while the manager of a tightly run operation usually continues to find additional methods to curtail costs, even when costs are already well below those of its competitors. No one has demonstrated this latter ability better than Gene Abegg."[35]

Tenet: Favorable Long-Term Prospects

Wells Fargo is not Coca-Cola, Buffett says. Under most circumstances, it is hard to imagine how Coca-Cola could fail as a business. But the banking business is different. Banks can fail and have, on many occasions. Most bank closures can be traced to management mistakes, Buffett points out, usually when they foolishly issue loans that a rational banker would never have considered. When assets are 20 times equity, which is common in the banking industry, any managerial foolishness involving even a small amount of assets can destroy a company's equity.

Still, it is not impossible for banks to be good investments, Buffett says. If management does its job, banks can generate a 20 percent return on equity. Although this is below what a Coca-Cola might earn, it is above the average return for most businesses. It is not necessary to be number one in your industry if you are a bank, Buffett explains. What counts is how you manage your assets, liabilities, and costs. Like insurance, banking is very much a commodity business. And as we know, in a commodity-like business, the actions of management are frequently the most distinguishing trait. In this respect, Buffett picked the best management team in banking. "With Wells Fargo," he states, "we think we have obtained the best managers in the business, Carl Reichardt and Paul Hazen. In many ways, the combination of Carl and Paul reminds me of another—Tom Murphy and Dan Burke at Capital Cities/ABC. Each pair is stronger than the sum of the parts."[36]

Tenet: Rationality

When Carl Reichardt became chairman of Wells Fargo in 1983, he began to transform the sluggish bank into a profitable business. From 1983 through 1990, Wells Fargo averaged returns of 1.3 percent on assets and 15.2 percent on equity. By 1990, it had become the tenth-largest bank in the country, with $56 billion in assets. Reichardt, like many managers that Buffett admires, is rational. Although he had not instigated stock buy-back programs or passed along special dividends, all of which reward shareholders, he does run Wells Fargo for the benefit of its owners. Like Tom Murphy at Capital Cities/ABC, he was legendary when it came to controlling costs. Once costs were under control, Reichardt never let up. He constantly searched for ways to improve profitability.

One measure of a bank's operating efficiency is the ratio of its operating (i.e., noninterest) expense to net interest income.[37] Wells Fargo's operating efficiencies were 20 to 30 percent better than First Interstate or Bank of America. Reichardt manages Wells Fargo like an entrepreneur. "We try to run this company like a business," he said. "Two and two is four. It's not seven or eight."[38]

When Buffett was buying Wells Fargo in 1990, the bank ended that year with the highest percentage of commercial real estate loans of any major bank in the country. Wells Fargo's $14.5 billion in commercial loans was five times its equity. Because California's recession was worsening, analysts figured that a large portion of the bank's commercial loans would sour. It was this that caused Wells Fargo's share price to decline in 1990 and 1991.

In the wake of the Federal Savings and Loan Insurance Corporation (FSLIC) debacle, bank examiners rigorously reviewed Wells Fargo's loan portfolio. They pressured the bank to set aside $1.3 billion in reserves for bad loans in 1991 and another $1.2 billion the following year. Because reserves were set aside every quarter, investors began to feel squeamish with each subsequent announcement. Instead of taking one large charge for loan reserves, the bank strung out the charges over a period of two years. Investors began to wonder whether the bank would ever reach the end of its problem loans.

After Berkshire announced its ownership of Wells Fargo in 1990, the stock price climbed briefly, reaching $98 in early 1991 and providing Berkshire with a $200 million profit. But then, in June 1991, the bank announced another charge to reserves and the stock price fell 13 points in two days to $74. Although the stock price recovered slightly in the fourth quarter of 1991, it became clear that Wells Fargo would have to take yet another charge against earnings for additions to its loan loss reserves. At year-end, the stock closed at $58 per share. After a roller coaster ride, Berkshire's investment was breaking even. "I underestimated the severity of both the California recession and the real estate troubles of the company," Buffett confessed.[39]

Tenet: Determine the Value

In 1990, Wells Fargo earned $711 million, an 18 percent increase over 1989. The next year, because of loan loss reserves, the bank earned $21 million. A year later, earnings increased slightly to $283 million—still less than half the earnings just two years earlier. Not surprisingly, there is an inverse relationship between a bank's earnings and its loan loss provisions. But if you remove Wells Fargo's loan loss provisions from the income statement, you uncover a company with dynamic earnings power. Since 1983, the bank's net interest income had grown at an 11.3 percent rate, and its noninterest income (investment fees, trust income, deposit charges) had grown at a 15.3 percent rate. If you exclude the unusual loan loss provisions in 1991 and 1992, the bank would have had approximately $1 billion in earnings power.

The value of a bank is the function of its net worth plus its projected earnings as a going concern. When Berkshire Hathaway began purchasing Wells Fargo in 1990, the company, in the previous year, had earned $600 million. The average yield on the 30-year U.S. government bond in 1990 was approximately 8.5 percent. To remain conservative, we can discount Wells Fargo's 1989 earnings of $600 million by 9 percent and value the bank at $6.6 billion. If the bank never earned another dime over $600 million in annual earnings during the next 30 years, it was worth at least $6.6 billion. When Buffett purchased Wells Fargo in 1990, he paid $58 per share for its stock. With 52 million shares outstanding, this was equivalent to buying the company for $3 billion, a 55 percent discount to its value.

Of course, the debate over Wells Fargo centered on whether the company, after taking into consideration all of its loan problems, even had earnings power. The short sellers said it did not; Buffett said it did. He knew that ownership of Wells Fargo was not riskless. This is how he rationalized his purchase: "California banks face the specific risk of a major earthquake, which might wreak enough havoc on borrowers to in turn destroy the banks lending to them," Buffett said. "A second risk is systemic—the possibility of a business contraction or financial panic so severe that it would endanger almost every highly-leveraged institution, no matter how intelligently run."[40] Now, the possibility of these two events occurring, in Buffett's judgment, was low. But there still remained one viable risk, he said. "The market's major fear of the moment is that West Coast real estate values will tumble because of overbuilding and deliver huge losses to banks that financed the expansion. Because it is a leading real estate lender, Wells Fargo is thought to be particularly vulnerable."[41]

Buffett knew that Wells Fargo earned $1 billion pretax annually after expensing an average $300 million for loan losses. He figured if 10 percent of the bank's $48 billion in loans (not just commercial loans, but all of the bank's loans) were problem loans in 1991 and produced losses, including interest, averaging 30 percent of the principal, Wells Fargo would break even. He calculated that this was unlikely. Even if Wells Fargo earned no money for a year, that would not be distressing. "At Berkshire," Buffett said, "we would love to acquire businesses or invest in capital projects that produce no return for a year, but that could then be expected to earn 20% on growing equity."[42] The attraction of Wells Fargo intensified when Buffett was able to purchase shares at a 50 percent discount to value.

"Banking doesn't have to be a bad business, but it often is," Buffett said, adding that "bankers don't have to do stupid things, but they often do."[43] He describes a high-risk loan as any loan made by a stupid banker. When Buffett purchased Wells Fargo, he bet that Reichardt was not a stupid banker. "It's all a bet on management," said Charlie Munger. "We think they will fix the problems faster and better than other people."[44] Berkshire's bet paid off. By the end of 1993, Wells Fargo's price per share had reached $137.

American Express Company

"I find that a long-term familiarity with a company and its products is often helpful in evaluating it," Buffett said.[45] With the exception of selling bottles of Coca-Cola for a nickel, delivering copies of the *Washington Post*, and recommending that his father's clients buy shares of GEICO, Buffett has had a longer history with American Express than any other company Berkshire owns. You may recall that in the mid-1960s, the Buffett Limited Partnership invested 40 percent of its assets in American Express shortly after the company's losses in the salad oil scandal. Thirty years later, Berkshire accumulated 10 percent of American Express shares for $1.4 billion.

Tenet: Consistent Operating History

Although the company has weathered a cycle of changes, American Express is essentially the same business it was when Buffett first purchased the company in his Partnership. There were three divisions. Travel Related Services (TRS), which issues the American Express charge card and American Express Travelers Cheques, contributed about 72 percent of American Express's sales. American Express Financial Advisors (formerly IDS Financial Services), a financial planning, insurance, and investment product division, contributed 22 percent of sales. The American Express Bank contributed a modest 5 percent of sales. The bank had long been the local representative for the American Express card with a network of 87 offices in 37 countries worldwide.

American Express Travel Related Services continues to be a predictable provider of profits. The division had always generated substantial owner earnings and easily funded the company's growth. But when a company generates more cash than it requires for operations, it often becomes a test of management to allocate this capital responsibly. Some managers pass this test by investing only that capital that is required and returning the balance to the company's owners either by increasing the dividend or by repurchasing shares. Other managers, unable to resist the institutional imperative, constantly find ways to spend cash and expand the corporate empire.

Unfortunately, this was the fate of American Express for several years under the leadership of James Robinson.

Robinson's plan was to use TRS's excess cash to acquire related businesses and thus build American Express into a financial services powerhouse. IDS proved to be a profitable purchase. However, Robinson's purchase of Shearson-Lehman was disappointing. Not only was Shearson unable to fund itself, but it also required increasing amounts of TRS's excess cash for its own operation. Over time, Robinson invested $4 billion in Shearson. It was this financial drain that prompted Robinson to contact Buffett. Berkshire purchased $300 million in preferred shares. Although Buffett was willing to invest in American Express at that time via preferred shares, it was not until rationality finally surfaced at the company that he felt confident to become a common stock shareholder.

Tenet: Rationality

It is no secret that the company's crown jewel is the famed American Express Card. What seemed to be lacking at American Express was a management team that recognized and appreciated the economics of this business. Fortunately, this realization occurred in 1992, when Robinson unceremoniously resigned and Harvey Golub became chief executive. Golub, striking a familiar tone with Buffett, began to use terms such as *franchise* and *brand value* when he referred to the American Express Card. Golub's immediate task was to strengthen the brand awareness of TRS and shore up the capital structure at Shearson-Lehman to ready it for sale.

Over the next two years, Golub began the process of liquidating American Express's underperforming assets and restoring profitability and high returns on equity. In 1992, Golub initiated a public offering for First Data Corporation (the company's information data service division), which netted American Express over $1 billion. The following year, the company sold The Boston Company, its money management division, to Mellon Bank for $1.5 billion. Soon after, Shearson-Lehman was separated into two businesses. Shearson's retail accounts were sold and Lehman

Brothers was spun off to American Express shareholders via a tax-free distribution, but not before Golub had to pump a final $1 billion into Lehman.

By 1994, American Express was beginning to show signs of its old profitable self. The resources of the company were now firmly behind TRS. The goal of management was to build the American Express Card into the "world's most respected service brand." Every communication from the company emphasized the franchise value of the name American Express. Even IDS Financial Services was renamed American Express Financial Advisors.

Now that everything was in place, Golub set the financial targets for the company: to increase earnings per share by 12 to 15 percent annually and to achieve an 18 to 20 percent return on equity. Then American Express, in September 1994, issued a statement that demonstrated clearly the rationality of the company's new management. Subject to market conditions, the board of directors authorized management to repurchase 20 million shares of its common stock. That was music to Buffett's ears.

During the summer of 1994, Buffett converted Berkshire's preferred issue into American Express common stock. Soon thereafter, he began to acquire even more shares of common stock. By year-end, Berkshire owned 27 million shares at an average price of $25 per share. With the completion of the stock purchase plan it had announced in the fall of 1994, the following spring American Express announced it would repurchase an additional 40 million shares, representing 8 percent of the total stock outstanding.

Clearly, American Express was a changed company. After jettisoning Shearson-Lehman with its massive capital needs, American Express had a powerful ability to generate excess cash. For the first time, the company had more capital and more shares than needed. Buffett, appreciating the economic changes that were under way at American Express, dramatically increased Berkshire's position in the company. By March 1995, he had added another 20 million shares, bringing Berkshire's ownership of American Express to slightly less than 10 percent.

Tenet: Determine the Value

Since 1990, the noncash charges, depreciation, and amortization have roughly equaled American Express's acquisition of land, buildings, and equipment. When depreciation and amortization charges approximate capital spending, owner earnings equal net income. However, because of the company's erratic history, it is difficult to ascertain the growth rate of American Express's owner earnings. Under these circumstances, it is best to use a very conservative growth projection.

By the end of 1994, reflecting the results of American Express's net of the subsidiaries sold in 1993, the company's owner earnings were approximately $1.4 billion. Golub's goal, you will remember, was to grow earnings at a 12 to 15 percent rate going forward. Using a 10 percent growth in earnings for the next 10 years followed by a 5 percent residual growth thereafter (which is decidedly below management's forecast) and discounting the earnings by 10 percent (which is a conservative discount factor considering the 30-year U.S. Treasury bond was yielding 8 percent), the intrinsic value of American Express was $43.4 billion, or $87 per share. If the company was able to grow its earnings at 12 percent, the intrinsic value of American Express was closer to $50 billion, or $100 per share. At the more conservative valuation, Buffett was purchasing American Express at a 70 percent discount to intrinsic value—a significant margin of safety.

International Business Machines

When Buffett announced during a CNBC interview in October 2011 that Berkshire Hathaway had been purchasing shares of IBM, I am sure more than a few Berkshire shareholders were scratching their heads. After all, this was the man who had repeatedly confessed that he was not interested in buying technology companies. "I could spend all my time thinking about technology for the next year and still not be the 100th, 1,000th or even the 10,000th smartest guy in the country in analyzing those businesses," he once said.[46]

What prevented Buffett from buying technology companies was not that he didn't understand these companies; he understood them all too well. What had always troubled him was the difficulty of predicting their future cash flows. The constant disruption and innovation that is inherent in the industry made the life spans of technology franchises very short. Buffett could see a future that included Coca-Cola, Wells Fargo, American Express, Johnson & Johnson, Procter & Gamble, Kraft Foods, and Wal-Mart, and think confidently. A future that included Microsoft, Cisco, Oracle, Intel, and—so we thought—IBM was just too unpredictable.

But by year-end 2011, Berkshire Hathaway had purchased 63.9 million shares of IBM, about 5.4 percent of the company. It was a bold $10.8 billion purchase, the single biggest purchase of an individual stock Buffett had ever made.

Tenet: Rationality

When Buffett introduced the IBM purchase to Berkshire shareholders in the 2011 annual report, many might have thought they would be getting a crash course on the competitive advantages of IBM's advance information processing technology. But what they got instead was a tutorial on the value of common stock repurchases and how to think intelligently about this corporate strategy over the long term.

Buffett began, "All business observers know, CEOs Lou Gerstner and Sam Palmisano did a super job in moving IBM from near-bankruptcy twenty years ago to its prominence today. Their operational accomplishments were truly extraordinary."[47] It is hard to imagine that 20 years ago, the hundred-year-old IBM was near collapse. But in 1992, the company lost $5 billion, the most money any U.S. company had ever lost in a single year. The next year Lou Gerstner was brought in to turn the company around. In his book *Who Says Elephants Can't Dance?* (HarperCollins, 2002), Gerstner outlined his strategies, including selling low-margin hardware technology assets and moving more into software and services. Later, when Sam Palmisano became CEO in 2002, he sold off the personal computer business and kept IBM growing for the next 10 years by focusing its business on services, the Internet, and software.

"Their financial management was equally brilliant," Buffett continued. "I can think of no major company that has had better financial management, a skill that has materially increased the gains enjoyed by IBM shareholders. The company has used debt wisely, made value-adding acquisitions almost exclusively for cash and aggressively repurchased its own stock."[48]

In 1993, IBM had 2.3 billion shares outstanding. Ten years later, when Gerstner retired and Palmisano became CEO, the company had 1.7 billion shares outstanding. Over the 10 years, Gerstner bought back 26 percent of the shares outstanding while raising the dividends by 136 percent. This lesson was not lost on Palmisano. During his 10-year reign as CEO, IBM reduced shares outstanding from 1.7 billion to 1.1 billion, a 36 percent reduction. Combined, Gerstner and Palmisano repurchased over half of the shares outstanding. And if that was not enough, Palmisano, in the decade he ran the company, increased the dividend from $0.59 to $3.30, a 460 percent increase.

Of the four technology horsemen—IBM, Microsoft, Intel, and Cisco—only one company has seen its recent share price surpass its 1999 high—the peak of the tech bubble. And that is IBM. At year-end 1999, IBM was selling at $112 per share and by the end of 2012 it was trading for $191. Compare this to Cisco ($54 to $19), Intel ($42 to $20), and Microsoft ($52 to $27). It was not that IBM grew the company faster than the others, but rather that its share price went up because it grew the per-share value faster. Between 1999 and 2012, Microsoft reduced shares by 19 percent and Intel and Cisco both reduced shares outstanding by 23 percent, but IBM reduced its shares outstanding by 36 percent.

Remember Buffett's notion: that after he begins buying shares in a company, he likes the stock market to delay its recognition, for that gives him the opportunity to buy more shares at bargain prices. The same is true for a company that is in the midst of a share repurchase program. "When Berkshire buys stock in a company that is repurchasing shares, we hope for two events: First, we have the normal hope that earnings of the business will increase at a good clip for a long time to come; and second, we also hope that the stock *underperforms* in the market for a long time as well." As Buffett explains, IBM will likely spend $50 billion over the next five years to repurchase stock. He then asks, "What should a long-term shareholder, such as Berkshire, cheer for during that period? We should wish for IBM's stock price to languish throughout the five years."[49]

In a world that is obsessed with short-term performance, wishing for a stock to underperform the market for a long time sounds backward, to say the least. But if one is truly a long-term investor, such thinking is actually quite rational. Buffett walks us through the math. "If IBM's stock price averages say $200, the company will acquire 250 million shares for its $50 billion. There would consequently be 910 million shares outstanding and we would own about 7% of the company. If the stock conversely sells for an average of $300 during the five-year period, IBM will acquire only 167 million shares. That would leave about 990 million shares outstanding after five years, of which we would own 6.5%."[50] The difference to Berkshire is significant. At the lower stock price, Berkshire would increase its share of earnings by $100 million, which five years down the road might mean an increase in value of $1.5 billion.

Tenet: Favorable Long-Term Prospects

Buffett confessed that he came late to the IBM party. Like Coca-Cola in 1988 and Burlington Northern Santa-Fe in 2006, he had been reading the annual reports for 50 years before his epiphany. It arrived, he said, one Saturday in March 2011. Quoting Thoreau, Buffett says, "It's not what you look at that matters; it's what you see." Buffett admitted to CNBC that he had been "hit between the eyes" by the competitive advantages IBM possesses in finding and keeping clients.[51]

The information technology (IT) services industry is a dynamic and global industry within the technology sector, and no one is bigger in this industry than IBM.[52] Information technology is an $800 billion plus market that covers a broad spectrum of services broken down into four different buckets: consulting, systems integration,

IT outsourcing, and business process outsourcing. The first two, combined, contribute 52 percent of IBM's revenues; 32 percent comes from IT outsourcing; and 16 percent from business process outsourcing. In the consulting and systems integration space, IBM is the number-one global provider—38 percent bigger than the next competitor, Accenture. In the IT outsourcing space, IBM is also the number-one global provider—78 percent larger than the next competitor, Hewlett-Packard. In business process outsourcing, IBM is the seventh-largest provider, behind Teleperformance, Atento, Convergys, Sitel, Aegis, and Genpact.

Information technology services are considered to be a growth-defensive industry within the technology sector. Whereas technology sectors like hardware and semiconductors are more cyclical in nature, the services sector benefits from relatively stable growth prospects. The IT industry is more resilient because its revenues are both recurring and tied to the nondiscretionary budgets of larger corporations and governments. So important are IT services that consulting, systems integration, and IT outsourcing are thought to have "moatlike" qualities. According to Grady Burkett, associate director of technology at Morningstar, the intangible assets like reputation, track record, and client relationships are the sources of a moat in consulting and systems integration. In IT outsourcing, switching costs and scale advantages create their own moat, ensuring that once IBM lands a customer, that customer is likely to remain a loyal client for many years to come. Only one area, the relatively small business process outsourcing, is not protected by either the intangible assets or the cost of switching.

According to Gartner, the world's leading information technology research and advisory company, the total market for IT services is expected to grow at a compounded annual rate of 4.6 percent, from an estimated $844 billion in 2011 to $1.05 trillion in 2016.

Tenets: Profit Margins; Return on Equity; One-Dollar Premise

The move away from hardware technology to consulting and software begun by Lou Gerstner and accelerated by Sam Palmisano transformed IBM away from the low-margin, commoditized part of the technology industry to the higher-margin, moat-protected business of consulting, systems integration, and IT outsourcing. When Gerstner righted the ship in 1994, the return on equity at IBM was 14 percent. When he retired in 2002, return on equity had increased to 35 percent. Palmisano kept the ball rolling by moving return on equity even higher; it had reached 62 percent by the time he retired in 2012.

Part of the increase in return on equity can be attributed to the dramatic reduction in equity shares outstanding. But the more significant reason was the decision to leave behind low-margin businesses while dramatically growing the higher-margin businesses of consulting and outsourcing. In 2002, net profit margins at IBM were 8.5 percent. Ten years later, net margins had almost doubled to 15.6 percent.

Over 10 years (2002–2011), IBM generated a net profit for shareholders of $108 billion. It paid $20 billion to shareholders in the form of dividends, leaving it with $88 billion to run its business, which included capital reinvestments, acquisitions, and share repurchases. During this same period, the market capitalization of IBM gained $80 billion. This is not quite the one dollar of market value for each dollar retained that Buffett would prefer to see in his companies, but considering that the past 10 years had been a dreadful period for the performance of large-capitalization stocks, it is still respectable.

Tenet: Determine the Value

In 2010, IBM generated a net profit for shareholders of $14.8 billion. That year it spent $4.2 billion in capital expenditures, more than offset by $4.8 billion in depreciation and amortization charges. The net result was $15.4 billion in owner earnings. What is a business that in a year generates $15.4 billion in cash worth? According to John Burr Williams (and Warren Buffett), the value is the future cash flows of the business discounted back to the present value. The future cash flows will be determined by the growth of the company, and the discount rate that Buffett uses is the long-term U.S. government bond yield, his definition of a risk-free rate. Remember, Buffett does not use an equity risk premium in his calculations. Instead, he adjusts for riskiness by the margin of safety represented by the price he is willing to pay.

Using this theory, we can make our own calculation of IBM's value. Using a two-stage dividend discount model, I assumed IBM would grow its cash earnings at 7 percent for 10 years and 5 percent after that. I then discounted these cash flows by 10 percent—substantially higher than the 2 percent of the 10-year U.S. Treasury note. The higher discount rate simply builds in a greater margin of safety. Based on these calculations, IBM is worth $326 per share, much higher than the average $169 price Buffett paid. If we adjust the growth rate for the next 10 years down to 5 percent, closer to Gartner's estimate of the IT services industry's growth, the value is $279 per share, still $100 per share higher than what Buffett paid.

Another way to look at the valuation question is to ask what growth rates are embedded in a $169 share price. To be worth $169 per share, IBM would have to grow its owner earnings at 2 percent in perpetuity. Readers might quibble at a $326 or $279 estimate of fair value for a share of IBM. But just as many, I suspect, would argue that IBM will grow faster than 2 percent per year over the next decade. The fair value answer, I am sure, lies somewhere in between these two estimates, reminding us again of one of Buffett's favorite maxims: "I would rather be approximately right than precisely wrong."

In many ways, the IBM purchase reminds me of Buffett's purchase of the Coca-Cola Company. At the time, many critics were puzzled. Buffett had bought the stock near its all-time high (just like IBM). Many believed Coca-Cola was a boring, slow-growing company whose best days were behind it (just like IBM). When Buffett purchased Coca-Cola, the company's share price was 15 times earnings and 12 times cash flow, a 30 percent and 50 percent premium to the market average. When we ran the dividend discount model on Coca-Cola's owner earnings using various growth rates, we found the company was selling for a significant discount to fair value despite the premium price-to-earnings and price-to-cash-flow ratios.

Assuming an unbelievably low 5 percent growth rate for Coca-Cola, the dividend discount model said Coca-Cola was worth $20.7 billion—far higher than its current market value of $15.1 billion.

Over the next 10 years, Coca-Cola's share price went up tenfold versus the Standard & Poor's 500 index, which increased threefold. A caution flag: I am certainly not saying that IBM can go up tenfold over the next 10 years, only that Wall Street's method of using accounting ratios to determine value may capture the here and now but does a woefully poor job of calculating sustainable long-term growth. Or, put differently, more often than not, sustainable long-term growth is mispriced by the market.

Make no mistake—the greatest impact on IBM's future success will be the company's future earnings. Toni Sacconaghi, technology analyst at Sanford C. Bernstein, calls the company "fortress IBM, a company whose profit performance seems all but impervious to industry cycles." Toni has gone so far as to call IBM, the largest global supplier of information technology to corporations and governments, "boringly predictable."[53] Boringly predictable was what they said about Coca-Cola in 1989. Boringly predictable is just the kind of company Buffett likes best.

We have also learned that financial management is a very important secondary factor in determining a company's success. The legacy left by Gerstner and Palmisano will no doubt have a big influence on Ginni Rometty, IBM's new CEO. Already, IBM's Financial Model and Business Perspective (a five-year plan) includes $50 billion for future share repurchases. At IBM's current share repurchase rate, the company may be down to less than 100 million shares outstanding by 2030. Of course, no one can say for sure that IBM will maintain its current share repurchase rate. But that doesn't stop Buffett from dreaming. He told shareholders. "If repurchases ever reduce the IBM shares outstanding to 63.9 million, I will abandon my famed frugality and give Berkshire employees a paid holiday."[54]

H.J. Heinz Company

On February 14, 2013, Berkshire Hathaway and 3G Capital purchased H.J. Heinz Company for $23 billion. At $72.50 per share, the deal was a 20 percent premium to Heinz's share price the day before.

It was easy to see how Heinz fit the Berkshire Hathaway mold. One of the best-known food companies in the world, it has global recognition that approaches that of Coca-Cola and IBM. Heinz's deep red ketchup bottles can be found in millions of homes alongside Ore-Ida french fries and Lea & Perrins Worcestershire sauce. In 2012, the company reported $11.6 billion in revenue with a majority of ıles coming from Europe and the rapidly expanding emerging markets. "It's our kind of company," said Buffett.[55]

Tenet: Consistent Operating History

Eighteen years before the pharmacist John Pemberton invented the formula for Coca-Cola, Henry J. Heinz was packing foodstuffs in Sharpsburg, Pennsylvania. The company first began selling horseradish sauce in 1869 but turned to tomato ketchup in 1876. Henry Heinz bought out his two partners in 1888 and renamed the company H.J. Heinz Company. The company's famous slogan "57 varieties" was introduced in 1896. It is said Henry Heinz was riding an elevated train in New York City one day when he spotted a shoe store that claimed it had "21 styles." Heinz picked the number "57" at random but selected the number "7" specifically because of its positive psychological influence. Buffett noted that 1869, when Heinz was started, was the same year his great-grandfather Sidney founded a grocery store.

Tenet: Favorable Long-Term Prospects

Heinz is number one in ketchup globally and second in sauces. The future of Heinz depends on not only maintaining its market share leadership but also positioning itself in the rapidly growing emerging markets. Here Heinz is well positioned. The company bought Foodstar of China in 2010 and an 80 percent stake in Brazilian Coniexpress SA Industrias Alimeticias in 2011. Today, emerging markets account for seven of the company's top 10 markets. Already, the value of Foodstar in China has doubled.

How important are emerging markets to Heinz? Over the past five years, these rapidly growing markets have accounted for over 80 percent of the company's sales growth. In fiscal 2012, 21 percent of revenue came from emerging markets; estimates for fiscal year 2013 are for close to 25 percent. According to CEO William Johnson, the company's organic growth rate in emerging markets is among the best in its peer group.

Tenet: Determine the Value

In 2012, Heinz reported $923 million in net income, $342 million in depreciation and amortization charges, and $418 million in capital expenditures, leaving shareholders with $847 million in owner earnings. But in the company's annual report we note that $163 million was an after-tax charge for severance, asset writedowns, and other implementation costs. Adding back these nonoperational expenses, we can estimate that the company generated about $1 billion in owner earnings.

Using a two-stage dividend discount model, we estimated the company would grow its $1 billion in owner earnings at a 7 percent rate for 10 years, then 5 percent thereafter. Discounting the cash flows at 9 percent (which is the cost of the preferred stock Berkshire contributed to the deal) produces an estimated per-share value of $96.40. At a slower 5 percent constant growth rate in perpetuity, the company's shares would be worth $82.10. Considering that the company has grown its earnings per share at an 8.4 percent compounded annual growth rate over the past five years, and knowing that the next five years will see a larger portion of its earnings coming from the rapidly growing emerging markets, I would argue these valuation estimates are very conservative.

Tenet: Buy at Attractive Prices

If the company can grow at 7 percent for 10 years then 5 percent thereafter, Buffett bought the shares at a 25 percent discount to intrinsic value. At the very conservative estimated growth rate of 5 percent, he bought the company at a 12 percent discount.

Admittedly, these are not the margin-of-safety discounts we usually see in Buffett's purchases. But the attractiveness of the Heinz purchase goes beyond the usual discount formula.

Berkshire Hathaway and the Brazilian private equity firm 3G Capital will each own half of Heinz for $4 billion in equity. To that, Berkshire invested $8 billion in redeemable preferred stock yielding 9 percent. The preferred shares also have two other attractive features for Berkshire. First, at some point in the future the preferred will be redeemed at a significant premium; second, the preferred shares come with warrants that will allow Berkshire to buy 5 percent of the company's common stock for a nominal amount. All in all, Berkshire Hathaway will earn a 6 percent annual return on its blended investment, excluding the value of the warrants, the premium conversion of the preferred shares, and any future growth in the intrinsic value of the company. Even if Heinz loses money, Berkshire Hathaway will be paid its preferred dividend. And even in the remote possibility that Heintz would go bankrupt, Berkshire would be in a position to wipe out other creditors and position itself favorably in a newly and cheaply reorganized Heinz.

Tenet: Rationality

It is easy to see how Heinz fits the profile of the type of company Buffett likes to purchase. The business is simple and understandable; it has had a consistent operating history; and, because it has positioned itself to benefit from the growth of emerging markets, the company has favorable long-term prospects. The return on investable capital (including debt) is 17 percent, with a return on shareholders' equity of 35 percent.

But there are two caveats to the Heinz deal that make this purchase unique. First, the company will carry $6 of debt for every $1 of equity. Interest on the debt along with the 9 percent preferred dividend paid to Berkshire Hathaway will command much of the company's owner earnings. In a word, the company is now highly leveraged. Second, the company will be run by a new management team at 3G Capital led by Brazil's richest man, Jorge Paulo Lemann.

In the past, when Buffett bought a company, he preferred to have the existing management team continue to run the business. But in this case, a new management team will be responsible for the future of Heinz.

Buffett first met Lemann when both were on the board of Gillette in the 1990s. Although Lemann and 3G Capital are not well known in the United States, this team has had tremendous success with fast-food restaurants, banks, and brewers. In 2004, in what is considered his watershed deal, Lemann merged his smaller Brazilian beer company AmBev with Belgium's much larger Interbrew, the maker of Stella Artois and Beck's. Even though AmBev was smaller, it was Lemann's associates who took the senior jobs at the combined company. Then in 2008, this newly merged company paid $52 billion for Anheuser-Busch in what is now the largest beer merger ever.

In 2010, 3G Capital bought Burger King for $3.3 billion. Within weeks, the company had fired half the 600 employees at its Miami headquarters, sold off the executive wing, and henceforth required employees to get permission to make color printouts. Since the acquisition, 3G Capital has cut the operating costs by 30 percent. In the meantime, each restaurant introduced new products, including smoothies and snack wraps, and orchestrated a remodeling campaign paid for by the franchise owners. In its fourth quarter 2012 report, Burger King noted a doubled profit and improved cash flows.

In studying the management profile of 3G Capital and the success it has had with each of its deals, I am reminded of another manager whom Buffett considered one of the best in the world, Tom Murphy. The same passion that drove Murphy to slash unnecessary costs and improve the productivity of Cap Cities/ABC businesses is evident in the management team at 3G Capital.

Some have suggested that 3G Capital, being a private equity firm, will look to sell its Heinz investment sooner rather than later. But Lemann insists that 3G Capital intends to hold Heinz for the long term in much the same way it has become a long-term owner of Anheuser-Busch InBev N.V. Just as AmBev served as a platform for the consolidation and future growth of the beer business, so too could Heinz serve as an early platform for the consolidation and future growth of the food industry.

Whether 3G Capital stays or not, Buffett is happy to be a long-term owner. "Heinz will be 3G's baby," says Buffett. But of course he adds that "we may increase our ownership if any members of the 3G Group want to sell out later."[56]

A Common Theme

You may have noticed a standard refrain in these case studies: Warren Buffett is in no hurry to sell, even when the stocks he purchases are doing well. Short-term appreciation doesn't interest him. Philip Fisher taught him that either the investment you hold is a better investment than cash or it is not. Buffett says that he is "quite content to hold any security indefinitely, so long as the prospective return on equity capital of the underlying business is satisfactory, management is competent and honest, and the market does not overvalue the business."[57] (Recognize the tenets in that statement?) As he reminds shareholders, his favorite holding period is "forever."

And with that memorable statement, Buffett takes us to the other side of the coin: Having made rational decisions about which stocks to buy, how should we think about managing the portfolio? That is the subject of the next chapter.

CHAPTER 5

Portfolio Management

THE MATHEMATICS OF INVESTING

Let's recap: So far we have studied Warren Buffett's approach to buying a business or selecting stocks (he, of course, considers them the exact same thing). It is an approach built on timeless principles codified into 12 tenets. We have seen how these principles were applied in many Berkshire purchases, including the well-known classic purchase of Coca-Cola and the recent one of IBM. And we have taken the time to understand how the insights from others helped shape his philosophy of investing.

But, as every investor knows, deciding which stocks to buy is only half the story. The other half of the story is managing the portfolio, which, in turn, is a combination of portfolio construction and ongoing management.

When we think about managing our portfolios, we often believe it is a simple process of deciding what to buy, sell, or hold. These decisions are (or should be, if you want to think like Buffett) determined by the margin of safety, which he measures by comparing today's stock price to its intrinsic value. You buy great businesses when the price is far below that value, hold them when the price is modestly below, and sell them when the price is significantly higher.

However, the margin-of-safety approach, while crucial, is not sufficient in itself. We must also take into account three important portfolio management constructs that Buffett has developed:

1. His way of building a portfolio for long-term growth.
2. His alternative measuring stick for judging the progress of a portfolio.
3. His techniques for coping with the emotional roller coaster that inevitably accompanies portfolio management. (The psychological challenges of managing a Warren Buffett portfolio are fully discussed in Chapter 6.)

Hollywood has given us a visual cliché of what money managers look like: talking into two phones at once, frantically taking notes while trying to keep an eye on a bank of computer screens that blink and blip endlessly, and showing pained expressions whenever one of those computer blinks shows a minuscule drop in a stock price.

Warren Buffett is far from that kind of frenzy. He moves with the calm that comes with great confidence. He has no need to watch a dozen computer screens at once; the minute-by-minute changes in the market are of no interest to him. Warren Buffett does not think in seconds, minutes, days, months, or quarters, but in years. He doesn't need to keep up with hundreds of companies, because his common stock investments are focused in a select few. He refers to himself as a "focus investor"—"We just focus on a few outstanding companies."[1] This approach, called focus investing, greatly simplifies the task of portfolio management.

Focus investing is a remarkably simple idea, and yet, like most simple ideas, it rests on a complex foundation of interlocking concepts. In this chapter, we look more closely at the effects focus investing produces. The goal here is to give you a new way of thinking about portfolio management. Fair warning: In all likelihood, this new way is the opposite of what you have always been told about investing in the stock market.

The current state of portfolio management appears to be locked into a tug-of-war between two competing strategies: (1) active portfolio management and (2) index investing.

Active portfolio managers are constantly at work buying and selling a great number of common stocks. Their job is to try to keep their clients satisfied, or risk losing clients and ultimately their jobs. To stay on top, active managers try to predict what will happen with stocks in the coming months so at the end of the quarter the portfolio is in good relative shape and the client is happy.

Index investing, in contrast, is a buy-and-hold approach. It involves assembling and then holding a broadly diversified portfolio of common stocks deliberately designed to mimic the behavior of a specific benchmark index, such as the Standard & Poor's 500.

Active portfolio managers argue that, by virtue of their superior stock-picking skills, they can do better than any index. Index strategists, for their part, have history on their side. Annually, from 1980 through 2011, only 41 percent of large-cap mutual funds beat the S&P 500 index.[2]

From an investor's point of view, the underlying attraction of both strategies is the same: to minimize risk through diversification. By holding a large number of stocks representing many industries and many sectors of the market, investors hope to build in a warm blanket of protection against horrific loss that could occur if they had all their money in one arena and that arena suffered some disaster. In a normal period, so the thinking goes, some stocks in a diversified portfolio will go down and others will go up, so let's keep our fingers crossed that the latter will compensate for the former.

Active managers achieve this protection by loading up their portfolios. In their view, the more stocks the portfolio contains, the better their chances. Ten stocks are better than one, and 100 stocks are better than 10. An index fund, by definition, affords this kind of diversification if the index it mirrors is also diversified. So does the traditional stock mutual fund, which has upwards of 100 stocks.

There's just one problem: We have all heard this mantra of diversification for so long that we have become intellectually numb to its inevitable consequence: mediocre results. Both active and index funds do offer diversification, but, in general, neither strategy will give you exceptional returns.

What does Buffett say about this ongoing debate? Given these two particular choices, indexing versus an active strategy, he would unhesitatingly pick indexing. So would investors who have a low tolerance for risk, and people who know very little about the economics of a business but still want to participate in the long-term benefits of investing in common stocks. "By periodically investing in an index fund," Buffett says in his inimitable style, "the know-nothing investors can actually outperform most investment professionals."[3]

Buffett, however, would be quick to point out that there is a third alternative, a very different kind of active portfolio strategy that significantly increases the odds of beating the index. That alternative is *focus* investing. Reduced to its essence, focus investing means this: Choose a few stocks that are likely to produce above-average returns over the long haul, concentrate the bulk of your investments in those stocks, and have the fortitude to hold steady during any short-term market gyrations.

The Warren Buffett tenets, if followed closely, lead inevitably to good companies that make sense for a focus portfolio. The companies chosen will have a long history of superior performance and a stable management, and that stability points toward a high probability that they will perform in the future as they have in the past. That is the heart of focus investing: concentrating your investments in companies with the highest probability of above-average performance. (Probability theory, which comes to us from the field of mathematics, is one of the underlying concepts that make up the rationale for focus investing. We will learn more about probability theory later in this chapter.)

Remember Buffett's advice to a "know-nothing" investor, to stay with index funds? What is more interesting is what he said next: "If you are a know-something investor, able to understand business economics, and can locate five to ten sensibly priced companies that possess important long-term competitive advantages, conventional diversification makes no sense for you."[4]

What's wrong with conventional diversification? For one thing, it greatly increases the chances that you will buy something you don't know enough about. "Know-something" investors, applying the Buffett tenets, would do better to focus their attention on just a few companies—five to 10, Buffett suggests. For the average investor, a legitimate case can be made for investing in 10 to 20 companies.

As we know from Chapter 2, Buffett's thinking was greatly influenced by Philip Fisher, and we clearly see Fisher's hand in this area—portfolio management. Fisher was known for his focus portfolios; he always said he preferred owning a small number of outstanding companies that he understood well, rather than a large number of average companies, many of which he understood poorly. As we have seen, Fisher generally limited his portfolios to fewer than 10 companies, of which three or four represented 75 percent of the total investment.

Fisher's influence on Buffett can also be seen in his belief that the only reasonable course, when you encounter a strong opportunity, is to make a large investment. Today, Buffett echoes that thinking. "With each investment you make, you should have the courage and conviction to place at least ten percent of your net worth in that stock."[5]

You can see why Buffett says the ideal portfolio should contain no more than 10 stocks, if each is to receive a 10 percent weighting. Yet focus investing is not a simple matter of finding 10 good stocks and dividing an investment pool equally among them. Even though all the stocks in a focus portfolio are high-probability bets, some will inevitably be higher-probability than others, and they should be allowed a greater proportion of the investment.

Blackjack players understand this strategy intuitively; when the odds are strongly in their favor, they put down a big bet. Investors and gamblers draw from the same science: mathematics. Along with probability theory, mathematics provides another piece of the focus investing rationale: the Kelly optimization model, which is described in detail later in the chapter. The Kelly formula uses probability to calculate optimization—in this case, the optimal size bet one should make in the portfolio.

Focus investing is the antithesis of a broadly diversified high-turnover approach. Although focus investing stands the best chance, among all active strategies, of outperforming an index return over time, it does require investors to patiently hold their portfolios when it appears that other strategies are marching ahead. In shorter periods, we realize that changes in interest rates, inflation, or near-term expectations for a company's earnings can affect share prices. But as the time horizon lengthens, the trendline economics of the underlying business will increasingly dominate its share price.

How long is that ideal time? There is no hard-and-fast rule, although Buffett would probably say five years since this is the time period he is focusing on for Berkshire Hathaway's results. The goal is not a zero turnover ratio; that's foolish in the opposite direction, for it would prevent you from taking advantage of something better when it comes along. I suggest that, as a general rule of thumb, we should be thinking of a turnover rate between 10 and 20 percent. A 10 percent turnover rate suggests that an investor holds the stock for 10 years; a 20 percent rate implies a five-year period.

Focus investing pursues above-average results, and, as we will see, there is strong evidence, both academic research and actual case histories, that the approach is successful when thoughtfully applied. There can be no doubt, however, that the ride is bumpy, for an increased level of price volatility is a necessary by-product of the focus approach. Focus investors tolerate the bumpiness because they know that, in the long run, the underlying economics of the companies will more than compensate for any short-term price fluctuations.

Buffett is the master bump ignorer. So is his partner Charlie Munger, who came to the fundamental concept of focus investing by a slightly different route. "Back in the 1960s," he explained, "I actually took a compound interest rate table, and I made various assumptions about what kind of edge I might have in reference to the behavior of common stocks generally."[6] Charlie worked through several scenarios to determine the number of stocks he would need in the portfolio of his investment partnership and what kind of volatility he could expect.

"I knew from being a poker player that you have to bet heavily when you've got huge odds in your favor," Charlie said. He concluded that as long as he could handle the price volatility, owning as few as three stocks would be plenty. "I knew I could handle the bumps psychologically, because I was raised by people who believed in handling bumps."[7]

Maybe you also come from a long line of people who can handle bumps. But even if you were not born so lucky, you can acquire some of their traits. You need to consciously decide to change how you think and behave. Acquiring new habits and thought patterns does not happen overnight, but gradually teaching yourself not to panic or act rashly in response to the vagaries of the market is certainly doable.

The Mathematics of Focus Investing

It is a vast oversimplification, but not an overstatement, to say that the stock market is a giant warehouse full of countless probabilities. In this warehouse are thousands of single forces that combine to set prices, all of which are in constant motion, any one of which can have a dramatic impact, and none of which is predictable to an absolute certainty. The task for investors, then, is to narrow the field by identifying and removing that which is most unknown, and then focusing on the least unknown. That task is an exercise in probability.

When we are unsure about the situation but still want to express our opinion, we often preface our remarks by saying "the chances are," or "probably," or "it's not very likely but. . . ." When we go one step further and attempt to quantify those general expressions, we then are dealing with probabilities. Probabilities are the mathematical language of risk.

What is the probability of a cat giving birth to a bird? Zero. What is the probability the sun will rise tomorrow? That event, which is considered certain, is given a probability of 1. All events that are neither completely certain nor completely impossible have a probability somewhere between 0 and 1, expressed as a fraction. Determining the fraction is what probability theory is all about.

In 1654, Blaise Pascal and Pierre de Fermat exchanged a series of letters that formed the basis of probability theory. Pascal, a child prodigy gifted in both mathematics and philosophy, had been challenged by the Chevalier de Méré, a philosopher and gambler, to solve the riddle that had stumped many mathematicians. How should two card players decide the stakes of the game if they had to leave before the game was completed? Pascal approached Fermat, a mathematical genius in his own right, about Méré's challenge.

"The 1654 correspondence between Pascal and Fermat on this subject," said Peter Bernstein in *Against the Gods,* his wonderfully written treatise on risk, "signaled an epochal event in the history of mathematics and the theory of probability."[8] Although they attacked the problem differently (Fermat used algebra whereas Pascal turned to geometry), they were able to construct a system to determine the probability of several possible outcomes. Indeed, Pascal's triangle of numbers solves many problems, including the probability that your favorite baseball team will win the World Series after losing the first game.

The work by Pascal and Fermat marks the beginning of the theory of decision making. Decision theory is the process of deciding what to do when you are uncertain what will happen. "Making that decision," wrote Bernstein, "is the essential first step in any effort to manage risk."[9]

■ ■ ■

Although Pascal and Fermat were both credited with developing probability theory, another mathematician, Thomas Bayes, wrote the piece that laid the groundwork for putting probability theory to practical action.

Born in England in 1701, exactly 100 years after Fermat and 78 years after Pascal, Bayes lived an unremarkable life. He was a member of the Royal Society, but published nothing in mathematics during his lifetime. After his death, his paper titled "Essays Towards Solving a Problem in the Doctrine of Chances" appeared. At the time, no one thought much of it. However, according to Bernstein, the essay was a "strikingly original piece of work that immortalized Bayes among statisticians, economists, and other social scientists."[10] It provides a way for investors to make use of the mathematical theory of probability.

Bayesian analysis gives us a logical way to consider a set of outcomes of which all are possible but only one will actually occur. It is conceptually a simple procedure. We begin by assigning a probability to each of the outcomes, on the basis of whatever evidence is then available. If additional evidence becomes available, the initial probability is revised to reflect the new information. Bayes's theorem gives a mathematical procedure for updating our original beliefs, thus changing our relevant odds.

How does this work? Let's imagine that you and a friend have spent the afternoon playing your favorite board game, and now, at the end of the game, you are chatting about this or that. Something your friend says leads you to make a friendly wager: that with one roll of a die from the game, you will get a 6. Straight odds are one in six, a 16 percent probability. But then suppose your friend rolls the die, quickly covers it with his hand, and takes a peek. "I can tell you this much," he says; "it's an even number." Now you have new information and your odds change dramatically to one in three, a 33 percent probability. While you are considering whether to change your bet, your friend teasingly adds: "And it is not a 4." With this additional bit of information, your odds have changed again, to one in two, a 50 percent probability.

With this very simple example, you have performed a Bayesian analysis. Each new piece of information affected the original probability, and that is a Bayesian inference.

Bayesian analysis is an attempt to incorporate all available information into a process for making inferences, or decisions, about the underlying state of nature. Colleges and universities use Bayes's theorem to help their students study decision making. In the classroom, the Bayesian approach is more popularly called the decision tree theory; each branch of the tree represents new information that, in turn, changes the odds in making decisions. "At Harvard Business School," explains Charlie Munger, "the great quantitative thing that bonds the first-year class together is what they call decision tree theory. All they do is take high school algebra and apply it to real life problems. The students love it. They're amazed to find that high school algebra works in life."[11].

As Charlie points out, basic algebra is extremely useful in calculating probabilities. But to put probability theory to practical use in investing, we need to look a bit deeper at how the numbers are calculated. In particular, we need to pay attention to the notion of frequency.

What does it mean to say that the probability of guessing heads on a single coin toss is one in two? Or that the probability that an odd number will appear on a single throw of the dice is one in two? If a box is filled with 70 red marbles and 30 blue marbles, what does it mean that the probability is three in 10 that a blue marble will be picked? In all these examples, the probability of the event is what is referred to as a frequency interpretation, and it is based on the law of averages.

If an uncertain event is repeated countless times, the frequency of the event's occurrence is reflected in its probability. For example, if we toss a coin 100,000 times, the number of times that are expected to be heads is 50,000. Note I did not say it would be equal to 50,000. The law of large numbers says the relative frequency and the probability need be equal only for an infinite number of repetitions. Theoretically, we know that, in a fair coin toss, the chance of getting heads is one in two, but we will never be able to say the chance is equal until an infinite number of tosses have passed.

In any problem that deals with uncertainty, we will, quite obviously, never be able to make a definitive statement. However, if the problem is well defined, we should be able to list all the possible outcomes. If an uncertain event is repeated often enough, the frequency of the outcomes should reflect the probability of the different possible outcomes. The difficulty arises when we are concerned with an event that happens only once.

How do we estimate the probability of passing tomorrow's science test or the probability of the Green Bay Packers winning the Super Bowl? The problem we face is that each of these events is unique. We can look back at all the statistics on the Green Bay games, but we don't have enough exact matchups with the exact personnel who played each other repeatedly under identical circumstances. We can recall previous science exams to get an idea of how well we test, but all tests are not identical and our knowledge is not constant.

Without repeated tests that would produce a frequency distribution, how can we calculate probability? We cannot. Instead we must rely on subjective interpretation of probabilities. We do it all the time. We might say the odds of the Packers' winning the Lombardi trophy are two to one, or the possibility of passing that difficult science test is one in 10. These are probabilistic statements; they describe our *degree of belief* about the event. When it isn't possible to do enough repetitions of a certain event to get an interpretation of probability based on frequency, we have to rely on our own good sense.

You can immediately see that many subjective interpretations of those two events would lead you in the wrong direction. In subjective probability, the burden is on you to analyze your assumptions. Stop and think them through. Are you assuming a one-in-10 chance of doing well on the science test because the material is more difficult and you haven't adequately prepared, or because of false modesty? Is your lifelong loyalty to the Packers blinding you to the superior strength of the other team?

According to the textbooks on Bayesian analysis, if you believe that your assumptions are reasonable, it is "perfectly acceptable" to make your subjective probability of a certain event equal to a frequency probability.[12] What you have to do is sift out the unreasonable and illogical and retain the reasonable. It is helpful to think about subjective probabilities as nothing more than extensions of the frequency probability method. In fact, in many cases, subjective probabilities add value because this approach allows you to take operational issues into account rather than depend on long-run statistical regularity.

Probability Theory and the Market

Whether or not investors recognize it, virtually all the decisions they make are exercises in probability. For them to succeed, it is critical that their probability statement combines the historical record with the most recent data available. And that is Bayesian analysis in action.

"Take the probability of loss times the amount of possible loss from the probability of gain times the amount of possible gain. That is what we're trying to do," says Buffett. "It's imperfect but that's what it is all about."[13]

A useful example to clarify the link between investing and probability theory is the practice of risk arbitrage. Pure arbitrage is nothing more than profiting from the discrepancy in the price of a security quoted in two different markets. For example, commodities and currencies are quoted in several different markets around the world. If two separate markets quote a different price on the same commodity, you could buy in one market, sell in another market, and pocket the difference.

Risk arbitrage, which is the form more commonly practiced today, involves announced corporate mergers or acquisitions. There are individuals who practice risk arbitrage on unannounced corporate events, but this is an area that Buffett avoids and so will we. In a speech to a group of Stanford University students, Buffett shared his views on risk arbitrage. "My job," he said, "is to assess the probability of the events [announced mergers] actually transpiring and the gain/loss ratio."[14]

Let's preface Buffett's next remarks to the Stanford students with this scenario. Suppose the Abbott Company began the day trading at $18 per share. Then, in midmorning, it is announced that sometime this year, perhaps in six months, Abbott will be sold to the Costello Company for $30 per share. Immediately, the share price of Abbott races to $27, where it settles in and begins to trade back and forth.

Buffett sees the announced merger and must make a decision. First of all, he tries to assess the degree of certainty. Some corporate deals don't materialize. The board of directors could unexpectedly resist the idea of the merger or the Federal Trade Commission might voice an objection. No one ever knows with certainty whether a risk arbitrage deal will close, and that is where the risk comes in.

Buffett's decision process is an exercise in subjective probability. He explains: "If I think there is a 90 percent chance of occurring and there is 3 points on the upside and there is a 10 percent chance that it will fall through and there is 9 points on the downside, then that's $0.90 off of $2.70, leaving $1.80 mathematical expectation."[15]

Next, said Buffett, you have to figure in the time span involved and then relate the return of the investment to other investments available to you. If you bought one share of Abbott Company at $27, there is, according to Buffett's mathematics, a potential 6.6 percent return ($1.80/$27). If the deal is expected to close in six months, the annualized return on the investment would be 13.2 percent. Buffett would then compare the return from this risk arbitrage with other returns available to him.

Buffett freely acknowledges that risk arbitrage carries the potential for loss. "We are perfectly willing to lose money on a given transaction," he said, "arbitrage being one example, but we're not willing to enter into any transaction in which we think the probability of a number of mutually independent events of similar type has an expectancy of loss. We hope," he added, "that we're entering into transactions where our calculations of those probabilities have validity."[16]

We can see quite clearly that Buffett's risk arbitrage estimates are subjective probabilities. There is no frequency distribution in risk arbitrage. Every deal is different. Every circumstance requires different estimations. Even so, there is value to approaching the risk arbitrage deal with some rational mathematical calculation. The process, we shall learn, is no different when you invest in common stocks.

Kelly Optimization

Each time you step foot inside a casino, the probability of coming out a winner is pretty low. You shouldn't be surprised; after all, we all know the house has the best odds. But one game, if played correctly, gives you a legitimate chance to beat the house: blackjack. In a worldwide best seller called *Beat the Dealer: A Winning Strategy for the Game of Twenty-One*, Edward O. Thorp, a mathematician by training, outlined a process for outsmarting the casino.[17]

Thorp's strategy was based on a simple concept. When the deck is rich with 10s, face cards, and aces, the player—let's say it's you—has a statistical advantage over the dealer. If you assign a −1 for the high cards and a +1 for the low cards, it's quite easy to keep track of the cards dealt; just keep a running tally in your head, adding and subtracting as each card shows. When the count turns positive, you know there are more high cards yet to be played. Smart players save their biggest bets for when the card count reaches a high relative number.

Buried deep inside Thorp's book was a notation on the Kelly betting model.[18] Kelly, in turn, took his inspiration from Claude Shannon, the inventor of information theory.

A mathematician with Bell Laboratories in the 1940s, Shannon spent a good deal of his career trying to find the most optimal way to transmit information over copper lines without having the information become garbled by random molecular noise. In 1948, in an article called "A Mathematical Theory of Communication," he described what he had discovered.[19] Included in the article was the mathematical formula for the optimal amount of information that, considering the possibility of success, can be pushed through a copper wire.

A few years later, J. L. Kelly, another mathematician, read Shannon's article and realized the formula could just as easily work in gambling—another human endeavor that would be enhanced by knowing the possibilities of success. In 1956, in a paper titled "A New Interpretation of Information Rate," Kelly pointed out that Shannon's various transmission rates and possible outcomes of a chance event are essentially the same thing—probabilities—and the same formula could optimize both.[20]

The Kelly optimization model, often called the optimal growth strategy, is based on the concept that if you know the probability of success, you bet the fraction of your bankroll that maximizes the growth rate. It is expressed as a formula: $2p - 1 = x$ where 2 times the probability of winning (p) minus 1 equals the percentage of your total bankroll that you should bet (x). For example, if the probability of beating the house is 55 percent, you should bet

10 percent of your bankroll to achieve maximum growth of your winnings. If the probability is 70 percent, bet 40 percent. And if you know the odds of winning are 100 percent, the model would say: Bet it all.

The stock market, of course, is far more complex that the game of blackjack. In a card game, there are a finite number of cards and therefore a limited number of possible outcomes. The stock market, with many thousands of stocks and millions of investors, has an almost unlimited number of various outcomes. Using the Kelly approach requires constant recalculations and adjustments throughout the investment process. Nonetheless, the underlying concept—mathematically linking the degree of probability to investment size—carries important lessons.

I believe the Kelly model is an attractive tool for focus investors. However, it will benefit only those who use it responsibly. There are risks to employing the Kelly approach, and investors would be wise to understand its three limitations:

1. Anyone who intends to invest, using the Kelly model or not, should have a long-term horizon. Even if a blackjack player has a sound model that can beat the house, it does not always hold that success will be revealed in the first few hands dealt. The same is true for investing. How many times have investors seen that they have selected the right company but the market has taken its own sweet time in rewarding the selection?
2. Be wary of using leverage. The danger of borrowing to invest in the stock market (with a margin account) has been trumpeted loudly by both Ben Graham and Warren Buffett. The unexpected call on your capital can occur at the most unfortunate time in the game. If you use the Kelly model in a margin account, a stock market decline can force you to sell your stock, causing you to remove a high-probability bet.
3. The biggest danger in playing high-probability games is the risk of overbetting. If you judge that an event has a 70 percent chance of success when in fact it is only a 55 percent event,

> you run the risk of so-called gambler's ruin. The way to minimize that risk is to underbet, by using what is known as a *half-Kelly* or *fractional-Kelly* model. For example, if the Kelly model would tell you to bet 10 percent of your capital, you might choose to bet only 5 percent (half-Kelly) instead. Both the half-Kelly bet and the fractional-Kelly bet provide a margin of safety in portfolio management; that, together with the margin of safety we apply to selecting individual stocks, provides a double layer of protection.

Because the risk of overbetting far outweighs the penalties of underbetting, I believe that all investors, especially those who are just beginning to use a focus investment strategy, should use fractional-Kelly bets. Unfortunately, minimizing your bets also minimizes your potential gain. However, because the relationship in the Kelly model is parabolic, the penalty for underbetting is not severe. A half-Kelly bet, which reduces the amount you bet by 50 percent, reduces the potential growth rate by 25 percent.

Munger on Betting Odds

In 1994, Charlie Munger accepted an invitation from Dr. Guilford Babcock to address the student investment seminar at the University of Southern California's business school. He touched on several topics, including the "art of achieving worldly wisdom." He also explained, as only he can, what he thinks about probabilities and optimization.

"The model I like—to sort of simplify the notion of what goes on in a market for common stocks—is the pari-mutuel system at the racetrack," he said. "If you stop and think about it, a pari-mutuel system is a market. Everybody goes there and bets and the odds are changed based on what's bet. That's what happens in the stock market."

He continued, "Any damn fool can see that a horse carrying a light weight with a wonderful win rate and good position et cetera is way more likely to win than a horse with a terrible record and extra weight and so on and so on. But if you look at the odds, the bad horse pays 100 to 1, whereas the good horse pays 3 to 2. Then it's not clear which is statistically the best bet. The prices have changed in such a way that it's very hard to beat the system."[21]

Charlie's racetrack analogy is perfect for investors. Too often, investors are attracted to a long shot that pays incredible odds but, for any one of countless reasons, never finishes the race. Or sometimes they pick the sure thing without ever considering the payoff. It appears to me that the most sensible way to approach horse racing, or the stock market, is to wait until the good horse comes to the post with inviting odds.

The Element of Psychology

Andrew Beyer, the author of several books on Thoroughbred racing, has spent many years watching race goers bet and has seen far too many lose money through impetuosity. At the racetrack, as elsewhere, the casino mentality—the itch to get into the action: to put down the money, toss the dice, pull the lever, do something—compels people to bet foolishly, without taking the time to think through what they are doing.

Beyer, who understands the psychological urge to get into the game, advises players to accommodate it by dividing their strategy between action bets and prime bets. Prime bets are reserved for serious players when two conditions occur: (1) confidence in the horse's ability to win is high, and (2) payoff odds are greater than they should be. Prime bets call for serious money. Action bets, as the name implies, are reserved for the long shots and hunches that satisfy the psychological need to play. They are smaller bets and never are allowed to become a large part of the player's betting pool.

When a horseplayer starts blurring the distinction between prime bets and action bets, says Beyer, he or she "is taking a step that will inevitably lead toward helter-skelter betting with no proper balance between . . . strong and weak selections."[22]

From Theory to Reality

Now, let us move away from the racetrack and put all this theory together into the reality of the stock market. The chain of thinking is the same.

1. *Calculate probabilities.* This is the probability you are concerned with: What are the chances that this stock I am considering will, over time, achieve an economic return greater than the stock market?
2. *Wait for the best odds.* The odds of success tip in your favor when you have a margin of safety; the more uncertain the situation, the greater the margin you need. In the stock market, the margin of safety is provided by a discounted price. When the company you like is selling at a price that is below its intrinsic value, that is your signal to act.
3. *Adjust for new information.* Knowing that you are going to wait until the odds turn in your favor, pay scrupulous attention in the meantime to whatever the company does. Has management begun to act irresponsibly? Have the financial decisions begun to change? Has something happened to alter the competitive landscape in which the business operates? If so, the probabilities will likely change.
4. *Decide how much to invest.* Of all the money you have available for investing in the market, what proportion should go into a particular purchase? Start with the Kelly formula, then adjust downward, perhaps to a half-Kelly bet or a fractional-Kelly bet.

Thinking about probabilities may be new to you, but it is not impossible to learn how to use them. If you are able to teach yourself to think about stocks this way, you are well on your way to being able to profit from your own lessons. Recall Buffett's purchase of the Coca-Cola Company in 1988. He invested one-third of Berkshire's portfolio in the company. Coca-Cola was an outstanding business with above-average economics selling at a price substantially below intrinsic value. Opportunities like this do not often occur in the stock market. But when one does occur, those who understand probabilities will recognize it and will know what to do. As Charlie Munger puts it, "The wise [investors] bet heavily when the world offers them that opportunity. They bet big when they have the odds. And the rest of the time, they don't. It's just that simple."[23]

Focus Investors in Graham-and-Doddsville

In 1934, during the height of the Great Depression, a remarkable book with the unremarkable title of *Security Analysis* was published. Its coauthors, Benjamin Graham and David Dodd, had been working on it for five years. Their writing time had been interrupted by teaching at Columbia University and helping clients cope with the aftereffects of the 1929 crash. Graham later said the delay was providential, for it allowed him to include "wisdom acquired at the cost of much suffering."[24] *Security Analysis* is universally acclaimed as a classic; it is still in print after five editions and 80 years. It is impossible to overstate its influence on the modern world of investing.

Fifty years after the original publication, the Columbia University Business School sponsored a seminar marking the anniversary. Warren Buffett, one of the school's best-known alumni and the most famous modern-day proponent of Graham's value approach, was invited to address the gathering. His speech, titled "The Superinvestors of Graham-and-Doddsville," has become, in its own way, as much a classic as the book it honored.[25]

Most in the audience that day in 1984—university professors, researchers, and other academicians—still held firmly to modern portfolio theory and the validity of the efficient market hypothesis. Buffett, to no one's surprise, firmly disagreed, and in his speech he quietly demolished the platform on which rested the efficient market theory.

He began by recapping the central argument of modern portfolio theory—that the stock market is efficient, all stocks are priced correctly, and therefore anyone who beats the market year after year is simply lucky. Maybe so, he said, but I know some folks who have done it, and their success can't be explained away as simply random chance.

And he proceeded to lay out the evidence. All the examples he presented that day were of people who had managed to beat the market over time, and who had done so not because of luck but because they followed principles learned from the same source: Ben Graham. They all reside, he said, in the "intellectual village" of Graham-and-Doddsville.

Although they may make specific decisions differently, Buffett explained, they are linked by a common approach that seeks to take advantage of discrepancies between the market price and intrinsic value. "Needless to say, our Graham and Dodd investors do not discuss beta, the capital asset pricing model or covariance of returns," Buffett said. "These are not subjects of any interest to them. In fact, most of them would have trouble defining those terms."

In a published article based on his 1984 speech, Buffett included tables that presented the impressive performance results of the residents of Graham-and-Doddsville.[26] But it was not just the Graham approach to value investing that united these great investors. Each of these great investors—Charlie Munger, Bill Ruane, and Lou Simpson—also managed focused portfolios just like Buffett did. From their performance records there is much we can learn. But before we start this investigation, let us begin with the very first focus investor.

John Maynard Keynes

Most people recognize John Maynard Keynes for his contributions to economic theory. Few know that he was also a legendary investor. Proof of his investment prowess can be found in the performance record of the Chest Fund at King's College in Cambridge, England.

Before 1920, King's College investments were restricted to fixed income securities. When Keynes was appointed the Second Bursar in late 1919, he persuaded the trustees to begin a separate fund that would contain only common stocks, currency, and commodity futures. This separate account became the Chest Fund. From 1927, when he was named First Bursar, until his death in 1945, Keynes had sole responsibility for this account. In all that time, he kept its holdings focused on just a few companies. In 1934, the same year that *Security Analysis* was published, Keynes wrote to a colleague, explaining his reasoning.

> It is a mistake to think one limits one's risk by spreading too much between enterprises which one knows little and has no reason for special confidence. . . . One's knowledge and experience are definitely limited and there are seldom more than two or three enterprises at any given time in which I personally feel myself entitled to put full confidence.[27]

Four years later, Keynes prepared a full policy report for the Chest Fund, outlining his principles:

1. A careful selection of a few investments having regard to their cheapness in relation to their probable actual and potential *intrinsic* [emphasis his] value over a period of years ahead and in relation to alternative investments at the time;
2. A steadfast holding of these fairly large units through thick and thin, perhaps several years, until either they have fulfilled their promise or it is evident that they were purchased on a mistake;
3. A *balanced* [emphasis his] investment position, i.e., a variety of risks in spite of individual holdings being large, and if possible opposed risks.[28]

Although he did not use the term, I believe it is clear from Keynes's investment policy that he was a focus investor. He purposely limited his stocks to a select few and relied on fundamental analysis to estimate the value of his picks relative to their price. He liked to keep portfolio turnover at a very low rate. And he aimed to include "opposed risks" by introducing a variety of economic positions concentrated in high-quality, predictable businesses.

How well did Keynes perform? During his 18-year stewardship, the Chest Fund achieved an average annual return of 13.2 percent, at a time when the overall UK market remained basically flat. Considering that the time period included both the Great

Depression and World War II, we would have to say that Keynes's performance was extraordinary.

Even so, the Chest Fund endured some painful periods; in three separate years (1930, 1938, and 1940), its value dropped significantly more than that of the overall UK market. Reviewing Keynes's performance record in 1983, two modern analysts commented, "From the large swings in the Fund's fortune, it is obvious that the Fund must have been more volatile than the market."[29] Indeed, if we measure the standard deviation of the Chest Fund, we find it was almost two and a half times more volatile than the general market. Without a doubt, investors in the fund occasionally had a bumpy ride but, in the end, outscored the market by a significant degree.

■ ■ ■

Lest you think Keynes, with his macroeconomic background, possessed marketing timing skills, take further note of his investment policy. "We have not proved able to take much advantage of a general systematic movement out of and into ordinary shares as a whole at different phases of the trade cycle," he wrote. "As a result of these experiences I am clear that the idea of a wholesale shift is for various reasons impracticable and indeed undesirable. Most of those who attempt to [do so] sell too late and buy too late, and do both too often, incurring heavy expenses and developing too unsettled and speculative state of mind, which if it is widespread has besides the grave social disadvantage of aggravating the scale of the fluctuations."[30]

High turnover produces heavy expenses, fuels a speculative state of mind, and makes the overall market fluctuations worse. True then, true now.

Charles Munger Partnership

Although Berkshire Hathaway's investment performance is usually tied to its chairman, we should never forget that vice chairman Charlie Munger is an outstanding investor himself. "I ran into him in about 1960," said Buffett, "and I told him law was a fine hobby but he could do better."[31] As you may recall from Chapter 2, Munger at the time had a thriving law practice in Los Angeles, but gradually shifted his energies to a new investment partnership bearing his name.

"His portfolio was concentrated in very few securities and, therefore, his record was much more volatile," Buffett explained, "but it was based on the same discount-from-value approach." In making investment decisions for his partnership, Charlie followed the Graham methodology and would only look at companies that were selling below their intrinsic value. "He was willing to accept greater peaks and valleys in performance, and he happens to be a fellow whose psyche goes toward concentration."[32]

Notice that Buffett does not use the word *risk* in describing Charlie's performance. Using the conventional definition of risk as found in modern portfolio theory, where risk arises from price volatility, some would say that, over its 13-year history, Charlie's partnership was extremely risky. Its standard deviation was almost twice that of the market. But beating the average annual return of the market by 18 points over that time period was an achievement not of a risk taker but of an astute investor.

Sequoia Fund

Buffett first met Bill Ruane in 1951, when both were attending Ben Graham's security analysis class at Columbia. The two classmates stayed in contact, and Buffett watched Ruane's investment performance over the years with admiration. When Buffett closed his investment partnership in 1969, he asked Ruane to handle the funds of some of the partners. That was the beginning of the Sequoia Fund.

Both men knew it was a difficult time to set up a mutual fund, but Ruane plunged ahead. The stock market was splitting into a two-tier market. Most of the hot money was gravitating to the new Nifty Fifty (high-flying growth companies), leaving value stocks far behind. Although, as Buffett pointed out, comparative performance for value investors in the early 1970s was difficult, "I am happy to say that my partners, to an amazing degree, not only stayed with him but added money, with happy results."[33]

The Sequoia Fund was a true pioneer, the first mutual fund run on the principles of focus investing. The public record of Sequoia's holdings demonstrates clearly that Bill Ruane and Rick Cuniff, his partner at Ruane, Cuniff & Company, managed a tightly focused, low-turnover portfolio. On average, well over 90 percent of the fund was invested in a group of six to 10 companies. Even so, the economic diversity of the portfolio was, and continues to be, broad. Ruane has often pointed out that even though Sequoia is a focused portfolio, it has always owned a variety of different businesses.

Early on, Bill Ruane was unique among money managers. Generally speaking, most investment managers put together a portfolio of stocks that is not too far different from the index they are measured against. The portfolio manager understands the industry sector weightings of the index and then goes about populating the portfolio with stocks that fit in each sector. At Ruane, Cuniff & Company, the partners begin with the idea of selecting the best possible stocks; then they let the portfolio form around those selections.

Selecting the best possible stocks, of course, requires a high level of research. The firm has built a reputation as one of the brightest shops in money management. The principals eschew Wall Street's broker-fed research reports. Instead, they rely on their own intensive company investigations. "We don't go in much for titles at our firm," Ruane once said, "[but] if we did, my business card would read Bill Ruane, Research Analyst."

Such thinking is unusual on Wall Street, he explained. "Typically, people start out their careers in an analyst function but aspire to get promoted to the more prestigious portfolio manager designation. To the contrary, we have always believed that if you are a long-term investor, the analyst function is paramount and the portfolio management follows naturally."[34]

How well has this unique approach served Sequoia's shareholders? From 1971 through 2013 the Sequoia Fund earned an average annual return of 14.46 percent, compared to 10.65 percent for the Standard & Poor's 500 index.

Like other focus portfolios, the Sequoia Fund achieved this above-average return with a slightly bumpier ride. The standard deviation of the market during this period was 16.1 percent compared to Sequoia's 21.2 percent. Those who adhere to the modern portfolio theory definition of risk might conclude, as with the Munger Partnership, that Sequoia took on more risk to get its excess return. But those who recognized the care and diligence that embodied the Sequoia research effort would be hard-pressed to conclude its approach was risky.

Lou Simpson

About the time Warren Buffett began acquiring the stock of the GEICO insurance company in the late 1970s, he also made an acquisition that would have a direct effect on GEICO's financial health. His name was Lou Simpson.

Simpson, who earned a master's degree in economics from Princeton University, worked for both Stein Roe & Farnham and Western Asset Management before Buffett lured him to GEICO in 1979. Recalling the job interview, Buffett remembers that Lou had "the ideal temperament for investing." He was an independent thinker who was confident of his own research and "who derived no particular pleasure from operating with or against the crowd."[35]

Lou developed a reputation as a voracious reader who ignored Wall Street research reports and pored over annual reports instead. His common-stock selection process was similar to Buffett's. He purchased only high-return businesses that were run by able management and that were available at reasonable prices. Lou had something else that was in common with Buffett: He focused his portfolio on only a few stocks. GEICO's billion-dollar equity portfolio typically owned fewer than 10 stocks.

Between 1980 and 2004, GEICO's portfolio achieved an average annual return of 20.3 percent compared to the market's 13.5 percent. Buffett commented, "Lou has consistently invested in undervalued common stocks that, individually, were unlikely to present him with a permanent loss and that, collectively, were close to risk-free."[36]

Here again we see Buffett's sense of risk: It has nothing to do with stock price volatility, but rather with the certainty that the individual stocks will, over time, produce a profit.

Simpson's performance and investment style fit neatly inside Buffett's way of thinking. "Lou takes the same conservative concentrated approach to investments that we do at Berkshire and it is an enormous plus for us to have him on board," said Buffett. "There are very few people who[m] I will let run money and businesses that we have control over, but we are delighted in the case of Lou."[37]

Buffett, Munger, Ruane, Simpson. It is clear the superinvestors of Buffettville have a common intellectual approach to investing. They are united in their belief that the way to reduce risk is to buy stocks only when the margin of safety (that is, the favorable discrepancy between the intrinsic value of the company and today's market price) is high. They also believe that concentrating their portfolios around a limited number of these high-probability events not only reduces risk, but helps to generate returns far above the market rate of return.

Still, when we point out these successful focus investors, there are some people who remain skeptical. They wonder: Are all of these people successful because of their close professional relationships? As it turns out, these stock pickers owned different stocks. Buffett didn't own exactly what Munger owned, and Munger didn't own what Ruane owned; Ruane didn't own what Simpson owned; and nobody knows what Keynes owned.

Well, that may be true, say the skeptics, but you have offered only five examples of focus investors, and five observations are not enough to draw a statistically meaningful conclusion. In an industry that has thousands of portfolio managers, these five success stories could have been completely random.

Fair enough. To eliminate any notion that the five superinvestors of Buffettville are nothing more than statistical aberrations, we need to examine a wider field. Unfortunately, the population of focus investors is very small. Among the thousands of portfolio managers who manage money, there are only a scant few who manage concentrated portfolios. Thus we are left with the same challenge.

We were faced with this same problem when I wrote *The Warren Buffett Portfolio: Mastering the Power of the Focus Investing Strategy* (John Wiley & Sons, 1999). There were simply not enough focus investors to study and draw a statistically meaningful conclusion. So what did we do? We went inside a statistical laboratory and designed a universe with 3,000 focus portfolios.[38]

Using the Compustat database of common stock returns, we isolated 1,200 companies that displayed measurable data—including revenues, earnings, and return on equity. We then asked the computer to randomly assemble, from these 1,200 companies, 12,000 portfolios of various sizes, forming four portfolio groups:

1. Three thousand portfolios containing 250 stocks.
2. Three thousand portfolios containing 100 stocks.
3. Three thousand portfolios containing 50 stocks.
4. Three thousand portfolios containing 15 stocks—the focus portfolio group.

Next, we calculated the average annual return of each portfolio in each group over a 10-year period (1987–1996). Then we compared the returns of the four portfolio groups to the overall stock market (defined as the Standard & Poor's 500 index) for the same period.

- Among the portfolios containing 250 stocks, the standard deviation was 0.65 percent; the best portfolio returned 16.0 percent annually, and the worst was 11.4 percent.
- Among the 100-stock portfolios, the standard deviation was 1.11 percent—18.3 percent best, 10 percent worst.
- Among the 50-stock portfolios, the standard deviation was 1.54 percent—19.1 percent best, 8.6 percent worst.
- Among the 15-stock portfolios, the standard deviation was 2.78 percent—26.6 percent best, 6.7 percent worst.

From all this, one key finding emerged: When we reduced the number of stocks in a portfolio, we began to increase the probability of generating returns that were higher than the market's rate of return. But, not surprisingly, at the same time we also increased the probability of generating lower returns.

To reinforce the first conclusion, we found some remarkable statistics when we sorted the data:

- Out of 3,000 250-stock portfolios, 63 beat the market.
- Out of 3,000 100-stock portfolios, 337 beat the market.
- Out of 3,000 50-stock portfolios, 549 beat the market.
- Out of 3,000 15-stock portfolios, 808 beat the market.

With a 250-stock portfolio, you have a one-in-50 chance of beating the market. With a 15-stock portfolio your chances increase dramatically, to one in four.

Another important consideration: In this study, I did not factor in the effect of trading expenses. Obviously, where the portfolio turnover ratio is high, so are the costs. These costs work to lower the return for investors.

As to the second conclusion, it simply reinforces the critical importance of intelligent stock selection. It is no coincidence that the superinvestors of Buffettville are also superior stock pickers. If you run a focus portfolio and do not have good stock-picking skills, the underperformance could be striking. However, if you develop the skill set to pick the right companies, then outsized returns can be achieved by focusing your portfolio on your best ideas.

When we isolated our 3,000 focus portfolios in the statistical laboratory 15 years ago, it was a simple and straightforward exercise. Since then, academia has delved further into the concept of focus investing, examining the behavior of different sized portfolios and studying the performance returns over much longer time periods. Most notably, K. J. Martijn Cremers and Antti Petajisto have together conducted a thorough research investigation into focus investing based on a concept they call "active share."[39]

Active share represents the percentage share of a portfolio that is different from the benchmark index holdings the portfolio is measured against. It is stated as a percentage and takes into account not only security selection but also the overweighting and underweighting of the stocks in the portfolio compared to the weighting in the benchmark. According to Cremers and Petajisto, portfolio managers with an active share of 60 percent or less are closet indexers. That is, their portfolios closely resemble the index they are being measured against. A portfolio within active share of 80 percent or more is a portfolio that is truly different from the index.

Cremers and Petajisto computed the active share for domestic equity mutual funds from 1980 to 2003. They were able to relate the active share to the fund's characteristics, including size, expenses, turnover ratios, and performance. What did they discover? Active share predicts fund performance. The mutual funds with the highest active share, funds that were the most different from the index, significantly outperformed their benchmark, whereas those with the lowest active share underperformed their benchmarks.

Interestingly, Cremers reports that in 1980, 50 percent of large-cap mutual funds had an active share score of 80 percent or more. That is, half the mutual funds had a portfolio that was significantly different from their benchmark. Today, just 25 percent of mutual funds are considered truly active. "Both investors and fund managers have become more benchmark-aware," says Cremers. "As a manager, you want to avoid being in the bottom 20% or 40% (of your peer group). The safest way to do that, especially when you're evaluated over the shorter time periods, is to hug the index."[40]

Because investors habitually take money away from underperforming mutual funds, portfolio managers have increasingly made their portfolios more similar to indexes, thereby reducing the chance they will significantly underperform the index. Of course, as we learned, the more your portfolio resembles the index, the less likely you are to outperform it. It is important to remember that any portfolio manager who has a portfolio that is different from the benchmark, however small a difference, is an active portfolio manager. The only question that remains is: How active is your portfolio?

The Real Measure of Worth

In that famous speech about Graham-and-Doddsville, Warren Buffett said many important things, none more profound than this: "When the price of a stock can be influenced by a 'herd' on Wall

Street with prices set at the margin by the most emotional person, or the greediest person, or the most depressed person, it is hard to argue that the market always prices rationally. In fact, market prices are frequently nonsensical."[41]

It is profound because of where it leads us. If we accept the idea that prices are not always rational, then we are freed from the shortsightedness of using them as the sole basis for decisions. If we accept the idea that share price is not everything, we can broaden our horizon to focus on what counts: the thoughtful research and analysis of the underlying business. Of course, we always want to be aware of prices, so we can recognize when they dip below value, but we need no longer be strangled by this one-dimensional measure that can so seriously lead us in the wrong direction.

Making this shift will not be easy. Our entire industry—money managers, institutional investors, and all manner of individual investors—is price myopic. If the price of a particular stock is going up, we assume good things are happening; if the price starts to go down, we assume something bad is happening, and we act accordingly.

It's a poor mental habit, and it is exacerbated by another: evaluating price performance over very short periods of time. Not only are we depending solely on the wrong thing (price), Buffett would say, but we're looking at it too often and we're too quick to jump when we don't like what we see.

This double-barreled foolishness—this price-based, short-term mentality—is a flawed way of thinking, and it shows up at every level in our business. It is what prompts some people to check stock quotes every day, sometimes every hour. It is why institutional investors, with responsibility for billions of dollars, are ready to buy and sell at the snap of a finger. It is the reason managers of mutual funds churn the stocks in the fund's portfolio at dizzying rates: They think it is their job to do so.

Amazingly, those same money managers are the first to urge their clients to remain calm when things start to look shaky. They send out reassuring letters lauding the virtue of staying the course. So why don't they practice what they preach?

It is especially easy to observe this contradiction in the handling of mutual funds because their actions are so thoroughly documented and scrutinized by the financial press. Because so much information is available, and because mutual funds are so familiar and well understood, I believe we can learn a great deal about the folly of a price-based measure by looking at how it works in mutual funds.

The financial writer Joseph Nocera has pointed out the inconsistencies between what mutual fund managers recommend shareholders do—namely, "buy and hold"—and what managers actually do with their own portfolios—namely, buy-sell, buy-sell, buy-sell. Reinforcing his own observations of this double standard, Nocera quoted Morningstar's Don Phillips: "There is huge disconnect between what the fund industry does and what it tells investors to do."[42]

The obvious question becomes: If investors are counseled to buy and hold, why do managers frenetically buy and sell stocks each year? The answer, says Nocera, "is that the internal dynamics of the fund industry make it almost impossible for fund managers to look beyond the short term."[43] Why? Because the business of mutual funds has turned into a senseless short-term game of who has the best performance, measured totally by price.

Today, there is substantial pressure on portfolio managers to generate eye-catching short-term performance numbers. These numbers attract a lot of attention. Every three months, leading publications such as the *Wall Street Journal* and *Barron's* publish quarterly performance rankings of mutual funds. The funds that have done the best in the past three months move to the top of the list, are praised by financial commentators on television and in newspapers, rush to put out self-congratulatory advertising and promotional pieces, and attract a flurry of new deposits. Investors, who have been waiting to see which fund manager has the so-called hot hand, pounce on these rankings. Indeed, quarterly performance rankings are increasingly used to separate those managers deemed gifted from those who are mediocre.

The fixation on short-term price performance, while acutely obvious in mutual funds, is not limited to them; it dominates thinking throughout the investment industry. We are no longer in an environment where managers are measured over the long term. Even people who function as their own manager are infected by the unhealthy nuances of this environment. In many ways, we have become enslaved to a marketing machine that all but guarantees underperformance.

Caught in a vicious circle, there appears to be no way out. But of course, as we have learned, there is a way to improve investment performance. What we must do now is find a better way to measure performance. The cruel irony is that the strategy most likely to provide above-average returns over time appears to be incompatible with how we judge performance.

In 1986, V. Eugene Shahan, a Columbia University Business School alumnus and portfolio manager at U.S. Trust, wrote a follow-up article to Buffett's "The Superinvestors of Graham-and-Doddsville." In his piece, titled "Are Short-Term Performance and Value Investing Mutually Exclusive?," Shahan took on the same question that we are now asking: How appropriate is it to measure a money manager's skill on the basis of short-term performance?

He noted that, with the exception of Buffett himself, many of the people Buffett described as "Superinvestors"—undeniably skilled, undeniably successful—faced periods of short-term underperformance. In a money-management version of the tortoise and the hare, Shahan commented: "It may be another of life's ironies that investors principally concerned with short-term performance may very well achieve it, but at the expense of long-term results. The outstanding records of Superinvestors of Graham-and-Doddsville were compiled with the apparent indifference to short-term performance."[44] In today's mutual fund performance derby, Shahan explains, the Superinvestors of Graham-and-Doddsville would have been overlooked. The same is also true of the Superinvestors of Buffettville.

John Maynard Keynes, who managed the Chest Fund for 18 years, underperformed the market one-third of the time. Indeed, he underperformed the market the first three years he managed the fund, which put him behind the market by 18 percentage points.

The story is similar at the Sequoia Fund. In the marking period, Sequoia underperformed 37 percent of the time. Like Keynes, Ruane also had difficulty coming of age. "Over the years," he confessed, "we have periodically qualified to be the Kings of Underperformance. We had the blurred vision to start the Sequoia Fund in mid-1970 and suffered the Chinese water torture of underperforming the S&P four straight years." By the end of 1974, Sequoia was a whopping 36 percentage points behind the market. "We hid under the desk, didn't answer the phones and wondered if the storm would ever clear."[45] But of course the storm did clear. Seven years after inception, Sequoia had gained 220 percent, versus a gain of 60 percent for the Standard & Poor's 500 index.

Even Charlie Munger couldn't escape the inevitable bumps of focus investing. Over 14 years, Charlie underperformed 36 percent of the time. Like other focus investors, he had a string of short-term bad luck. From 1972 through 1974, Munger fell behind the market by 37 percentage points. Over 17 years, Lou Simpson underperformed the market 24 percent of the time. His worst relative performance, which occurred in a one-year period, put him 15 percentage points behind the market.

Incidentally, we saw the same performance trends when we analyzed our laboratory of 3,000 focus portfolios. Of the 808 portfolios that beat the market over the 10-year period, an astonishing 95 percent endured some prolonged period of underperformance—three, four, five, or even six years out of 10.

What do you think would have happened to Keynes, Munger, Ruane, or Simpson if they were rookie managers starting their careers in today's environment, which can see only the value of one year's performance?

Yet, following the argument that using a focus strategy will likely result in periods of underperformance, how can we tell, just using price performance as our measure, whether we are looking at a very bright investor who is having a poor year (or even a poor three years) but will do well over the long haul, or a manager who perhaps lacks the skills to be a good focus investor?

We can well imagine what Warren Buffett might say. For him, the moral of the story is clear: We have to drop our insistence on price as the only measuring stick, and we have to break ourselves of the counterproductive habit of making short-term judgments.

But if price is not the measuring stick, what are we to use instead? "Nothing" is not a good answer. Even buy-and-hold strategists don't recommend keeping your eyes shut. We just have to find another benchmark for measuring performance. Fortunately, there is one, and it is the cornerstone of how Buffett judges his performance and the performance of his operating units at Berkshire Hathaway.

Warren Buffett once said he "wouldn't care if the stock market closed for a year or two. After all, it closes on Saturday and Sunday and that hasn't bothered me yet."[46] It is true that "an actively trading market is useful, since it periodically presents us with mouthwatering opportunities," said Buffett. "But by no means is it essential."[47]

To fully appreciate this statement, you need to think carefully about what Buffett said next. "A prolonged suspension of trading in securities we hold would not bother us any more than does the lack of daily quotations for [Berkshire's wholly owned subsidiaries]. Eventually our economic fate will be determined by the economic fate of the business we own, whether our ownership is partial [in the form of shares of stock] or total."[48]

If you owned a business and there were no daily quotes to measure its performance, how would you determine your progress? Likely you would measure the growth in earnings, the increase in return on capital, or the improvement in operating margins. You simply would let the economics of the business dictate whether you were increasing or decreasing the value of your investment. In Buffett's mind, the litmus test for measuring the performance of a publicly traded company is no different. "Charlie and I let our marketable equities tell us by their operating results—not by their daily, or evenly yearly, price quotations—whether our investments are successful," he explains. "The market may ignore a business success for a while, but it eventually will confirm it."[49]

But can we count on the market to reward us for picking the right companies? Can we draw a significantly strong correlation between the operating earnings of a company and its share price? The answer appears to be yes, if we are given the appropriate time horizon.

When we set out to determine how closely price and earnings are connected, using our laboratory group of 12,000 companies, we learned that the longer the time period, the stronger the correlation. With stocks held three years, the degree of correlation between stock price and operating earnings ranged from .131 to .360. (A correlation of .360 means that 36 percent of the variance in the price was explained by the variance in earnings.) With stocks held for five years, the correlation ranged from .374 to .599. In the 10-year holding period, the correlation between earnings and stock price increased to a range of .593 to .695.

This bears out Buffett's thesis that, given enough time, the price of a business will align with the company's economics. He cautions, though, that translation of earnings into share price is both "uneven" and "unpredictable." Although the relationship between earnings and price strengthens over time, it is not always prescient. "While market values track business values quite well over long periods," Buffett notes, "in any given year the relationship can gyrate capriciously."[50] Ben Graham gave us the same lesson: "In the short run the market is a voting machine but in the long run it is a weighing machine."[51]

A Variety of Measuring Sticks

It is clear that Buffett is in no hurry to have the market affirm what he already believes is true. "The speed at which a business's success is recognized, furthermore, is not that important as long as the company's intrinsic value is increasing at a satisfactory rate," he says. "In fact, delayed recognition can be an advantage: It may give you a chance to buy more of a good thing at a bargain price."[52]

To help shareholders appreciate the value of Berkshire Hathaway's large common stock investments, Buffett coined the term *look-through* earnings. Berkshire's look-through earnings are made up of the operating earnings of its consolidated businesses (its subsidiaries), the retained earnings of its large common stock investments, and allowance for the tax that Berkshire would have to pay if the retained earnings were actually paid out.

The notion of look-through earnings was originally devised for Berkshire's shareholders, but it also represents an important lesson for focus investors who seek a way to understand the value of their portfolio when, as will happen from time to time, share prices disengage from underlying economics. "The goal of each investor," says Buffett, "should be to create a portfolio (in effect, a company), that will deliver him or her the highest possible look-through earnings a decade or so from now."[53]

According to Buffett, since 1965 (the year Buffett took control of Berkshire Hathaway), the company's look-through earnings have grown at almost the identical rate of the market value of its securities. However, the two have not always moved in lockstep. On many occasions, earnings moved ahead of prices; at other times, prices moved far ahead of earnings. What is important to remember is that the relationship works over time. "An approach of this kind," counsels Buffett, "will force the investor to think about long-term business prospects rather than short-term market prospects, a perspective that will likely improve results."[54]

When Buffett considers adding an investment, he first looks at what he already owns to see whether the new purchase is any better. What Berkshire owns today is an economic measuring stick used to compare possible acquisitions. "What Buffett is saying is something very useful to practically any investor," Charlie Munger stresses. "For an ordinary individual, the best thing you already have should be your measuring stick." What happens next is one of the most critical but widely overlooked secrets to increasing the value of a portfolio. "If the new thing you are considering purchasing is not better than what you already know is available," says Charlie, "then it hasn't met your threshold. This screens out 99 percent of what you see."[55]

You already have at your disposal, with what you now own, an economic benchmark—a measuring stick. You can define your own personal economic benchmark in several different ways: look-through earnings, return on equity, or margin of safety, for example. When you buy or sell stock of a company in your portfolio, you have either raised or lowered your economic benchmark. The job of a portfolio manager who is a long-term owner of securities, and who believes future stock prices eventually will match with underlying economics, is to find ways to raise your benchmark.

If you step back and think for a moment, the Standard & Poor's 500 index is a measuring stick. It is made up of 500 companies and each has its own economic return. To outperform the S&P 500 index over time—to raise that benchmark—we have to assemble and manage a portfolio of companies with economics that are superior to the average weighted economics of the index.

"If my universe of business possibilities was limited, say, to private companies in Omaha, I would, first, try to assess the long-term economic characteristics of each business," says Buffett. "Second, assess the quality of the people in charge of running it; and third, try to buy into a few of the best operations at a sensible price. I certainly would not wish to own an equal part of every business in town. Why, then, should Berkshire take a different tack when dealing with the larger universe of public companies? And since finding great businesses and outstanding managers is so difficult, why should we discard proven products? Our motto is: If at first you do succeed, quit trying."[56]

Focus investing is necessarily a long-term approach to investing. If we were to ask Buffett what he considers an ideal holding period, he would answer, "Forever"—so long as the company continues to generate above-average economics and management allocates the earnings of the company in a rational manner. "Inactivity strikes us as an intelligent behavior," he explains. "Neither we nor most business managers would dream of feverishly trading highly profitable subsidiaries because a small move in the Federal Reserve's discount rate was predicted or because some Wall Street pundit has reversed his views on the market. Why, then, should we behave differently with our minority positions in wonderful businesses?"[57]

Of course, if you own a lousy company, you require turnover. Otherwise, you end up owning the economics of a subpar business for a long time. But if you own a superior company, the last thing you want to do is sell it.

This slothlike approach to portfolio management may appear quirky to those accustomed to actively buying and selling stocks on a regular basis, but it does have two important economic benefits, in addition to growing capital at an above-average rate. It works to reduce transaction costs and to increase after-tax returns. Each advantage by itself is extremely valuable; their combined benefit is enormous.

In a review of 3,650 domestic stock funds, Morningstar, the Chicago-based researcher of mutual funds, discovered that funds with low turnover ratios generated superior returns compared to funds with higher turnover ratios. The Morningstar study found that, over a 10-year period, funds with turnover ratios of less than 20 percent were able to achieve returns 14 percent higher than funds with turnover rates of more than 100 percent.

This is one of those commonsense dynamics that is so obvious it is easily overlooked. The problem with high turnover is that all that trading adds brokerage costs to the fund, which works to lower your net returns.

Except in the case of nontaxable accounts, taxes are the biggest expense that investors face—higher than brokerage commissions and often higher than the expense ratio of running a fund. In fact, taxes have become one of the principal reasons why funds generate poor returns. "That is the bad news," according to money managers Robert Jeffrey and Robert Arnott. They are the authors of "Is Your Alpha Big Enough to Cover Its Taxes?" which appeared in the well-respected *Journal of Portfolio Management*. "The good news," they write, "is that there are trading strategies that can minimize these typically overlooked tax consequences."[58]

In a nutshell, the key strategy involves another of those commonsense notions that is often underappreciated: the enormous value of the unrealized gain. When a stock appreciates in price but is not sold, the increase in value is an unrealized gain. No capital gains tax is owed until the stock is sold. If you leave the gain in place, your money compounds more forcefully.

Overall, investors have too often underestimated the enormous value of this unrealized gain—what Buffett calls an "interest-free loan from the Treasury." To make his point, Buffett asks us to imagine what happens if you buy a $1 investment that doubles in price each year. If you sell the investment at the end of the first year, you would have a net gain of $0.66 (assuming you're in the 34 percent tax bracket). Let's say you reinvest the $1.66 and it doubles in value by the second year-end. If the investment continues to double each year, and you continue to sell, pay the tax, and reinvest the proceeds, at the end of 20 years you have a net gain of $25,200 after paying taxes of $13,000. If, instead, you purchase a $1 investment that doubles each year and is not sold until the end of 20 years, you would gain $692,000 after paying taxes of approximately $356,000.

The Jeffrey-Arnott study concluded that to achieve high after-tax returns, investors need to keep their average annual portfolio ratio somewhere between 0 and 20 percent. What strategies lend themselves best to low turnover rates? One possible approach is a low-turnover index fund. Another is a focus portfolio. "It sounds like premarital counseling advice," say Jeffrey and Arnott, "namely, to try to build a portfolio that you can live with for a long, long time."[59]

Before we end this chapter, it is critically important that you think seriously about what exactly a focus investing approach entails:

- Do not approach the market unless you are willing to think about stocks, first and always, as part-ownership interests in businesses.
- Be prepared to diligently study the businesses you own, as well as the companies you compete against, with the idea that no one will know more about your business than you do.
- Do not even start a focus portfolio unless you are willing to invest a minimum of five years (10 years would even be better).

- Never leverage your focus portfolio. An unleveraged focus portfolio will help you reach your goals fast enough. Remember, an unexpected margin call on our capital will likely wreck a well-tuned portfolio.
- Accept the need to acquire the right temperament and personality to become a focus investor.

As a focus investor, your goal is to reach a level of understanding about your business that is unmatched on Wall Street. You may protest that this is unrealistic, but, considering what Wall Street promotes, it may not be as hard as you think. Wall Street sells short-term performance, emphasizing what may happen from quarter to quarter. Business owners, in contrast, are more interested in the long-term competitive advantages of the companies they own. If you are willing to work hard at studying businesses, you will likely get to know, over time, more about the companies whose stocks you own than the average investor, and that is all you need to gain an advantage.

Some investors would rather chatter about "what the market is doing" than bother to read an annual report. But a cocktail conversation about the future direction of the stock market and interest rates will be far less profitable than spending 30 minutes reading the last communication provided by the company in which you are invested.

Does that seem like too much effort? It's easier than you might think. There are no computer programs to learn or two-inch-thick investment banking manuals to decipher. You do not have to become an MBA-level authority on business valuation to profit from the focus approach. There is nothing scientific about valuing a business and then paying a price that is below this business value.

"You don't need to be a rocket scientist," confesses Buffett. "Investing is not a game where the 160 IQ guy beats the guy with the 130 IQ. The size of an investor's brain is less important than his ability to detach the brain from the emotions."[60] Changing the way you approach investing, including how you will, going forward, interact with the stock market, will involve some emotional and psychological adjustments. Even though you may fully accept the mathematical arguments for focus investing, and even though you see that other very smart people have been successful with it, you may still feel some hesitation—emotionally speaking.

The key is to keep the emotions in appropriate perspective, and that is much easier if you understand something of the basic psychology involved in applying the Warren Buffett Way—which brings us to the next chapter.

CHAPTER 6

The Psychology of Investing

Warren Buffett's first common stock investment was a disappointment, both financially and emotionally. I think we can excuse him, though; he was only 11 years old. You might remember from Chapter 1 that Buffett and his sister Doris pooled their savings and bought a total of six shares of Cities Service Preferred stock at $38.25 per share. A few months later, it was trading at $26.95, down 30 percent.

Even at that young age, Buffett had done his homework, which at the time included analyzing the price charts and piggybacking on one of his dad's favorite stocks. Still, Doris was beside herself at the thought of losing money. Not a day went by that she didn't pester her younger brother about their investment. As soon as Cities Service Preferred recovered and their investment was safely in the black, Buffett sold the stock, then watched in disbelief as it later soared to more than $200 per share.

Despite this painful experience, Buffett's first at-bat in the stock market was not a total waste of time. He did learn two very important lessons. First was the value of patience; second, although short-term changes in stock prices may have little to do with value, they can have a lot do with emotional discomfort. In the next chapter, we will examine the role of patience in long-term investing. For now, we will study the debilitating effect that short-term changes in stock prices often have on investor behavior. This takes us into the fascinating realm of psychology.

Few aspects of human existence are more emotion-laden than our relationship to money, and this is particularly important when we are talking about the stock market. Much of what drives the decisions that people make about stock purchases can be explained only by principles of human behavior. And since the market is, by definition, the collective decisions made by all stock purchasers, it is not an exaggeration to say that the entire market is pushed and pulled by psychological forces.

The Intersection of Psychology and Economics

The study of what makes us all tick is endlessly fascinating. It is particularly intriguing to me that it plays such a strong role in investing, a world that is generally presumed to be dominated by cold numbers and soulless data. When it comes to investment decisions, our behavior is sometimes erratic, often contradictory, and occasionally goofy.

What is particularly alarming, and what all investors need to grasp, is that they are often unaware of their bad decisions. To fully understand the markets and investing, we now know we have to understand our own irrationalities. The study of the psychology of misjudgment is every bit as valuable to an investor as the analysis of a balance sheet and an income statement.

In recent years we have seen what amounts to a revolution, a new way of looking at issues of finance through the framework of human behavior. This blending of economics and psychology is known as behavioral finance, and it has slowly moved down from the universities' ivory towers to become part of the informed conversation among investment professionals . . . who, if they look over their shoulders, will find the shadow of a smiling Ben Graham.

Meet Mr. Market

Ben Graham, widely known as the father of financial analysis, has taught three generations how to navigate the stock market with a mathematical road map. But what is often overlooked is Graham's teachings on psychology and investing. In both *Security Analysis* and *The Intelligent Investor*, Graham devoted considerable space to explaining how investor emotions trigger stock market fluctuations.

Graham figured that an investor's worst enemy was not the stock market but oneself. They might have superior abilities in mathematics, finance, and accounting, but people who could not master their emotions were ill suited to profit from the investment process.

As Warren Buffett, his most famous student, explains, "There are three important principles to Graham's approach." The first is simply looking at stocks as businesses, which "gives you an entirely different view than most people who are in the market." The second is the margin-of-safety concept, which "gives you the competitive edge." And the third is having a true investor's attitude toward the stock market. "If you have that attitude," says Buffett, "you start out ahead of 99 percent of all the people who are operating in the stock market—it is an enormous advantage."[1]

Developing an investor's attitude, Graham said, is a matter of being prepared, both financially and psychologically, for the market's inevitable ups and downs—not merely knowing intellectually that a downturn will happen, but having the emotional ballast needed to react appropriately when it does. In Graham's view, an investor's appropriate reaction to a downturn is the same as a business owner's response when offered an unattractive price: ignore it. "The true investor," says Graham, "scarcely ever is forced to sell his shares and at all other times is free to disregard the current price quotation."[2]

To drive home his point, Graham created an allegorical character he named "Mr. Market." The well-known story of Mr. Market is a brilliant lesson on how and why stock prices periodically depart from rationality.

Imagine that you and Mr. Market are partners in a private business. Each day, without fail, Mr. Market quotes a price at which he is willing to either buy your interest or sell you his.

The business you both own is fortunate to have stable economic characteristics, but Mr. Market's quotes are anything but. You see,

Mr. Market is emotionally unstable. Some days he is cheerful and can only see brighter days ahead. On these days, he quotes a very high price for shares in your business. At other times, Mr. Market is discouraged and, seeing nothing but trouble ahead, quotes a very low price.

Mr. Market has another endearing characteristic, said Graham. He does not mind being snubbed. If Mr. Market's quotes are ignored, he will be back again tomorrow with a new quote. Graham warned that it is Mr. Market's pocketbook, not his wisdom, that is useful. If Mr. Market shows up in a foolish mood, you are free to ignore him or take advantage of him, but it will be disastrous if you fall under his influence.

More than 60 years have passed since Ben Graham created Mr. Market. Yet the mistakes of judgment that Graham warned against are very much with us. Investors still act irrationally. Fear and greed still permeate the marketplace. Foolish mistakes are still the order of the day. Along with good business judgment, then, investors need to understand how to protect themselves from the emotional whirlwind that Mr. Market unleashes. To do that, we must become familiar with behavioral finance, that place where finance intersects with psychology.

Behavioral Finance

Behavioral finance is an investigative study that seeks to explain market inefficiencies by using psychological theories. Observing that people often make foolish mistakes and illogical assumptions when dealing with their own financial affairs, academics began to dig deeper into psychological concepts to explain the irrationalities in people's thinking. It is a relatively new field of study, but what we are learning is fascinating, as well as eminently useful to smart investors.

Overconfidence

Several psychological studies have pointed out that errors in judgment occur because people in general are overconfident. Ask a large sample of people to describe their skills at driving a car, and an overwhelming majority will say they are above average. Another example: Doctors believe they can diagnose pneumonia with 90 percent confidence when in fact they are right only 50 percent of the time. "One of the hardest things to imagine is that you are not smarter than average," said Daniel Kahneman, professor of psychology and public affairs at Princeton University's Woodrow Wilson School of Public and International Affairs and winner of the Nobel Prize in economics.[5] But the sobering reality is that not everyone can be better than average.

Confidence per se is not a bad thing. But overconfidence is another matter, and it can be particularly damaging when we are dealing with our financial affairs. Overconfident investors not only make silly decisions for themselves but also have a powerful effect on the market as a whole.

Investors, as a rule, are highly confident they are smarter than everyone else. They have a tendency to overestimate their skills and their knowledge. They typically rely on information that confirms what they believe, and disregard contrary information. In addition, the mind works to assess whatever information is readily available rather than to seek out information that is little known. Too often, investors and money managers are endowed with a belief that they have better information and therefore can profit by outsmarting other investors.

Overconfidence explains why so many money managers make wrong calls. They take too much confidence from the information they gather, and think they are more right than they actually are. If all the players think their information is correct and they know something that others do not, the result is a great deal of trading.

Overreaction Bias

One of the most important names in the field of behavioral finance is Richard Thaler, professor of behavioral science and economics, who moved from Cornell to the University of Chicago with the sole purpose of questioning the rational behavior of investors. He points to several recent studies that demonstrate that people put too much emphasis on a few chance events, thinking that they spot a trend. In particular, investors tend to fix on the most recent information they received and extrapolate from it; the last earnings report thus becomes in their mind a signal of future earnings. Then, believing that they see what others do not, they make quick decisions based on superficial reasoning.

Overconfidence is at work here, of course; people believe they understand the data more clearly than others and interpret it better. But there is more to it. Overconfidence is exacerbated by overreaction. The behaviorists have learned that people tend to overreact to bad news and react slowly to good news. Psychologists call this overreaction bias. Thus, if the short-term earnings report is not good, the typical investor response is an abrupt, ill-considered overreaction, with its inevitable effect on stock prices. Thaler describes this overemphasis on the short term as investor "myopia" (the medical term for nearsightedness), and believes most investors would be better off if they didn't receive monthly statements.

To illustrate his ideas about overreaction, Thaler developed a simple analysis. He took all the stocks on the New York Stock Exchange and ranked them by performance over the preceding five years. He isolated the 35 best performers (those that went up in price the most) and the 35 worst performers (those that went down the most) and created hypothetical portfolios of those 70 stocks. Then he held those portfolios for a subsequent five years, and watched as "losers" outperformed "winners" 40 percent of the time. In the real world, Thaler believes, few investors would have had the fortitude to resist overreacting at the first sign of a price downturn, and would have missed the benefits when the losers began to move in the other direction.[4]

Overreaction bias, as a concept, has been understood for some time now. But in the past few years it has been profoundly exacerbated by modern technology. Before the advent of the Internet and cable financial news programs, most investors looked at stock prices infrequently. They might check their brokerage statement at the end of each month, check their quarterly results after three months, and then tabulate their annual performance at year-end.

Today, with the advancements in communication technology, investors are able to stay connected, continuously, to the stock market. Mobile devices allow people to check their portfolios while riding in a car or train. They can check their performance walking to and from meetings or standing in a checkout line. Online brokerage accounts can tell you how well your portfolio has been performing since the opening bell. These accounts can calculate your relative performance for trailing one-day, five-day, 10-day, monthly, quarterly, and yearly returns. In short, investors can check the prices of their stocks every second of every 24-hour day.

Is this constant fixation on stock prices healthy for investors? Richard Thaler has a crisp answer. He lectures frequently at the Behavioral Conference sponsored by the National Bureau of Economic Research and the John F. Kennedy School of Government at Harvard University, and he always includes this advice: "Invest in equities and then don't open the mail."[5] To which we might add, "And don't check your computer or your phone or any other device every minute."

Loss Aversion

When Doris Buffett badgered her younger brother about their investment in Cities Service Preferred, it was a clear demonstration that it was difficult for her to endure the discomfort associated with declining stock prices. But let's not be too harsh on Doris. She was suffering from an emotional condition that affects millions of investors each and every day. It is called loss aversion, and it is, in my opinion, the single most difficult hurdle that prevents most investors from successfully applying the Warren Buffett approach to investing.

This psychological condition was discovered 35 years ago by two giants in the field, Nobel laureate Daniel Kahneman, whom we met earlier in the chapter, and Amos Tversky, professor of psychology at Stanford University. The two men, longtime collaborators, were interested in the theory of decision making.

In 1979, Kahneman and Tversky wrote a paper titled "Prospect Theory: An Analysis of Decision under Risk." It would later become the most cited paper ever to appear in *Econometrica*, the prestigious academic journal of economics. Up until that point, the utility theory of decision making, popularized by John von Neumann and Oskar Morgenstern in their book *Theory of Games and Economic Behavior* (Princeton University Press, 1944), was the accepted dogma in economics. Utility theory states that it should not matter how the alternatives are presented to someone making a decision. What matters most is for that person to do what is best for himself or herself. For example, if presented with a game that gives a 65 percent chance of winning and a 35 percent chance of losing, a person following utility theory should play, because the game has a positive sum outcome.

The utility theory is mathematically pristine. In an ideal world it's the perfect approach to decision making. However, Kahneman and Tversky were trained as psychologists, not economists, and they weren't so sure. They had spent their careers studying specific errors in human judgment, and they had learned that individuals weight gains and losses differently. Under utility theory, value is assigned to the final asset. Under Kahneman and Tversky's prospect theory, value is assigned individually to gains and losses. Kahneman and Tversky were able to prove that people do not look at final wealth, as dictated by utility theory, but rather they focus on the incremental gains and losses that contribute to their final wealth. The most important discovery in prospect theory was the realization that people are loss averse. In fact, Kahneman and Tversky were able to prove mathematically that people regret losses more than they welcome gains of the same size—two to two and one-half times more.

In other words, the pain of a loss is far greater than the enjoyment of a gain. Many experiments have demonstrated that people need twice as much positive to overcome a negative. On a 50/50 bet, with precisely even odds, most people will not risk anything unless the potential gain is twice as high as the potential loss.

This is known as asymmetric loss aversion: The downside has a greater impact than the upside, and it is a fundamental bit of human psychology. Applied to the stock market, it means that investors feel twice as bad about losing money as they feel good about picking a winner. The impact of loss aversion on investment decisions is obvious, and it is profound. We all want to believe we made good decisions. To preserve our good opinion of ourselves, we hold on to bad choices far too long, in the vague hope that things will turn around. By not selling our losers, we never have to confront our failures.

This aversion to loss makes investors unduly conservative. Participants in 401(k) plans whose time horizons are decades still keep large amounts of their money invested in the bond market. Why? Only a deeply felt aversion to loss would make anyone allocate so conservatively. But loss aversion can affect you in a more immediate way, by making you irrationally hold on to losing stocks. No one wants to admit making a mistake. But if you don't sell a mistake, you are potentially giving up a gain that you could earn by reinvesting smartly.

Mental Accounting

Over the years, Richard Thaler had the good fortune to study and collaborate with Kahneman and Tversky as well as several other academics in the field of behavioral finance. He has written several articles on decision making, many of which can be found in his popular book, *The Winner's Curse: Paradoxes and Anomalies of Economic Life* (Free Press, 1992). However, Thaler is best known for his 1995 article titled "Myopic Loss Aversion and the Equity Risk Premium," cowritten with Shlomo Benartzi, professor and cochair of the behavioral decision-making group at the University of California at Los Angeles Anderson School of Management. In their article, Thaler and Benartzi took loss aversion described in Kahneman and Tversky's prospect theory and connected it directly to the stock market.

Thaler and Benartzi were puzzled by one central question: Why would anyone with a long-term horizon want to own bonds over stocks when they know that stocks have consistently outperformed? The answer, they believed, rested on two central concepts from

Kahneman and Tversky. The first was loss aversion, which we have already explored. The second was a behavioral concept called mental accounting, which describes the methods people use to code financial outcomes. It refers to our habit of shifting our perspective on money as surrounding circumstances change. We tend to mentally put money into different "accounts," and that determines how we think about using it.

A simple situation will illustrate. Let us imagine that you have just returned home from an evening out with your spouse. You reach for your wallet to pay the babysitter, but discover that the $20 bill you thought was there is not. So, when you drive the sitter home you stop by an ATM machine and get another $20. Then the next day you discover the original $20 bill in your jacket pocket.

If you're like most people, you react with something like glee. The $20 in the jacket is found money. Even though the first $20 and the second $20 both came from your checking account, and both represent money you worked hard for, the $20 bill you hold in your hand is money you didn't expect to have, and you feel free to spend it frivolously.

Once again, Richard Thaler provides an interesting academic experiment to demonstrate this concept. In his study he started with two groups of people. People in the first group were given $30 in cash and told they had two choices: (1) pocket the money and walk away, or (2) gamble on a coin flip in which if they won they would get $9 extra and if they lost they would have $9 deducted. Most (70 percent) took the gamble because they figured they would at the very least end up with $21 of found money. Those in the second group were offered a different choice: (1) try a gamble on a coin toss: if they win they'd get $39 and if they lost they'd get $21, or (2) get an even $30 with no coin toss. More than half (57 percent) decided to take the sure money. Both groups of people stood to win the exact same amount of money with the exact same odds, but the situation was perceived differently.[6]

The implications are clear: how we decide to invest, and how we choose to manage those investments, has a great deal to do with how we think about money. For instance, mental accounting has been suggested as one further reason why people don't sell stocks that are doing badly: In their minds the loss doesn't become real until it is acted on. It also helps us understand our risk tolerance: We are far more likely to take risks with found money.

Myopic Loss Aversion

Thaler and Benartzi weren't through. Thaler remembered a financial riddle first proposed by the Nobel laureate Paul Samuelson. In 1963, Samuelson asked a colleague if he would be willing to accept the following bet: a 50 percent chance of winning $200 or a 50 percent chance of losing $100. According to Samuelson, the colleague turned down the initial offer but then reconsidered. He would happily play the game, he said, if he could play 100 times and did not have to watch each individual outcome. The willingness to play the game under a new set of rules sparked an idea for Thaler and Benartzi.

Samuelson's colleague was willing to accept the wager with two qualifiers: lengthen the time horizon for the game and reduce the frequency in which he was forced to watch the outcomes. Moving that observation into investing, Thaler and Benartzi reasoned that the longer the investor holds an asset, the more attractive the asset becomes but only if the investment is not evaluated frequently.

When analyzing historical investment returns, we find that the vast majority of long-term returns are a result of just 7 percent of all trading months. The return of the remaining 93 percent averages out to approximately zero.[7] What is clear, then, is that evaluating performance over shorter periods of time increases the chances that you will see a loss in your portfolio. If you check your portfolio daily, there is a 50/50 chance you will experience a loss. The odds don't improve much if you extend the evaluation period to a month.

But if you don't check your portfolio every day, you will be spared the angst of watching daily price gyrations; the longer you hold off, the less likely you will be confronted with volatility and therefore the more attractive your choices seem. Put differently, the two factors that contribute to an investor's emotional turmoil are loss aversion and a frequent evaluation period. Using the medical word for short-sightedness, Thaler and Bernatzi coined the term *myopic loss aversion* to reflect a combination of loss aversion and frequency.

Next, Thaler and Bernatzi sought to determine the ideal time frame. We know that over short periods, stock prices are much more volatile than bond prices. We also know that if we're willing to extend the period in which we measure changes in stock prices, the standard deviation of stock returns will diminish. What Thaler and Bernatzi wanted to know was this: How long would investors need to hold stocks without checking their performance to reach the point of being indifferent to the myopic loss aversions of stocks versus bonds? The answer: one year.

Thaler and Bernatzi examined the return, standard deviation, and positive return probability for stocks with time horizons of one hour, one day, one week, one month, one year, 10 years, and 100 years. Next they employed a simple utility function based on Kahneman and Tversky's loss-aversion factor of 2 (utility = probability of price increase − probability of decline × 2). Based on the math, an investor's emotional utility factor did not cross over to a positive number until it reached a one-year observable time period. I have often wondered whether Warren Buffett's preference that the stock market be opened only once a year for trading dovetailed with the psychological findings of myopic loss aversion.

Thaler and Bernatzi argue that any time we talk about loss aversion we must also consider the frequency with which returns are calculated. If investors evaluate their portfolios over shorter and shorter time periods, then it is clear that they will be less attracted to volatile stocks. "Loss aversion is a fact of life," explain Thaler and Benartzi. "In contrast, the frequency of evaluations is a policy choice that presumably could be altered, at least in principle."[8]

The Lemming Factor

One other psychological trap that beckons investors is the temptation to follow what everyone else is doing, whether or not it makes sense. We might call it the lemming fallacy.

Lemmings are small rodents indigenous to the tundra region and are noted for their mass exodus to the sea. In normal periods, lemmings move about during the spring migration in search of food and new shelter. Every three to four years, however, something odd happens. Because of high breeding and low mortality, the population of lemmings begins to rise. Once their ranks have swollen, lemmings begin an erratic movement under darkness. Soon, this bold group begins to move in daylight. When confronted by barriers, the number of lemmings in the pack increases until a panic-like reaction drives them through or over the obstacle. As this behavior intensifies, lemmings begin to challenge other animals they normally would avoid. Although many lemmings die from starvation, predators, and accidents, most reach the sea. There they plunge in and swim until they die from exhaustion.

The behavior of lemmings is not fully understood. Zoologists theorize that the mass migration occurs because of changes in their food supply and/or stressful conditions. The crowding and competition among lemmings possibly evoke a hormonal change that induces an alteration in behavior.

Why do so many investors behave like lemmings? To help us understand, Buffett shared one of Ben Graham's favorite stories in Berkshire Hathaway's 1985 annual report.

An oil prospector, moving to his heavenly reward, was met by St. Peter with bad news. "You're qualified for residence," said St. Peter, "but as you can see, the compound for oilmen is packed. There's no way to squeeze you in." After thinking for a moment, the prospector asked if he might say just four words to the present occupants. That seemed harmless to St. Peter, so he gave his okay. The prospector cupped his hand and yelled, "Oil discovered in hell." Immediately the gates to the compound opened and all the oilmen rushed out. Impressed, St. Peter invited the prospector to move in and make himself comfortable. The prospector paused. "No," he said, "I think I'll go along with the rest of the boys. There might be some truth to that rumor after all."

To help investors avoid this trap, Buffett asks us to think about professional money managers, who are too often compensated by a system that equates safe with average and rewards adherence to standard practices over independent thinking. "Most managers," Buffett has said, "have very little incentive to make the intelligent-but-with-some-chance-of-looking-like-an-idiot decision. Their personal gain/loss ratio is all too obvious; if an unconventional decision works out well, they get a pat on the back, and if it works out poorly, they get a pink slip. Failing conventionally is the route to go; as a group, lemmings may have a rotten image, but no individual lemming has ever received bad press."[9]

Managing the Emotional Traps

Each of these common ways of thinking about money creates problems for investors unable to escape their harmful repercussions, but in my opinion the most serious one is myopic loss aversion. I believe it is the single greatest psychological obstacle that prevents investors from successfully applying the Warren Buffett Way. In my almost three decades of professional experience, I have observed firsthand the difficulty investors, portfolio managers, consultants, and committee members of large institutional funds have with internalizing losses made all the more painful by tabulating those losses on a frequent basis. Overcoming this psychological burden penalizes all but a very few select individuals.

Perhaps it is not surprising that one person who has mastered myopic loss aversion is also the world's greatest investor—Warren Buffett. I have always believed that Buffett's long-term success has had much to do with the unique structure of his company. Berkshire Hathaway owns both common stocks and wholly owned businesses, so Buffett has observed firsthand how inextricably linked are the growth in value of these businesses and the prices of their common stocks. He does not need to look at stock prices every day, because he does not need the market's affirmation to convince him he has made the right investment. As he often states, "I don't need a stock price to tell me what I already know about value."

A side observation as to how this works for Buffett can be found in Berkshire's $1 billion investment in the Coca-Cola Company in 1988. At the time it was the single-largest investment Berkshire had ever made in a stock. Over the next 10 years, the stock price of Coca-Cola went up tenfold while the S&P 500 index went up threefold. Looking back, we might think Coca-Cola was one of the easiest investments an investor could have made. In the late 1990s, I participated in numerous investment seminars and I always asked the audience, "How many of you owned Coca-Cola over the past 10 years?" Practically all the hands would immediately go up. I then asked, "How many of you got the same rate of return on your Coca-Cola investment as Buffett did?" Sheepishly, people in the audience slowly dropped their hands.

Then I would ask the real question: "Why?" If so many in the audience owned shares of Coca-Cola (they actually made the same investment as Buffett), why did none of them get the same return? I think the answer comes back to myopic loss aversion. During the 10-year period (1989–1998) Coca-Cola did outperform the market, but on an annual basis it outperformed the stock market only six years. By the mathematics of loss aversion, investing in Coca-Cola had a negative emotional utility (six positive emotional units – four negative emotional units × 2). I can only imagine that those individuals who owned Coca-Cola came into a year when the stock was underperforming the market and they decided to sell. What did Buffett do? He first checked the economic progress of Coca-Cola—still excellent—and continued to own the business.

Ben Graham reminded us that "most of the time common stocks are subject to irrational and excessive price fluctuations in both directions, as the consequence of the ingrained tendency of most people to speculate or gamble—i.e., to give way to hope, fear, and greed."[10] Investors must be prepared, he cautioned, for ups and downs in the market. And he meant prepared psychologically as well as financially—not merely knowing intellectually that a downturn will happen, but having the emotional wherewithal to act appropriately when it does.

"The investor who permits himself to be stampeded or unduly worried by unjustified market declines in his holdings is perversely transforming his basic advantage into a basic disadvantage," said

Graham. "That man would be better off if his stocks had no market quotation at all, for he would then be spared the mental anguish caused him by another person's mistakes of judgment."[11]

And on the Other Side, Warren Buffett

Warren Buffett's approach to investing, thinking of stocks as businesses and managing a focus portfolio, is directly at odds with the financial theories taught to thousands of business students each and every year. Collectively, this financial framework is known as modern portfolio theory. As we will discover, this theory of investing was built not by business owners but by ivory tower academicians. And it is an intellectual house that Buffett refuses to reside in. Those who follow Buffett's principles will quickly find themselves emotionally and psychologically disconnected from how a majority of investors behave.

Harry Markowitz—Covariance

In March 1952, Harry Markowitz, a University of Chicago graduate student, published a 14-page article in the *Journal of Finance* entitled "Portfolio Selection."[12] In it, Markowitz explained what he believed was a rather simple notion, that return and risk are inextricably linked, and presented the calculations that supported his conclusion that no investor can achieve above-average gains without assuming above-average risk. It seems almost ridiculously obvious today, but it was a revolutionary concept in the 1950s, a time when portfolios were constructed haphazardly. Today that brief article is credited with launching modern finance.

Seven years later, Markowitz published his first book, *Portfolio Selection: Efficient Diversification of Investments* (John Wiley & Sons, 1959). In what many believe was his greatest contribution, he now turned his attention to measuring the riskiness of an entire portfolio. He called it *covariance*, a method for measuring the direction of a group of stocks. The more they move in the same direction, the greater is the chance that economic shifts will drive them down at the same time. By the same token, a portfolio composed of risky stocks might actually be a conservative selection if the individual stock prices move differently. Either way, Markowitz said, diversification is the key. The smart course for investors, he concluded, is first to identify the level of risk they are comfortable handling, and then to construct an efficient diversified portfolio of low-covariance stocks.

Eugene Fama—The Efficient Market

In 1965, Eugene Fama of the University of Chicago published his PhD dissertation, "The Behavior of Stock Market Prices," in the *Journal of Business*, proposing a comprehensive theory of the behavior of the stock market. His message was very clear: Predictions about future stock prices are pointless because the market is too efficient. In an efficient market, as information becomes available, a great many smart people aggressively apply that information in a way that causes prices to adjust instantaneously, before anyone can profit. At any given point, prices reflect all available information and hence we say the market is efficient.

Bill Sharpe—Capital Asset Pricing Model

About 10 years after Markowitz's paper first appeared, a young PhD student named Bill Sharpe talked with him at length about his work in portfolio theory and the need for countless covariances. The next year, in 1963, Sharpe's dissertation was published: "A Simplified Model of Portfolio Analysis." While fully acknowledging his reliance on Markowitz's ideas, Sharpe suggested a simpler method. Sharpe believed that all securities bore a common relationship with some underlying base factor, and therefore analysis was simply a matter of measuring the volatility of an individual security to its base factor. He gave his volatility measure a name: beta factor.

A year later, Sharpe introduced a far-reaching concept called the capital asset pricing model (CAPM), a direct extension of his single-factor model for composing efficient portfolios. CAPM says that stocks carry two distinct risks. One risk is simply the risk of being in the market, which Sharpe called *systemic risk*. Systemic risk is "beta" and it cannot be diversified away. The second type, called *unsystemic risk*, is the risk specific to a company's economic position. Unlike systemic risk, unsystemic risk can be diversified away by simply adding different stocks to the portfolio.

■ ■ ■

In the space of one decade, three academicians had defined important elements of what would later be called modern portfolio theory: Markowitz with his idea that the proper reward-risk balance depends on diversification, Fama with his theory of the efficient market, and Sharpe with his definition of risk. Thus for the first time in history, our financial destiny rested not with Wall Street or Washington, D.C., and not even in the hands of business owners. As we moved forward, the financial landscape would be defined by a group of university professors on whose doors the finance professionals had finally come knocking. From their ivory towers, they now became the new high priests of modern finance.

Buffett on Risk and Diversification

Now let's return to Warren Buffett. He had started an investment partnership with a few thousand dollars and turned that into $25 million. With the profits from his investment partnership, he had taken control of Berkshire Hathaway and was quickly heading toward a net worth that would soon exceed $1 billion. In all those 25 years, he had given little or no thought to the covariance of stocks, strategies to reduce the variability of a portfolio return, or—heaven forbid—the idea that the stock market was efficiently priced. Buffett did think deeply about the concept of risk, but his interpretation was far removed from what academicians were now saying about risk.

Recall that in modern portfolio theory, risk is defined by the volatility of the share price. But Buffett had always perceived a drop in share prices as an opportunity. If anything, a dip in price actually *reduces* risk. He points out, "For owners of a business—and that's the way we think of shareholders—the academic's definition of risk is far off the market, so much so that it produces absurdities."[13]

Buffett has a different definition of risk: the possibility of harm or injury. And that is a factor of the "intrinsic value risk" of a business, not the price behavior of the stock. The real risk, Buffett says, is whether after-tax returns from an investment "will give him [an investor] at least as much purchasing power as he had to begin with, plus a modest rate of interest on that initial stake."[14]

Risk, for Buffett, is inextricably linked to an investor's time horizon. This alone is the single greatest difference between how Warren Buffett thinks about risk and how modern portfolio theory frames risk. If you buy a stock today with the intention of selling it tomorrow, Buffett explains, then you have entered into a risky transaction. The odds are no better than the toss of a coin—you will lose about half the time. However, says Buffett, if you extend your time horizon out to several years, the probability of its being a risky transaction declines meaningfully, assuming of course that you have made a sensible purchase. "If you ask me to assess the risk of buying Coca-Cola this morning and selling it tomorrow morning," Buffett says, "I'd say that that's a very risky transaction."[15] But in Buffett's way of thinking, buying Coca-Cola this morning and holding it for 10 years, that's zero risk.

Buffett's unique view on risk also drives his portfolio diversification strategy; here, too, his thinking is the polar opposite of modern portfolio theory. According to the theory, remember, the primary benefit of a broadly diversified portfolio is to mitigate the price volatility of the individual stocks. But if you are unconcerned with short-term price volatility, as Buffett is, then you will also see portfolio diversification in a different light.

"Diversification serves as a protection against ignorance," explains Buffett. "If you want to make sure that nothing bad happens to you relative to the market, you should own everything. There is nothing wrong with that. It's a perfectly sound approach for somebody that doesn't know how to analyze businesses." In many ways, modern portfolio theory protects investors who have limited knowledge and understanding of how to value a business. But the protection comes with a price. According to Buffett, modern portfolio theory "will tell you how to do average. But I think almost anybody can figure out how to do average by fifth grade."[16]

Last, if the efficient market theory (EMT) is correct, there is no possibility, except a random chance, that any person or group could outperform the market, and certainly no chance that the same person or group could consistently do so. Yet Buffett's performance record for the past 48 years is prima facie evidence that it is possible, especially when combined with the experience of other bright individuals who also have beaten the market following Buffett's lead. What does this say about the efficient market theory?

Buffett's problem with the efficient market theory rests on one central point: It makes no provision for investors who analyze all the available information and gain a competitive advantage by doing so. "Observing correctly that the market is frequently efficient, they went on to conclude incorrectly that it was always efficient. The difference between these propositions is night and day."[17]

Nonetheless, the efficient market theory is still religiously taught in business schools, a fact that gives Warren Buffett no end of satisfaction. "Naturally, the disservice done students and gullible investment professionals who have swallowed EMT has been an extraordinary service to us and other followers of Graham," he wryly observed. "In any sort of a contest—financial, mental or physical—it's an enormous advantage to have opponents who have been taught it's useless to even try. From a selfish standpoint, we should probably endow chairs to ensure the perpetual teaching of EMT."[18]

Today, investors are caught at an intellectual and deeply emotional crossroads. To the left lies the pathway of modern portfolio theory. The theory has a 50-year history full of academic papers, neat formulas, and Nobel Prize winners. It seeks to get investors from point A to point B with as little price volatility as possible, thereby minimizing the emotional pain of a bumpy ride. Believing the market is efficient, hence price and intrinsic value are one and the same, adherents to modern portfolio theory focus on price first and asset value later—or sometimes not at all.

To the right lies the pathway that Warren Buffett and other successful investors have taken. It is a 50-year history that is full of life experiences, simple arithmetic, and long-term business owners. It seeks to get investors from point A to point B not by providing a smooth short-term price ride but by orchestrating an investment approach that seeks to maximize, on an economic risk-adjusted basis, the intrinsic-value rate of growth. Proponents of the Buffett approach do not believe the market is always efficient. Instead, they focus on asset values first and prices later—or sometimes not at all.

■ ■ ■

Now that you have an outline, albeit brief, of the concepts of modern portfolio theory, you can easily see how applying the Buffett approach will put you in conflict with its proponents. Not only are you intellectually at odds with modern portfolio theorists, but you are also vastly outnumbered, both in the classroom and the workspace. Embracing the Warren Buffett Way makes you a rebel looking out across the field at a much larger army of individuals who invest totally differently. As you will learn, being an outcast has its own emotional challenges.

I have written about Warren Buffett for over 20 years. Over that time period, I have not met anyone who has vehemently disagreed with the methodology outlined in *The Warren Buffett Way*. I have, however, met countless individuals who, although they wholeheartedly agree with Buffett's writings, were never emotionally able to apply his lessons. This, I have come to believe, is the single most important key to understanding his success, and it is one part of the puzzle that has not been fully explored. In a word, Warren Buffett is rational, not emotional.

Why Psychology Matters

In 2002 Daniel Kahneman—a psychologist—was awarded the Nobel Prize in economics "for having integrated insights from the psychological research into economic science, especially concerning human judgment and decision-making under certainty." That signaled the formal arrival of behavioral finance as a legitimate force in how to think about capital markets. Despite computer programs and black boxes, it is still people who make markets.

Because emotions are stronger than reason, fear and greed move stock prices above and below a company's intrinsic value. When people are greedy or scared, Buffett says, they often will sell stocks at foolish prices. In the short run, investor sentiment—human emotion—has a more pronounced impact on stock prices than a company's fundamentals.

Long before behavioral finance had a name, it was understood and accepted by a few renegades like Warren Buffett and Charlie Munger. Charlie points out that when he and Buffett left graduate school, they "entered the business world to find huge, predictable patterns of extreme irrationality."[19] He is not talking about predicting the timing, but rather the idea that when irrationality does occur it leads to predictable patterns of subsequent behavior.

Buffett and Munger aside, it is only quite recently that the majority of investment professionals have paid serious attention to the intersection of finance and psychology. When it comes to investing, emotions are very real, in the sense that they affect people's behavior and thus ultimately affect market prices. You have already sensed, I am sure, two reasons why understanding the human dynamic is so valuable in your own investing: (1) You will have guidelines to help you avoid the most common mistakes. (2) You will be able to recognize other people's mistakes in time to profit from them.

All of us are vulnerable to individual errors of judgment, which can affect our personal success. When a thousand or a million people make errors of judgment, the collective impact is to push the market in a destructive direction. Then, so strong is the temptation to follow the crowd, accumulated bad judgment only compounds itself. In a turbulent sea of irrational behavior, the few who act rationally may well be the only survivors.

In fact, the only antidote to emotion-driven misjudgment is rationality, especially when applied over the long haul with patient perseverance. And that is the subject of our next chapter.

CHAPTER 7

The Value of Patience

In his epic masterpiece *War and Peace*, Leo Tolstoy made this profound observation: "The strongest of all warriors are these two—time and patience." He of course was speaking from a military perspective, but the idea also brilliantly applies to economics, and it has great value to those who would deepen their understanding of capital markets.

All market activity lies on a time continuum. Moving from left to right, we observe buy-sell decisions that occur in microseconds, minutes, hours, days, weeks, months, years, and decades. Although it is unclear exactly where the demarcation line is located, it is generally agreed that activity on the left side (shorter time frame) is more likely to be speculation and activity on the right side (longer times) is considered investing. Warren Buffett, it probably goes without saying, sits comfortably on the right—quietly patient over the long term.

This prompts the question: Why are so many people frantically scrabbling on the far left, trying to make as much money as fast as possible? Is it greed? Is it a mistaken belief that they can predict changes in market psychology? Or could it be that they have lost faith in the possibility of achieving positive long-term investment returns after experiencing two bear markets and a financial crisis over the past decade? Truth be known, the answer to all three questions is yes. Although each is problematic, it is the last observation, a lack of confidence in long-term investing, that troubles me the most—because long-term investing lies at the heart of the Warren Buffett Way.

For the Long Term

The seminal work comparing short-term and long-term strategies was written over 20 years ago by Andrei Shleifer, a Harvard professor and winner of the John Bates Clark Medal, and Robert Vishny, professor of finance at the University of Chicago's Booth School of Business. In 1990, Shleifer and Vishny wrote a research paper for the *American Economic Review* titled "The New Theory of the Firm: Equilibrium Short Horizons of Investors and Firms."[1] In it, they compared the cost, risk, and return of short-horizon and long-horizon arbitrage.

The cost of arbitrage is the amount of time your capital is invested; risk is the amount of uncertainty over the outcome; and return is the amount of money made on the investment. In short-horizon arbitrage, all three elements are less. With long-horizon arbitrage, your capital is invested longer, the knowledge about when the payoff occurs is more uncertain, but the returns should be higher.

According to Shleifer and Vishny, "In equilibrium, the net expected return from arbitrage in each asset must be the same. Since arbitrage in long-term assets is more expensive than it is for short-term assets, the former must be more mispriced in equilibrium for net returns to be equal."[2] Put differently, because long-horizon arbitrage is more expensive than short-horizon arbitrage, the investment return must be greater.

Shleifer and Vishny point out that common stocks can be used for short-horizon arbitrage. For example, short-term speculators, acting as information arbitragers, may bet on the outcome of a takeover possibility, or an earnings release, or any other public announcement that would make the mispricing disappear quickly. Even if the stock price does not react as expected, the trader is able to exit the position rapidly with little financial repercussion. Following Shleifer and Vishny's train of thought, the speculator's cost is minimal (capital is invested for a short period of time) and the risk is small (the uncertainty over the outcome is settled quickly). However, the return is also small.

It should be noted that in order to generate substantial returns from short-term arbitrage, the strategy must be employed frequently, over and over again. Shleifer and Vishny also explain that, to increase your investment return beyond what a speculator would likely receive, you must be willing to increase the cost of the investment (the amount of time your money is invested) as well as take on more risk (uncertainty as to when the outcome will be resolved). The controlling variable for both speculators and investors is the time horizon. Speculators work in short-horizon periods and accept smaller returns. Investors operate over long-horizon periods and expect larger returns.

This leads us to the next question: In long-horizon arbitrage, do large returns from buying and holding common stocks actually exist? I decided to look closely at the evidence.

We calculated the one-year return, trailing three-year return, and trailing five-year return (price only) between 1970 and 2012. During this 43-year period, the average number of stocks in the S&P 500 index that doubled in any one year averaged 1.8 percent, or about nine stocks out of 500. Over three-year rolling periods, 15.3 percent of stocks doubled, about 77 stocks out of 500. In rolling five-year blocks, 29.9 percent doubled, about 150 out of 500.

So, back to the original question: Over the long term, do large returns from buying and holding stocks actually exist? The answer is indisputably yes. And unless you think a double over five years is trivial, this equates to a 14.9 percent average annual compounded return.

Of course, the value of that research is relevant only to the degree investors have the ability to select, beforehand, which stocks have the potential to double in five years. The answer obviously lies in the robustness of their stock selection process and portfolio management strategy. I am confident those investors who apply the investment tenets outlined in *The Warren Buffett Way* and stick to a low-turnover portfolio strategy stand a good chance of isolating a fair number of five-year doubles.

Finance theory tells us investors are rewarded for identifying mispricings. We can assume if the excess returns from any one stock are large enough, it should attract a larger number of investors who seek to close the gap between price and value. When the number of arbitrageurs increases, we also know the returns from arbitrage should decrease. However, examining the average percentage return from our basket of rolling five-year doubles between 1970 and 2012, we cannot point to any significant diminution in the excess returns. Yes, the absolute number of investment doubles does correlate to the performance of the overall market. Stronger markets beget a higher number of doubles, while weaker markets produce fewer. But the percentage outperformance of the doubles relative to the market, whatever the environment, remains impressive. In short, the army of long-horizon arbitrageurs one would expect to attack this mispricing pool remained largely absent.

Who is best positioned to close the price-value gap over rolling five-year periods? Answer: long-term investors. However, because that gap has remained wide for the past 43 years, perhaps the market's constituency has become dominated by short-term traders.

Between 1950 and 1970, the average holding period for stocks was between four and eight years. However, beginning in the 1970s, the holding period has persistently declined, to the point that today the average holding period for mutual funds is measured in months. Our research indicates that the greatest number of opportunities to bag high excess returns occurs after three years. No doubt, with portfolio turnover ratios in excess of 100 percent, this all but guarantees that most investors are excluded.

One can make a strong argument that the market is best served by having a balance between short-term traders and long-term investors. If the market comprised an equal force of arbitrageurs, half who attack short-term mispricing and half who seek to close the long-term price-value gap, then, so the argument goes, the market's short-term and long-term inefficiencies would largely be erased. But what happens to the market when this balance is disrupted? A market dominated by long-term investors would leave unattended the mispricing that occurs over short periods of time, and a market dominated by short-term traders is largely uninterested in long-term mispricing.

Why has the market lost so much of the diversity that once characterized it? Because of the slow migration of people who converted from long-term investing to short-term speculation. The results from this evolutionary shift are somewhat predictable. It's a question of simple arithmetic. With so many people now speculating, the difficulty of winning short-term bets has gone up while the returns have gone down. The powerful magnet that has pulled so many people into becoming short-term speculators has left but a rarefied few to close the inefficiencies, the excess returns, of long-term investing.

Rationality: The Critical Difference

Rationalism, according to the *Oxford American Dictionary*, is a belief that one's opinions or actions should be based on reason and knowledge rather than emotional responses. A rational person thinks clearly, sensibly, and logically.

The first thing to understand is that rationality is not the same as intelligence. Smart people can do dumb things. Keith Stanovich, a professor of human development and applied psychology at the University of Toronto, believes that intelligence tests like IQ tests or SAT/ACT exams do a very poor job of measuring rational thought. "It is a mild predictor at best," he says, "and some rational thinking skills are totally dissociated from intelligence."[3]

In his book, *What Intelligence Tests Miss: The Psychology of Rational Thought*, he coined the term *dysrationalia*—the inability to think and behave rationally despite high intelligence. Research in cognitive psychology suggests there are two principal causes of dysrationalia. The first is a processing problem. The second is a content problem. Let's look at them closely, one at a time.

Stanovich believes we humans process poorly. When solving a problem, he says, people have different cognitive mechanisms to choose from. At one end of the thinking spectrum are mechanisms that have great computational power. But this great computational power comes with a cost. It is a slower process of thinking and requires a great deal of concentration. At the opposite end of the thinking spectrum are mechanisms with very little computational power; they require very little concentration and permit quick decisions. "Humans are cognitive misers," writes Stanovich, "because our basic tendency is to default to the processing mechanisms that require less computational effort, even if they are less accurate."[4] In a word, humans are lazy thinkers. They take the easy way out when solving problems; as a result, their solutions are often illogical.

Slow-Moving Ideas

Let us now turn our attention to the role of information. The information we require speaks to the subject of this chapter—patience—and the value of a "slow-traveling idea."

Many readers may not know Jack Treynor. But he is an intellectual giant in the field of financial management. First trained as a mathematician at Haverford College, he graduated with distinction from Harvard Business School in 1955 and began his career in the research department at Arthur D. Little, a consulting firm. As a young analyst, Treynor generated 44 pages of mathematical notes on the issue of risk while on a three-week vacation in Colorado. A prolific writer, he eventually became editor of CFA Institute's *Financial Analysts Journal.*

Over the years, Treynor swapped papers with many of the leading finance academicians, including Nobel laureates Franco Modigliani, Merton Miller, and William Sharpe. A number of Treynor's articles won prestigious awards, including the *Financial Analysts Journal*'s Graham and Dodd Award and the Roger F. Murray Prize. In 2007, he won the prestigious CFA Institute Award for Professional Excellence. Fortunately, Treynor's writings, which were once loosely noted, are now available in a 574-page volume titled *Treynor on Institutional Investing.* It deserves a place on every serious investor's bookshelf.

My copy is a bit dog-eared and tired looking, because several times a year I reread my favorite parts. Tucked near the back, on page 424, is my favorite article—"Long-Term Investing." It first appeared in the May–June 1976 issue of the *Financial Analysts Journal.* Treynor begins by talking about the ever-present puzzle of market efficiency. Is it true, he wondered, that no matter how hard we try we'll never be able to find an idea that the market hasn't already discounted? To address the question, Treynor asks us to distinguish between "two kinds of investment ideas: (a) those whose implications are straightforward and obvious, take relatively little special expertise to evaluate, and consequently travel quickly and (b) those that require reflection, judgment, and special expertise for their evaluation, and consequently travel slowly."[5]

"If the market is inefficient," he concludes, "it will not be inefficient with respect to the first kind of idea, since by definition the first kind is unlikely to be misevaluated by the great mass of investors."[6] To say this another way, the simple ideas—price-to-earnings ratios, dividend yields, price-to-book ratios, P/E-to-growth ratios, 52-week-low lists, technical charts, and any other elementary ways we can think about a stock—are unlikely to provide easy profits. "If there is any market inefficiency, hence any investment opportunity," says Treynor, "it will arise with the second kind of investment idea—the kind that travels slowly. The second kind of idea—rather than the obvious, hence quickly discounted insight relating to 'long-term' business developments—is the only meaningful basis for long-term investing."[7]

You have, I'm sure, already realized that the investment tenets outlined in *The Warren Buffett Way* are the ideas that "travel slowly" and that relate to "'long-term' business developments," and thus are the basis for "long-term investing." Let's be clear: The slow-moving idea is not intellectually difficult to grasp, but it is more laborious than relying on the "straightforward and obvious."

System 1 and System 2

For years, psychologists have been interested in the idea that our cognition processes are divided into two modes of thinking, traditionally referred to as intuition, which produces "quick and associative" cognition, and reason, described as "slow and rule-governed." Today, psychologists routinely refer to these cognitive systems as System 1 and System 2 thinking. System 1 thinking is where simple and straightforward ideas travel quickly. It takes little time and not much intellectual work to calculate a price-earnings ratio or a dividend yield.

System 2 thinking is the reflective part of our cognition process. It operates in a controlled manner, slowly and with effort. Our "slow-moving ideas" that require "reflection, judgment, and special expertise" are housed in System 2 thinking.

In 2011, the Nobel laureate Daniel Kahneman wrote an important book titled *Thinking Fast and Slow*. It was a *New York Times* best seller and one of the top five nonfiction books that year—quite an accomplishment for a 500-page book on decision making. My favorite part of the book is Chapter 3, "The Lazy Controller." Kahneman reminds us that cognitive effort is mental work, and, as with all work, many of us have the tendency to get lazy when the task gets harder. He is surprised by the ease with which intelligent people appear satisfied enough with their initial answer that they stop thinking.

Kahneman tells us activities that put demands on System 2 thinking require self-control, and continuous exertion of self-control can be unpleasant. If we are continually forced to do something over and over that is challenging, there is a tendency to exert less self-control when the next challenge arrives. Eventually we simply run out of gas. In contrast, "those who avoid the sin of intellectual sloth could be called 'engaged.' They are more alert, more intelligently active, less willing to be satisfied with superficially attractive answers, more skeptical about their intuitions."[8]

Shane Frederick, associate professor of marketing at Yale University, has given us a fascinating look at how people with fairly high IQs navigate between System 1 and System 2 thinking. He gathered a group of Ivy League students from Harvard, Princeton, and MIT (presumably all highly intelligent) and asked them the following three questions:

1. A bat and ball cost $1.10. The bat costs one dollar more than the ball. How much does the ball cost?

2. If it takes five machines five minutes to make five widgets, how long would it take 100 machines to make 100 widgets?
3. In a lake, there is a patch of lily pads. Every day, the patch doubles in size. If it takes 48 days for the patch to cover the entire lake, how long will it take for the patch to cover half of the lake?[9]

To Frederick's surprise, over half of the students got the answers wrong, leading him to delineate two significant problems. First, people are not accustomed to thinking hard about problems and often rush to the first plausible answer that comes to mind so they don't have to engage the heavy burden of System 2 thinking. The second problem, which is disturbing in itself, was the realization that the System 2 process does a very poor job of monitoring System 1 thinking for errors. It seemed clear to Frederick that the students were stuck in System 1 thinking and could not, or would not, convert to System 2.

How do System 1 and System 2 thinking work in investing? Say an investor is considering making a common stock purchase. Using System 1 thinking, the investor would tabulate a company's price-to-earnings ratio, book value, and dividend yield. Seeing that the two ratios are trading near historical lows and the company has raised the dividend each year for the past 10 years, the investor might quickly conclude that the stock is a good value. Sadly, too many investors rely almost exclusively on System 1 thinking to make a decision, never stopping to engage System 2 thinking.

What does it mean to be engaged? Quite simply, it means your System 2 thinking is strong, vibrant, and less prone to fatigue. So distinct is System 2 thinking from System 1 thinking that the psychologist Keith Stanovich has termed the two as having "separate minds."

But a "separate mind" is separate only if it is distinguishable. Put in the context of investing, the "separate mind" that inhabits System 2 thinking is distinguishable from the "separate mind" in System 1 thinking only if it is adequately armed with the required understanding of a company's competitive advantages, the strength of a company's management team to rationally allocate the capital of the company, the important economic drivers that determine a company's value, and the psychological lessons that prevent the investor from making foolish decisions.

It appears to me that much of the decision making that goes on in Wall Street is System 1 thinking. It operates mainly by intuition. Decisions are made automatically and quickly with little or no time for thoughtful reflection. System 2 thinking is serious thought. It is deliberate and requires concentration. System 2 thinkers are naturally patient. For System 2 thinking to work effectively, you must allocate time for deliberation and, yes, even meditation. You will not be surprised when I point out that the tenets outlined in *The Warren Buffett Way* are best suited for slow thinking, not the rapid-fire decisions common to System 1.

The Mindware Gap

The second cause of dysrationalia, according to Stanovich, is lack of adequate content for System 2 thinking. Psychologists who study decision making refer to content deficiency as a *mindware gap*. First articulated by David Perkins, a Harvard cognitive scientist, mindware is all the rules, strategies, procedures, and knowledge people have at their mental disposal to help solve a problem. "Just as kitchenware consists of tools for working in the kitchen, and software consists in tools with your computer, mindware consists in the tools for the mind," explains Perkins. "A piece of mindware is anything a person can learn that extends the person's general powers to think critically and creatively."[10]

What mindware would you need to activate System 2 thinking? At a minimum, you would read a company's annual report and the annual reports of competitors. If it appears the company has a strong competitive position with a favorable long-term outlook, you would next run several dividend discount models that include different growth rates of the company's owner earnings over different time periods to get a sense of approximate valuation. Then you would study and understand management's long-term capital allocation strategy. Last, you might call a few friends, colleagues, or financial advisers to see if they have an opinion about your company or, better yet, your company's competitors. Take note: None of this requires a high IQ, but it is more laborious and requires more mental effort and concentration than simply figuring out the company's current price-to-earnings ratio.

Time and Patience

Even though there is ample evidence that long-term thinking, patiently applied, is the best course for investing success, it appears that nothing much has changed. Even the 2008–2009 financial crisis and bear market haven't changed our behavior. These days virtually all market activity is short-term. In 1960, the annualized value-weighted NYSE/AMEX turnover was less than 10 percent. Today, that ratio is greater than 300 percent—a 30-fold increase over the past 50 years.[11] It is hard to believe that this dramatic increase in activity has not had a transformative effect on both the market and its participants.

Theoretically, an increase in market participation coupled with higher trading volumes is thought to lead to better price discovery, which in turn leads to a narrowing of the price-value gap with a corresponding reduction in market noise and volatility. But in reality, we have learned that if the majority of the market participants are speculators, not investors, then we are likely to see the exact opposite: The increase in trading activity will work to widen the price-value gap, increase the noise in the system, and lead to spikes in volatility. In this world, an investor who is hostage to short-term performance pressures will feel nothing but discontent.

It doesn't have to be that way. The success of Warren Buffett is very much about his desire to play the game differently. And we are all invited to join him in that game. The only requirement for successful play is the willingness to adopt a different set of rules. Of these, none is more important than the value of patience.

Time and patience, two sides of the same coin—that is the essence of Buffett. His success lies in the patient attitude he quietly maintains toward both Berkshire's wholly owned businesses and the common stocks held in the portfolio. In this high-paced world of constant activity, Buffett purposefully operates at a slower speed. A detached observer might think this slothlike attitude means forgoing easy profits, but those who have come to appreciate the process realize that Buffett and Berkshire are accumulating mountains of wealth. The speculator has no patience. Buffett, the investor, lives for it. As he reminds us, "The best thing about time is its length."

And so we come back full circle, to the critical issue of emotion and its counterpoint, rationality. Intelligence alone is not enough to ensure investment success. The size of the investor's brain is less important than the ability to detach the brain from the emotions. "Rationality is essential when others are making decisions based on short-term greed or fear," says Buffett. "That is when the money is made."[12]

Buffett recognizes that he is neither richer nor poorer because of the market's short-term fluctuations in price, since his holding period is longer-term. Whereas most individuals cannot endure the discomfort associated with declining stock prices, Buffett is not unnerved, because he believes that he can do a better job than the market in valuing a company. Buffett figures that if you can't do a better job as well, you don't belong in the game. It's like poker, he explains—if you have been in the game for a while and don't know who the patsy is, you're the patsy.

Absent rationality, investors easily default to System 1 thinking, which is adequate for simple and predictable tasks but not for the complexity that is the stock market. Absent rationality, investors become enslaved to the basic emotions of fear and greed. Absent rationality, investors are destined to become the patsy in the game called investing.

CHAPTER 8

The World's Greatest Investor

He is often called the world's greatest investor, but how do we know for sure? How exactly would one go about determining such a claim? It seems to me all we need do is look at two simple variables: relative outperformance and duration. Both are needed. It is not enough to just beat the stock market over the short run. Countless people have done that at one time or another. Doing so over a long period of time is what counts. As Michael Mauboussin aptly describes in his book *The Success Equation* (Harvard Business School Press, 2012), there is a measure of both luck and skill in business, in sports—and in investing. And the only way to distinguish whether luck or skill prevails is by examining the results over time. Luck may play a role in the short run, but Father Time will let us know whether skill was involved. Here Buffett is unmatched.

Warren Buffett's career managing money spans nearly 60 years. It is divided between the time he managed the Buffett Investment Partnership, Ltd. (1956 to 1969) and the much longer period of managing Berkshire Hathaway, starting in 1965, the year he took control of the company.

At the relatively young age of 25 with a relatively small amount of money (his own investment was only $100), Buffett started his partnership. Although the objective of the partnership was to generate at least a 6 percent annual return, Buffett set himself a much tougher goal: to beat the Dow Jones Industrial Average by 10 percentage points a year. He did much better: Between 1965 and 1969, Buffett grew the partnership at a compound annual rate of 29.5 percent, 22 percentage points higher than the Dow. An investor who put $10,000 in Buffett's partnership at the beginning and held until the end would have netted, after Buffett's profit share, $150,270. The same amount invested in the Dow would have grown to $15,260. Over that time period, the Dow lost money five different years. Buffett made a profit and beat the index every single year.

In those days, there were very few hotshot managers Buffett could compare himself to. Gerald Tsai and Fred Carr, the two best-known mutual fund managers, burst on the scene in the mid-1960s near the time Buffett was thinking about shutting down the partnership. They built and then destroyed their reputations buying the 1960s "Go-Go" stocks. In one of Carol Loomis's earliest articles for *Fortune* magazine, titled "The Jones Nobody Keeps Up With" (April 1966), she compared Buffett's partnership performance to the famous hedge fund manager Alfred Winslow Jones. At the time, A.W. Jones & Company had a 10-year record but Buffett had only nine years managing money. Carol examined the trailing five-year returns for both investors and found that Buffett eked out the win, besting Jones 334 percent to 325 percent. But as Carol pointed out, Buffett soon shut down his partnership whereas Jones stayed in the game, suffering along with everyone else who could not see that stocks had become grossly overvalued.

Putting aside the incredible track record of the Buffett Investment Partnership, the claim that Buffett is the world's greatest investor could easily hang on what he has accomplished at Berkshire Hathaway, as Table 8.1 makes clear. Over 48 years, between 1965 and 2012, the book value of Berkshire Hathaway has grown from $19 per share to a staggering $114,214 per share, a 19.7 percent annual rate of return. By comparison, the S&P 500 index, with dividends included, grew at 9.4 percent. In those 48 years, the S&P 500 index lost money 11 years—nearly one in five years; Berkshire posted just two negative years.

Table 8.1 Berkshire's Corporate Performance versus the S&P 500

	Annual Percentage Change		
	in Per-Share Book Value of Berkshire	in S&P 500 with Dividends Included	Relative Results
Year	(1)	(2)	(1) – (2)
1965	23.8	10.0	13.8
1966	20.3	(11.7)	32.0
1967	11.0	30.9	(19.9)
1968	19.0	11.0	8.0
1969	16.2	(8.4)	24.6
1970	12.0	3.9	8.1
1971	16.4	14.6	1.8
1972	21.7	18.9	2.8
1973	4.7	(14.8)	19.5
1974	5.5	(26.4)	31.9
1975	21.9	37.2	(15.3)
1976	59.3	23.6	35.7
1977	31.9	(7.4)	39.3
1978	24.0	6.4	17.6
1979	35.7	18.2	17.5
1980	19.3	32.3	(13.0)
1981	31.4	(5.0)	36.4
1982	40.0	21.4	18.6
1983	32.3	22.4	9.9
1984	13.6	16.1	7.5
1985	48.2	31.6	16.6
1986	26.1	18.6	7.5
1987	19.5	5.1	14.4
1988	20.1	16.6	3.5
1989	44.4	31.7	12.7
1990	7.4	(3.1)	10.5
1991	39.6	30.5	9.1
1992	20.3	7.6	12.7
1993	14.3	10.1	4.2
1994	13.9	1.3	12.6
1995	43.1	37.6	5.5
1996	31.8	23.0	8.8
1997	34.1	33.4	0.7

(Continued)

Table 8.1 (Continued)

	Annual Percentage Change		
	in Per-Share Book Value of Berkshire	in S&P 500 with Dividends Included	Relative Results
Year	(1)	(2)	(1) – (2)
1998	48.3	28.6	19.7
1999	0.5	21.0	(20.5)
2000	6.5	(9.1)	15.6
2001	(6.2)	(11.9)	5.7
2002	10.0	(22.1)	32.1
2003	21.0	28.7	(7.7)
2004	10.5	10.9	(0.4)
2005	6.4	4.9	1.5
2006	18.4	15.8	2.6
2007	11.0	5.5	5.5
2008	(9.6)	(37.7)	27.4
2009	19.8	26.5	(6.7)
2010	13.0	15.1	(2.1)
2011	4.6	2.1	2.5
2012	14.4	16.0	(1.6)
Compounded Annual Gain, 1965–2012	19.7%	9.4%	10.3
Overall Gain, 1964–2012	586,817%	7,433%	

On sheer numbers, then—superior performance sustained over long periods—it's hard to argue with the statement that Warren Buffett is the world's greatest investor. But what if we look beyond the numbers?

The Private Buffett

How should we think about a man who began managing money when Dwight Eisenhower was president and continues to play the game well almost six decades later?

When he was not yet a teenager, young Buffett announced to anyone and everyone that he was going to be a millionaire by age 30 and if not he would jump off the tallest building in Omaha. He was joking, of course—about the jumping-off part—and even the millionaire ambition wasn't what we might expect. Today, he has far exceeded that youngster's goal, but those who know Buffett well know he cares little for the billionaire's lifestyle. He still lives in the same Omaha house he bought in 1958, he drives late-model American cars, and he much prefers cheeseburgers, Cokes, and ice cream to fancy cuisine. His only vice is his beloved private jet. "It's not that I want money," Buffett has said. "It's the fun of making money and watching it grow."[1] And, as we know from Chapter 1, these days he derives enormous pleasure from giving it away.

In a world where patriotism is too often turned into a shallow cliché, Warren Buffett is unabashedly bullish on the United States of America. He has never been shy to express his belief that the United States offers tremendous opportunity to anyone who is willing to work hard. He is upbeat, cheerful, and optimistic about life in general. Conventional wisdom holds that it is the young who are the eternal optimists and as you get older pessimism begins to tilt the scale. But Buffett appears to be the exception. And I think part of the reason is that for almost six decades he has managed money through a long list of dramatic and traumatic events, only to see the market, the economy, and the country recover and thrive.

It is a worthwhile exercise to Google the noteworthy events of the 1950s, 1960s, 1970s, 1980s, 1990s, and the first decade of the twenty-first century. Although too numerous to list here, the front-page headlines would include nuclear war brinkmanship; presidential assassination and resignation; civil unrest and riots; regional wars; oil crisis, hyperinflation, and double-digit interest rates; and terrorist attacks—not to mention the occasional recession and periodic stock market crash.

When asked how he navigates the treacherous episodes that can disrupt markets and inevitably scare away most investors, Buffett, with his folksy style, confesses he simply tries to be "greedy when others are fearful and fearful when others are greedy." But I think there is much more to it. Buffett has a well-developed ability not merely to survive the dangerous times that make headlines, but to aggressively invest through these rough periods.

The Buffett Advantage

For years, academicians and investment professionals have debated the validity of what has come to be known as the efficient market theory. As you may remember from Chapter 6, this controversial theory suggests that analyzing stocks is a waste of time because current prices already reflect all available information; so, in a sense, the market itself does all the research you need. Those who adhere to this theory claim, only partly in jest, that investment professionals could throw darts at a page of stock quotes and pick winners just as successfully as a seasoned financial analyst who spent hours poring over the latest annual reports or quarterly statements.

Yet the success of some who continually beat the major indexes—most notably Warren Buffett—suggests that the efficient market theory is flawed. Others, Buffett included, argue that the reason most money managers underperform the market is not because it is efficient, but because their methods are faulty.

Management consultants believe successful businesses have three distinct advantages: a behavioral advantage, an analytical advantage, and an organizational advantage.[2] Studying Warren Buffett, we can see each of these components at work.

Behavioral Advantage

Buffett tells us that successful investing does not require having a high IQ or taking the formal courses taught at most business schools. What matters most is temperament. And when Buffett talks about temperament he means rationality. The cornerstone to rationality is the ability to see past the present and analyze several possible scenarios, eventually making a deliberate choice. That, in a nutshell, is Warren Buffett.

Those who know Buffett agree it is rationality that sets him apart from the rest. "There were a thousand people in my Harvard law school class," Charlie Munger said. "I knew all the top students, and there was no one as able as Warren. His brain is a superbly rational mechanism."[3] Carol Loomis of *Fortune* magazine, who has known Warren Buffett for over 50 years, also believes rationality is the single most important trait in his investment success.[4] Roger Lowenstein, the author of *Buffett: The Making of an American Capitalist,* says, "Buffett's genius [is] largely a genius of character—of patience, discipline, and rationality."[5]

Bill Gates, a member of the Berkshire Hathaway board, likewise believes rationality is Buffett's distinguishing characteristic. This point was made demonstrably clear when the two friends spent an afternoon answering questions from students packed into an auditorium at the University of Washington in Seattle. One of the first questions a student asked was, "How did you get here? How did you become richer than God?" Buffett took a deep breath and began:

"How I got here is pretty simple in my case. It is not IQ, I'm sure you will be glad to hear. The big thing is rationality. I always look at IQ and talent as representing the horsepower of the motor, but that the output—the efficiency with which the motor works—depends on rationality. A lot of people start out with 400 horsepower motors but only get 100 horsepower of output. It's way better to have a 200 horsepower motor and get it all into output.

"So why do smart people do things that interfere with getting the output they're entitled to?" Buffett continued. "It gets into the habits and character and temperament, and behaving in a rational manner. Not getting in your own way. As I have said, everybody here has the ability absolutely to do anything I do and much beyond. Some of you will, and some of you won't. For those who won't, it will be because you get in your own way, not because the world doesn't allow you."[6]

All who know him, and Buffett himself, agree: The driving force of Warren Buffett is rationality. The driving force of his investment strategy is the rational allocation of capital. Determining how to allocate a company's earnings is the most important decision a manager will make; determining how to allocate one's savings is the most important decision an investor will make. Rationality—displaying rational thinking when making that choice—is the quality Buffett most admires. Despite its underlying vagaries, there is a line of reason that permeates the financial markets. Buffett's success is a result of locating that line of reason and never deviating from its path.

Analytical Advantage

When Buffett invests, he sees a business. Most investors see only a stock price. They spend far too much time and effort watching, predicting, and anticipating price changes and far too little time understanding the business they partly own. Elementary as this may be, it is the root of what distinguishes Buffett.

Owning and operating businesses has given him a distinct advantage in analytical thinking. He has experienced both success and failure in his business ventures and has applied to the stock market the lessons he has learned. Most professional investors have not been given the same beneficial education. While they were busy studying capital asset pricing models, beta, and modern portfolio theory, Buffett studied income statements, capital reinvestment requirements, and the cash-generating capabilities of his companies. "Can you really explain to a fish what it's like to walk on land?" Buffett asks. "One day on land is worth a thousand years of talking about it, and one day running a business has exactly the same kind of value."[7]

Buffett believes the investor and the businessperson should look at the company in the same way, because they both want essentially the same thing. The businessperson wants to buy the entire company, and the investor wants to buy portions of it. If you ask businesspeople what they think about when purchasing a company, they are likely to answer, "How much cash can be generated from the business." Finance theory dictates that, over time, there is a direct correlation between the value of a company and its cash-generating capability. So, to make a profit, the businessperson and the investor should be looking at the same variables.

"In our view," says Buffett, "investment students need only two well-taught courses: How to Value a Business, and How to Think about Market Prices."[8]

The stock market, remember, is manic-depressive. Sometimes it is wildly excited about future prospects and at other times it unreasonably depressed. Of course, this creates opportunities, particularly when shares of outstanding businesses are available at irrationally low prices. But just as you would not take direction from an adviser who exhibited manic-depressive tendencies, neither should you allow the market to dictate your actions. The stock market is not a preceptor; it exists merely to assist you with the mechanics of buying or selling shares of stock. If you believe that the stock market is smarter than you are, give it your money by investing in index funds. But if you have done your homework and are confident that you understand your business, turn off the market.

Buffett is not glued to a computer, watching every uptick or downtick on the screen, and he seems to get by just fine without it. If you plan on owning shares in an outstanding business for a number of years, what happens in the market on a day-to-day basis is inconsequential. You will be surprised to discover that your portfolio weathers nicely without you constantly looking at the market. If you don't believe it, give yourself a test. Try not to look at the market for 48 hours. Don't look at your computer or cell phone, don't check the newspaper, and don't listen to a stock market summary on television or radio. If after two days your companies are well, try turning off the stock market for three days, and then for a whole week. Pretty soon you will be convinced that your investment health will survive and your companies will continue to operate without your constant attention to stock quotes.

"After we buy a stock, we would not be disturbed if markets close for a year or two," says Buffett. "We don't need a daily quote on our 100 percent position in See's Candies to validate our well-being. Why then do we need a quote on our interest in Coke?"[9] Very clearly, Buffett is telling us that he does not need the market's price to validate Berkshire's common stock investments. The same holds true for individual investors. You know you have approached Buffett's level when your attention turns to the stock market and the only question on your mind is: "Has anybody done anything foolish lately that will allow me an opportunity to buy a good business at a great price?"

Just as people spend fruitless hours worrying about the stock market, so too do they needlessly worry about the economy. If you find yourself discussing and debating whether the economy is poised for growth or tilting toward a recession, whether interest rates are moving up or down, whether there is inflation or disinflation, *stop!* Give yourself a break. Buffett is a casual observer of the economy, but he dedicates no significant time or energy analyzing with the intent of predicting what the economy will do.

Often investors begin with an economic assumption and then go about selecting stocks that fit neatly within this grand design. Buffett considers this thinking foolish. First, no one has economic predictive powers any more than they have stock market predictive powers. Second, if you select stocks that will benefit only in a particular economic environment, you inevitably invite turnover and speculation. Whether you correctly predict the economy or not, you'll find yourself continuously adjusting your portfolio to benefit in the next economic scenario. Buffett prefers to buy a business that has the opportunity to profit regardless of the economy. Of course, macroeconomic forces may affect returns on the margin, but overall, Buffett's businesses are able to profit nicely despite the vagaries in the economy. Time is more wisely spent locating and owning a business that has the ability to profit in all economic environments than by renting a group of stocks that do well only if a guess about the economy happens to be correct.

Organizational Advantage

Winston Churchill, addressing the House of Commons in 1944 in a building that had sustained heavy damage from air strikes the day before, said, "We shape our dwellings, and afterwards the dwellings shape us." This eloquent truth, beloved by generations of architects, also helps us understand the shape of Berkshire Hathaway and its builder. As we dissect the Buffett advantage, it's helpful to look at the organizational structure of the company he has built.

When Buffett bought his first share of Berkshire Hathaway for $7, I am not sure he had a grand vision of what Berkshire would become a half-century later. But as Churchill predicted, the company did indeed reflect the characteristics of its architect, and Warren Buffett the investor epitomizes the characteristics of his company.

The success of Berkshire Hathaway rests on three fundamental pillars. First, the company's subsidiaries generate mountain-loads of cash that are sent upstream to corporate headquarters in Omaha. This cash comes from the float of its massive insurance operations as well as the cash-generating capabilities of its nonfinancial wholly owned subsidiaries.

Second, Buffett, the capital allocator, takes this cash and reinvests it into more cash-generating opportunities. This in turn allows him to buy still more cash-generating businesses, which generate cash, which allows him to . . . I am sure you the get the picture.

The last pillar is decentralization. Each of the subsidiaries is managed by very talented operators who need no help from Buffett to run their businesses. All for the better, as this allows Buffett to focus nearly 100 percent of his energies on capital allocation, his best talent. Buffett's management manifesto can be summarized as "hire well, manage little." Today, Berkshire Hathaway is a company with 80-plus subsidiaries and more than 270,000 employees, but the corporate headquarters is staffed by just 23 people.

The architecture of Berkshire Hathaway has led to something that is more powerful than a simple business strategy, says William Thorndike, author of *The Outsiders: Eight Unconventional CEOs and Their Radically Rational Blueprint for Success.* "Buffett has developed a *worldview* that at its core emphasizes the development of long-term relationships with excellent people and businesses and the avoidance of unnecessary turnover, which can interrupt the powerful chain of economic compounding that is the essence of long-term value creation," wrote Thorndike.[10]

Thorndike believes Buffett is best understood as a "manager/investor/philosopher whose primary objective is turnover reduction."[11] Why? Because there is a cost to turnover, and I am not speaking just of trading commissions and capital gains taxes.

In Buffett's mind, the cost of turnover is more human in nature. If you have assembled the best businesses, run by some of the best managers, financed by some of the best shareholders, why would anyone want to disrupt the long-term value creation that comes from this potent combination?

Learning to Think Like Buffett

In the 20-some years I have been writing and lecturing about Warren Buffett and his unparalleled success, one comment I hear often is some variation of this: "Well, if I had his millions I could make lots of money in the stock market, too." I never understood this thinking. If you follow the logic, what they are saying is you first have to be rich before you can achieve the talents of becoming rich. But I would remind readers that Buffett developed a unique investment process long before he made millions, much less billions.

I'm going to do my best to convince you that, within your own financial parameters, there is no reason you cannot achieve Buffett-style success, if you integrate his tenets into your thinking and base your investment decisions on them. I can't guarantee that you can start with $100 and end up many years later with billions, but I can guarantee that you will do better than someone with the same financial resources who depends on any one of the many speculator's schemes floating around.

So let's walk through the steps, using a hypothetical situation.

Let's pretend that you have to make a very important decision. Tomorrow you will be given an opportunity to pick one business—and only one—to invest in. To make it interesting, let us also pretend that once you have made your decision, it cannot be changed and, furthermore, you have to hold the investment for 10 years. Ultimately, the profit from this enterprise will support you in your retirement. Now what are you going to think about?

Business Tenets

Is the Business Simple and Understandable? You cannot make an intelligent guess about the future of your business unless you understand how it makes money. Too often people invest in stocks without a clue as to how a company generates sales, incurs expenses, and produces profits. If you can understand the economic process, you are ready to intelligently proceed further in your investigation.

Does the Business Have a Consistent Operating History? If you are going to invest your family's future in a company, you will need to know whether the company has stood the test of time. It is unlikely that you will bet your future on a new company that has not experienced different economic cycles and competitive forces. You should be assured that your company has been in business long enough to demonstrate an ability, over time, to earn significant profits.

Does the Business Have Favorable Long-Term Prospects? The best business to own, the one with the best long-term prospects, is what Warren Buffett terms a franchise—a business that sells a product or service that is needed or desired, that has no close substitute, and whose profits are not regulated. A franchise typically possesses a great amount of economic goodwill that allows the company to better withstand the effects of inflation. The worst business to own is a commodity business. A commodity business sells products or services that are indistinguishable from competitors. Commodity businesses have little or no economic goodwill. The only distinction in a commodity business is price. The difficulty of owning a commodity business is that sometimes competitors, using price as a weapon, will sell their product below the cost of business to temporarily attract customers in hopes that they will remain loyal. If you compete against other businesses that occasionally sell their products below cost, you are doomed.

Generally, most businesses fall somewhere in between: They are either weak franchises or strong commodity businesses. A weak franchise has more favorable long-term prospects than a strong commodity business. Even a weak franchise still has some pricing power that allows it to earn above-average returns on invested capital. Conversely, a strong commodity business will earn above-average returns only if it is the lowest-cost supplier. One advantage to owning a franchise is that a franchise can endure management incompetence and still survive, whereas in a commodity business, management incompetence is lethal.

Management Tenets

Is Management Rational? Since you do not have to watch the stock market or the general economy, watch your company's cash instead. How management reinvests cash earnings will determine whether you will achieve adequate returns on your investment. If your business generates more cash than is needed to remain operational, which is the kind of business you want, observe closely the actions of management. A rational manager will invest excess cash only in projects that produce earnings at rates higher than the cost of capital. If those rates are not available, the rational manager will return the money to shareholders by increasing dividends and buying back stock. Irrational managers constantly look for ways to spend excess cash rather than return the money to shareholders. They are ultimately revealed when they invest below the cost of capital.

Is Management Candid with Its Shareholders? Although you may never have the opportunity to sit down and talk to the chief executive officer of your business, you can tell much about CEOs by the way they communicate to their shareholders. Does your manager report the progress of the business in such a way that you understand how each operating division is performing? Does management confess its failures as openly as it trumpets its success? Most important, does management forthrightly proclaim that the company's prime objective is to maximize the total return of their shareholders' investment?

Does Management Resist the Institutional Imperative? There is a powerful unseen force that allows managers to act irrationally and supersede the interests of owners. The force is the institutional imperative—mindless, lemming-like imitation of other managers who justify their actions based on the logic that if other companies are doing it, it must be all right. One measure of managers' competence is how well they are able to think for themselves and avoid the herd mentality.

Financial Tenets

Focus on Return on Equity, Not Earnings per Share Most investors judge a company's annual performance by earnings per share, watching to see if they set a record or make a big increase over the previous year. But since companies continually add to their capital base by retaining a portion of their previous year's earnings, growth in earnings (which automatically increases earnings per share) is really meaningless. When companies loudly report "record earnings per share," investors are misled into believing that management has done a superior job year after year. A truer measure of annual performance, because it takes into consideration the company's ever-growing capital base, its return on equity—the ratio of operating earnings to shareholders' equity.

Calculate "Owner Earnings" The cash-generating ability of a business determines its value. Buffett seeks out companies that generate cash in excess of their needs as opposed to companies that consume cash. But when determining the value of a business, it is important to understand that not all earnings are created equal. Companies with a high ratio of fixed assets to profits will require a larger share of retained earnings to remain viable than companies with a lower ratio of fixed assets to profits, because some of the earnings must be earmarked to maintain and upgrade those assets. Thus accounting earnings need to be adjusted to reflect the business's cash-generating ability.

A more accurate picture is provided by what Buffett calls "owner earnings." To determine owner earnings, add depreciation, depletion, and amortization charges to net income and then subtract the capital expenditures the company needs to maintain its economic position and unit volume.

Look for Companies with High Profit Margins High profit margins reflect not only a strong business but management's tenacious spirit for controlling costs. Buffett loves managers who are cost-conscious and abhors managers who allow costs to escalate. Indirectly, shareholders own the profits of the business. Every dollar that is spent unwisely deprives the owners of the business a dollar of profit. Over the years, Buffett has observed that companies with high-cost operations typically find ways to sustain or add to their costs, whereas companies with below-average costs pride themselves on finding ways to cut expenses.

For Every Dollar Retained, Make Sure the Company Has Created at Least One Dollar of Market Value This is a quick financial test that will tell you not only about the strength of the business but how well management has rationally allocated the company's resources. From a company's net income, subtract all dividends paid to shareholders. What is left is the company's retained earnings. Now, add the company's retained earnings over a 10-year period. Next, determine the difference between the company's current market value and its market value 10 years ago. If your business has employed retained earnings unproductively over this 10-year period, the market will eventually catch up and set a lower price on the business. If the increase in the company's market value is less than the sum of the retained earnings, the company is going backward. But if your business has been able to earn above-average returns on retained capital, the gain in market value of the business should exceed the sum of the company's retained earnings, thus creating more than one dollar of market value for every dollar retained.

Market Tenets

What Is the Value of the Business? The value of a business is the estimated cash flows expected to occur over the life of the business, discounted at an appropriate interest rate. The cash flows of a business are the company's owner earnings. By measuring owner earnings over a long period, you will understand whether they are consistently growing at some average rate or merely bobbling around some constant value.

If the company has bob-around earnings, you should discount those earnings by the long-term interest rate. If owner earnings show some predictable growth pattern, the discount rate can be reduced by this rate of growth. Don't become overly optimistic about a company's future growth rate. It is better to use a conservative estimate than allow enthusiasm to inflate the value of the business. Buffett uses the long-term U.S. Treasury rate as his discount factor. He does not add an equity risk premium to this discount rate, but he will adjust the discount rate upward when interest rates are declining.

Can the Business Be Purchased at a Significant Discount to Its Value? Once you determine the value of a business, the next step is to look at the market price. Buffett's rule is to purchase the business only when its price is at a significant discount to its value. Take note: Only at his final step does Buffett look at the stock market price.

Calculating the value of a business is not mathematically complex. However, problems arise when an analyst wrongly estimates a company's future cash flow. Buffett deals with this problem in two ways. First, he increases his chances of correctly predicting future cash flows by sticking with businesses that are simple and stable in character. Second, he insists that with each company he purchases, there must be a margin of safety between the company's purchase price and its determined value. This margin of safety helps create a cushion that will protect him—and you—from companies whose future cash flows are changing.

■ ■ ■

Now that you are a business owner as opposed to a renter of stocks, you are ready to expand your theoretical portfolio from just one stock to several. Because you are no longer measuring your success solely by price change or comparing annual price change to a common stock benchmark, you have the liberty to select the best busi-

Buffett's Tenets

Business Tenets

Is the business simple and understandable?
Does the business have a consistent operating history?
Does the business have favorable long-term prospects?

Management Tenets

Is management rational?
Is management candid with its shareholders?
Does management resist the institutional imperative?

Financial Tenets

Focus on return on equity, not earnings per share.
Calculate "owner earnings."
Look for companies with high profit margins.
For every dollar the company retained, make sure the company has created at least one dollar of market value.

Market Tenets

What is the value of the business?
Can the business be purchased at a significant discount to its value?

nesses available. There is no law that says you must include every major industry within your portfolio, nor do you have to include 40, 50, 60, or 100 stocks in your portfolio to achieve adequate diversification.

Buffett believes that wide diversification is required only when investors do not understand what they are doing. If these "know-nothing" investors want to own common stocks, they should own a large number of securities and space out their purchases over time. In other words, the know-nothing investor should use an index fund and dollar-cost average purchases. There is nothing shameful about becoming an index investor. In fact, Buffett points out, the index investor will actually outperform the majority of investment professionals. "Paradoxically," he notes, "when 'dumb' money acknowledges its limitations, it ceases to be dumb."[12]

"On the other hand," says Buffett, "if you are a know-something investor, able to understand business economics and to find five to ten sensibly-priced companies that possess important long-term competitive advantages, conventional diversification makes no sense to you."[13] Buffett asks you to consider: If the best business you own presents the least financial risk and has the most favorable long-term prospects, why would you put money into your 20th favorite business rather than add money to the top choices?

Now, consider how your theoretical portfolio, now broader than one stock, is doing. You can measure the economic progress of the businesses you own by calculating their look-through earnings, just as Buffett does. Multiply the earnings per share by the number of shares you own to calculate the total earnings power of your companies. The goal of the business owner, Buffett explains, is to create a portfolio of companies that, in 10 years, will produce the highest level of look-through earnings.

Because the growth of look-through earnings, not price changes, now becomes the highest priority in your portfolio, many things begin to change. First, you are less likely to sell your best businesses just because you have a profit. Ironically, corporate managers understand this when they focus on their own business operation. "A parent company," Buffett explains, "that owns a subsidiary with superb long-term economics is not likely to sell that entity regardless of price."[14] A CEO wanting to increase the value of the business will not sell the company's crown jewel. Yet this same CEO will impulsively sell stocks in his or her personal portfolio with little more logic than the idea that "you can't go broke taking a profit." "In our view," Buffett explains, "what makes sense in business also makes sense in stocks: An investor should ordinarily hold a small piece of an outstanding business with the same tenacity that an owner would exhibit if he owned all of that business."[15]

Now that you are managing a portfolio of businesses, not only will you avoid selling your best businesses, but you will also pick new businesses for purchase with much greater care. As the manager of a portfolio of businesses, you must resist the temptation to purchase a marginal company just because you have cash reserves. If the company does not pass your tenet screen, do not purchase it. Be patient and wait for the right business. It is wrong to assume that if you are not buying and selling, you are not making progress. In Buffett's mind, it is too difficult to make hundreds of smart decisions in a lifetime. He would rather position his portfolio so he only has to make a few smart decisions.

Finding Your Own Way

"Something about the mind, wired to find patterns both real and imaginary, rebels at the notion of fundamental disorder."[16] Those words, written by George Johnson in his book *Fire in the Mind*, reveal the dilemma that all investors face. The mind craves patterns, Johnson believes; patterns suggest order, which allows us to plan and make sense of our resources.

What we have come to understand about Buffett is that he is continually seeking patterns—patterns that can be found when analyzing a business. He also knows that these business patterns will, at some point, reveal the future pattern of the stock price. Of course, a stock price pattern will not obligingly follow every change in the business pattern, but if your time horizon is long enough, it is remarkable how the price patterns eventually match up with the business patterns.

Too many investors are seeking patterns in the wrong places. They are certain that there is some predictable pattern for gauging short-term price changes. But they are mistaken. There simply are no predictable patterns for guessing the future direction of the stock market. The exact patterns do not repeat. Still, these investors keep trying.

How do investors maneuver in a world that lacks pattern recognition? The answer is to look in the right place at the right level. Although the economy and the market as a whole are too complex and too large to be predictable, there are recognizable patterns at the company level. Inside each company, there are business patterns, management patterns, and financial patterns.

If you study these patterns, in most cases you can make a reasonable prediction about the future of the company. Warren Buffett focuses on those patterns, not on the unpredictable behavioral patterns of millions of investors. "I have always found it easier to evaluate the weights dictated by fundamentals," said Buffett, "than votes dictated by psychology."[17]

One thing we can say with certainty is that knowledge works to increase our investment return and reduces overall risk. I believe we can also make the case that knowledge is what defines the difference between investment and speculation. In the end, the more you know about your companies, the less likely it is that pure speculation will dominate your thinking and your actions.

The financial writer Ron Chernow claims that "financial systems reflect the values of societies."[18] I believe that is largely true. From time to time, we seem to misplace our values, and then our markets succumb to speculative forces. Soon, we right ourselves and continue on with our financial walk, only to trip and fall back into destructive habits. One way to stop this vicious cycle is to educate ourselves about what works and what does not work.

Buffett has had his share of failures and no doubt will have a few more in the years ahead. But investment success is not synonymous with infallibility. Rather, it comes from doing more things right than wrong. The Warren Buffett Way is no different. Its success as an investment approach is as much a result of eliminating those things that you can easily get wrong, which are many and perplexing (predicting markets, economies, and stock prices), as requiring you to get certain thing right, which are few and simple (mainly, valuing a business). Wh n Buffett purchases stocks, he is focusing on two simple variables: the price of the business and its value. The price of the business can be found by looking up its quote. Determining the value requires some calculation, but it is not beyond the ability of those willing to do some homework.

Because you no longer worry about the stock market, the economy, or predicting stock prices, you are now free to spend more time understanding your businesses. More productive time can be spent reading annual reports and business and industry articles that will improve your knowledge as an owner. In fact, the degree to which you are willing to investigate your own business lessens your dependency on others who make a living advising people to take irrational actions.

Ultimately, the best investment ideas will come from you doing your own work. However, you should not feel intimidated. The Warren Buffett Way is not beyond the comprehension of most serious investors. You do not have to become an MBA-level authority on business valuation to use it successfully. Still, if you are uncomfortable applying these tenets yourself, nothing prevents you from asking your financial adviser these same questions. In fact, the more you enter into a dialogue on price and value, the more you will begin to understand and appreciate the Warren Buffett Way.

Over his lifetime, Buffett has tried different investment gambits. At a young age he even tried his hand at stock charting. He was tutored in securities analysis by the brightest financial mind in the industry, Benjamin Graham. He benefited early on by studying the investment strategies of Phil Fisher. And he was most fortunate to have partnered with Charlie Munger, putting into practice all he had learned. Over a career that is six decades and counting, Buffett has confronted countless economic, political, and military challenges and navigated his way to the other side. Through all the distractions, he found his niche, that point where all things make sense: where investment strategy cohabits with personality. "Our [investment] attitude," Buffett says, "fits our personalities and the way we want to live our lives."[19]

This harmony is easily found in Buffett's attitude. He is always upbeat and supportive. He is genuinely excited about coming to work every day. "I have in life all that I want right here," he says. "I love every day. I mean, I tap dance in here and work with nothing but people I like."[20] He adds, "There is no job in the world that is more fun than running Berkshire and I count myself lucky to be where I am."[21]

Appendix

Table A.1 Berkshire Hathaway 1977 Common Stock Portfolio

Number of Shares	Company	Cost	Market Value
934,300	The Washington Post Company	$ 10,628	$ 33,401
1,969,953	GEICO Convertible Preferred	19,417	33,033
592,650	Interpublic Group of Companies	4,531	17,187
220,000	Capital Cities Communications, Inc.	10,909	13,228
1,294,308	GEICO Common Stock	4,116	10,516
324,580	Kaiser Aluminum and Chemical Corp.	11,218	9,981
226,900	Knight-Ridder Newspapers	7,534	8,736
170,800	Ogilvy & Mather International	2,762	6,960
1,305,800	Kaiser Industries, Inc.	778	6,039
	Total	$ 71,893	$ 139,081
	All other common stocks	34,996	41,992
	Total common stocks	$ 106,889	$ 181,073

Source: Berkshire Hathaway 1977 Annual Report.

Note: Dollar amounts are in thousands.

Table A.2 Berkshire Hathaway 1978 Common Stock Portfolio

Number of Shares	Company	Cost	Market Value
934,000	The Washington Post Company	$ 10,628	$ 43,445
1,986,953	GEICO Convertible Preferred	19,417	28,314
953,750	SAFECO Corporation	23,867	26,467
592,650	Interpublic Group of Companies	4,531	19,039
1,066,934	Kaiser Aluminum and Chemical Corp.	18,085	18,671
453,800	Knight-Ridder Newspapers	7,534	10,267

(Continued)

Table A.2 (Continued)

Number of Shares	Company	Cost	Market Value
1,294,308	GEICO Common Stock	4,116	9,060
246,450	American Broadcasting Companies	6,082	8,626
	Total	$ 94,260	$ 163,889
	All other common stocks	39,506	57,040
	Total common stocks	$ 133,766	$ 220,929

Source: Berkshire Hathaway 1978 Annual Report.

Note: Dollar amounts are in thousands.

Table A.3 Berkshire Hathaway 1979 Common Stock Portfolio

Number of Shares	Company	Cost	Market Value
5,730,114	GEICO Corp. (common stock)	$ 28,288	$ 68,045
1,868,000	The Washington Post Company	10,628	39,241
1,007,500	Handy & Harman	21,825	38,537
953,750	SAFECO Corporation	23,867	35,527
711,180	Interpublic Group of Companies	4,531	23,736
1,211,834	Kaiser Aluminum and Chemical Corp.	20,629	23,328
771,900	F.W. Woolworth Company	15,515	19,394
328,700	General Foods, Inc.	11,437	11,053
246,450	American Broadcasting Companies	6,082	9,673
289,700	Affiliated Publications	2,821	8,800
391,400	Ogilvy & Mather International	3,709	7,828
282,500	Media General, Inc.	4,545	7,345
112,545	Amerada Hess	2,861	5,487
	Total	$ 156,738	$ 297,994
	All other common stocks	28,675	36,686
	Total common stocks	$ 185,413	$ 334,680

Source: Berkshire Hathaway 1979 Annual Report.

Note: Dollar amounts are in thousands.

Table A.4 Berkshire Hathaway 1980 Common Stock Portfolio

Number of Shares	Company	Cost	Market Value
7,200,000	GEICO Corporation	$ 47,138	$ 105,300
1,983,812	General Foods	62,507	59,889
2,015,000	Handy & Harman	21,825	58,435
1,250,525	SAFECO Corporation	32,063	45,177
1,868,600	The Washington Post Company	10,628	42,277
464,317	Aluminum Company of America	25,577	27,685
1,211,834	Kaiser Aluminum and Chemical Corp.	20,629	27,569
711,180	Interpublic Group of Companies	4,531	22,135
667,124	F.W. Woolworth Company	13,583	16,511
370,088	Pinkerton's, Inc.	12,144	16,489
475,217	Cleveland-Cliffs Iron Company	12,942	15,894
434,550	Affiliated Publications, Inc.	2,821	12,222
245,700	R.J. Reynolds Industries	8,702	11,228
391,400	Ogilvy & Mather International	3,709	9,981
282,500	Media General	4,545	8,334
247,039	National Detroit Corporation	5,930	6,299
151,104	The Times Mirror Company	4,447	6,271
881,500	National Student Marketing	5,128	5,895
	Total	$ 298,848	$ 497,591
	All other common stocks	26,313	32,096
	Total common stocks	$ 325,161	$ 529,687

Source: Berkshire Hathaway 1980 Annual Report.

Note: Dollar amounts are in thousands.

Table A.5 Berkshire Hathaway 1981 Common Stock Portfolio

Number of Shares	Company	Cost	Market Value
7,200,000	GEICO Corporation	$ 47,138	$ 199,800
1,764,824	R.J. Reynolds Industries	76,668	83,127
2,101,244	General Foods	66,277	66,714
1,868,600	The Washington Post Company	10,628	58,160
2,015,000	Handy & Harman	21,825	36,270
785,225	SAFECO Corporation	21,329	31,016
711,180	Interpublic Group of Companies	4,531	23,202

(Continued)

Table A.5 (Continued)

Number of Shares	Company	Cost	Market Value
370,088	Pinkerton's, Inc.	12,144	19,675
703,634	Aluminum Company of America	19,359	18,031
420,441	Arcata Corporation	14,076	15,136
475,217	Cleveland-Cliffs Iron Company	12,942	14,362
451,650	Affiliated Publications, Inc.	3,297	14,362
441,522	GATX Corporation	17,147	13,466
391,400	Ogilvy & Mather International	3,709	12,329
282,500	Media General	4,545	11,088
	Total	$ 335,615	$ 616,490
	All other common stocks	16,131	22,739
	Total common stocks	$ 351,746	$ 639,229

Source: Berkshire Hathaway 1981 Annual Report.

Note: Dollar amounts are in thousands.

Table A.6 Berkshire Hathaway 1982 Common Stock Portfolio

Number of Shares	Company	Cost	Market Value
7,200,000	GEICO Corporation	$ 47,138	$ 309,600
3,107,675	R.J. Reynolds Industries	142,343	158,715
1,868,600	The Washington Post Company	10,628	103,240
2,101,244	General Foods	66,277	83,680
1,531,391	Time, Inc.	45,273	79,824
908,800	Crum & Forster	47,144	48,962
2,379,200	Handy & Harman	27,318	46,692
711,180	Interpublic Group of Companies	4,531	34,314
460,650	Affiliated Publications, Inc.	3,516	16,929
391,400	Ogilvy & Mather International	3,709	17,319
282,500	Media General	4,545	12,289
	Total	$ 402,422	$ 911,564
	All other common stocks	21,611	34,058
	Total common stocks	$ 424,033	$ 945,622

Source: Berkshire Hathaway 1982 Annual Report.

Note: Dollar amounts are in thousands.

Table A.7 Berkshire Hathaway 1983 Common Stock Portfolio

Number of Shares	Company	Cost	Market Value
6,850,000	GEICO Corporation	$ 47,138	$ 398,156
5,618,661	R.J. Reynolds Industries	268,918	314,334
4,451,544	General Foods	163,786	228,698
1,868,600	The Washington Post Company	10,628	136,875
901,788	Time, Inc.	27,732	56,860
2,379,200	Handy & Harman	27,318	42,231
636,310	Interpublic Group of Companies	4,056	33,088
690,975	Affiliated Publications, Inc.	3,516	26,603
250,400	Ogilvy & Mather International	2,580	12,833
197,200	Media General	3,191	11,191
	Total	$ 558,863	$ 1,260,869
	All other common stocks	7,485	18,044
	Total common stocks	$ 566,348	$ 1,278,913

Source: Berkshire Hathaway 1983 Annual Report.

Note: Dollar amounts are in thousands.

Table A.8 Berkshire Hathaway 1984 Common Stock Portfolio

Number of Shares	Company	Cost	Market Value
6,850,000	GEICO Corporation	$ 47,138	$ 397,300
4,047,191	General Foods	149,870	226,137
3,895,710	Exxon Corporation	173,401	175,307
1,868,600	The Washington Post Company	10,628	149,955
2,553,488	Time, Inc.	89,237	109,162
740,400	American Broadcasting Companies	44,416	46,738
2,379,200	Handy & Harman	27,318	38,662
690,975	Affiliated Publications, Inc.	3,516	32,908
818,872	Interpublic Group of Companies	2,570	28,149
555,949	Northwest Industries	26,581	27,242
	Total	$ 573,340	$ 1,231,560
	All other common stocks	11,634	37,326
	Total common stocks	$ 584,974	$ 1,268,886

Source: Berkshire Hathaway 1984 Annual Report.

Note: Dollar amounts are in thousands.

Table A.9 Berkshire Hathaway 1985 Common Stock Portfolio

Number of Shares	Company	Cost	Market Value
6,850,000	GEICO Corporation	$ 45,713	$ 595,950
1,727,765	The Washington Post Company	9,731	205,172
900,800	American Broadcasting Companies	54,435	108,997
2,350,922	Beatrice Companies, Inc.	106,811	108,142
1,036,461	Affiliated Publications, Inc.	3,516	55,710
2,553,488	Time, Inc.	20,385	52,669
2,379,200	Handy & Harman	27,318	43,718
	Total	$ 267,909	$ 1,170,358
	All other common stocks	7,201	27,963
	Total common stocks	$ 275,110	$ 1,198,321

Source: Berkshire Hathaway 1985 Annual Report.
Note: Dollar amounts are in thousands.

Table A.10 Berkshire Hathaway 1986 Common Stock Portfolio

Number of Shares	Company	Cost	Market Value
2,990,000	Capital Cities/ABC, Inc.	$ 515,775	$ 801,694
6,850,000	GEICO Corporation	45,713	674,725
1,727,765	The Washington Post Company	9,731	269,531
2,379,200	Handy & Harman	27,318	46,989
489,300	Lear Siegler, Inc.	44,064	44,587
	Total	$ 642,601	$ 1,837,526
	All other common stocks	12,763	36,507
	Total common stocks	$ 655,364	$ 1,874,033

Source: Berkshire Hathaway 1986 Annual Report.
Note: Dollar amounts are in thousands.

Table A.11 Berkshire Hathaway 1987 Common Stock Portfolio

Number of Shares	Company	Cost	Market Value
3,000,000	Capital Cities/ABC, Inc.	$ 517,500	$ 1,035,000
6,850,000	GEICO Corporation	45,713	756,925
1,727,765	The Washington Post Company	9,731	323,092
	Total common stocks	$ 572,944	$ 2,115,017

Source: Berkshire Hathaway 1987 Annual Report.
Note: Dollar amounts are in thousands.

Table A.12 Berkshire Hathaway 1988 Common Stock Portfolio

Number of Shares	Company	Cost	Market Value
3,000,000	Capital Cities/ABC, Inc.	$ 517,500	$ 1,086,750
6,850,000	GEICO Corporation	45,713	849,400
14,172,500	The Coca-Cola Company	592,540	632,448
1,727,765	The Washington Post Company	9,731	364,126
2,400,000	Federal Home Loan Mortgage Corp.	71,729	121,200
	Total common stocks	$ 1,237,213	$ 3,053,924

Source: Berkshire Hathaway 1988 Annual Report.
Note: Dollar amounts are in thousands.

Table A.13 Berkshire Hathaway 1989 Common Stock Portfolio

Number of Shares	Company	Cost	Market Value
23,350,000	The Coca-Cola Company	$ 1,023,920	$ 1,803,787
3,000,000	Capital Cities/ABC, Inc.	517,500	1,692,375
6,850,000	GEICO Corporation	45,713	1,044,625
1,727,765	The Washington Post Company	9,731	486,366
2,400,000	Federal Home Loan Mortgage Corp.	71,729	161,100
	Total common stocks	$ 1,668,593	$ 5,188,253

Source: Berkshire Hathaway 1989 Annual Report.
Note: Dollar amounts are in thousands.

Table A.14 Berkshire Hathaway 1990 Common Stock Portfolio

Number of Shares	Company	Cost	Market Value
46,700,000	The Coca-Cola Company	$ 1,023,920	$ 2,171,550
3,000,000	Capital Cities/ABC, Inc.	517,500	1,377,375
6,850,000	GEICO Corporation	45,713	1,110,556
1,727,765	The Washington Post Company	9,731	342,097
2,400,000	Federal Home Loan Mortgage Corp.	71,729	117,000
	Total common stocks	$ 1,958,024	$ 5,407,953

Source: Berkshire Hathaway 1990 Annual Report.
Note: Dollar amounts are in thousands.

Table A.15 Berkshire Hathaway 1991 Common Stock Portfolio

Number of Shares	Company	Cost	Market Value
46,700,000	The Coca-Cola Company	$ 1,023,920	$ 3,747,675
6,850,000	GEICO Corporation	45,713	1,363,150
24,000,000	The Gillette Company	600,000	1,347,000
3,000,000	Capital Cities/ABC, Inc.	517,500	1,300,500
2,495,200	Federal Home Loan Mortgage Corp.	77,245	343,090
1,727,765	The Washington Post Company	9,731	336,050
31,247,000	Guinness plc	264,782	296,755
5,000,000	Wells Fargo & Company	289,431	290,000
	Total common stocks	$ 2,828,322	$ 9,024,220

Source: Berkshire Hathaway 1991 Annual Report.

Note: Dollar amounts are in thousands.

Table A.16 Berkshire Hathaway 1992 Common Stock Portfolio

Number of Shares	Company	Cost	Market Value
93,400,000	The Coca-Cola Company	$ 1,023,920	$ 3,911,125
34,250,000	GEICO Corporation	45,713	2,226,250
3,000,000	Capital Cities/ABC, Inc.	517,500	1,523,500
24,000,000	The Gillette Company	600,000	1,365,000
16,196,700	Federal Home Loan Mortgage Corp.	414,527	783,515
6,358,418	Wells Fargo & Company	380,983	485,624
4,350,000	General Dynamics	312,438	450,769
1,727,765	The Washington Post Company	9,731	396,954
38,335,000	Guinness plc	333,019	299,581
	Total common stocks	$ 3,637,831	$ 11,442,318

Source: Berkshire Hathaway 1992 Annual Report.

Note: Dollar amounts are in thousands.

Table A.17 Berkshire Hathaway 1993 Common Stock Portfolio

Number of Shares	Company	Cost	Market Value
93,400,000	The Coca-Cola Company	$ 1,023,920	$ 4,167,975
34,250,000	GEICO Corporation	45,713	1,759,594
24,000,000	The Gillette Company	600,000	1,431,000
2,000,000	Capital Cities/ABC, Inc.	345,000	1,239,000
6,791,218	Wells Fargo & Company	423,680	878,614
13,654,600	Federal Home Loan Mortgage Corp.	307,505	681,023
1,727,765	The Washington Post Company	9,731	440,148
4,350,000	General Dynamics	94,938	401,287
38,335,000	Guinness plc	333,019	270,822
	Total common stocks	$ 3,183,506	$ 11,269,463

Source: Berkshire Hathaway 1993 Annual Report.

Note: Dollar amounts are in thousands.

Table A.18 Berkshire Hathaway 1994 Common Stock Portfolio

Number of Shares	Company	Cost	Market Value
93,400,000	The Coca-Cola Company	$ 1,023,920	$ 5,150,000
24,000,000	The Gillette Company	600,000	1,797,000
20,000,000	Capital Cities/ABC, Inc.	345,000	1,705,000
34,250,000	GEICO Corporation	45,713	1,678,250
6,791,218	Wells Fargo & Company	423,680	984,272
27,759,941	American Express Company	723,919	818,918
13,654,600	Federal Home Loan Mortgage Corp.	270,468	644,441
1,727,765	The Washington Post Company	9,731	418,983
19,453,300	PNC Bank Corporation	503,046	410,951
6,854,500	Gannett Co., Inc.	335,216	365,002
	Total common stocks	$ 4,280,693	$ 13,972,817

Source: Berkshire Hathaway 1994 Annual Report.

Note: Dollar amounts are in thousands.

Table A.19 Berkshire Hathaway 1995 Common Stock Portfolio

Number of Shares	Company	Cost	Market Value
49,456,900	American Express Company	$ 1,392.70	$ 2,046.30
20,000,000	Capital Cities/ABC, Inc.	345.00	2,467.50
100,000,000	The Coca-Cola Company	1,298.90	7,425.00
12,502,500	Federal Home Loan Mortgage Corp.	260.10	1,044.00
34,250,000	GEICO Corporation	45.70	2,393.20
48,000,000	The Gillette Company	600.00	2,502.00
6,791,218	Wells Fargo & Company	423.70	1,466.90
	Total common stocks	$ 4,366.10	$ 19,344.90

Source: Berkshire Hathaway 1995 Annual Report.

Note: Dollar amounts are in millions.

Table A.20 Berkshire Hathaway 1996 Common Stock Portfolio

Number of Shares	Company	Cost	Market Value
49,456,900	American Express Company	$ 1,392.70	$ 2,794.30
200,000,000	The Coca-Cola Company	1,298.90	10,525.00
24,614,214	The Walt Disney Company	577.00	1,716.80
64,246,000	Federal Home Loan Mortgage Corp.	333.40	1,772.80
48,000,000	The Gillette Company	600.00	3,732.00
30,156,600	McDonald's Corporation	1,265.30	1,368.40
1,727,765	The Washington Post Company	10.60	579.00
7,291,418	Wells Fargo & Company	497.80	1,966.90
	Total common stocks	$ 5,975.70	$ 24,455.20

Source: Berkshire Hathaway 1996 Annual Report.

Note: Dollar amounts are in millions.

Table A.21 Berkshire Hathaway 1997 Common Stock Portfolio

Number of Shares	Company	Cost	Market Value
49,456,900	American Express Company	$ 1,392.70	$ 4,414.00
200,000,000	The Coca-Cola Company	1,298.90	13,337.50
21,563,414	The Walt Disney Company	381.20	2,134.80
63,977,600	Freddie Mac	329.40	2,683.10

Table A.21 (Continued)

Number of Shares	Company	Cost	Market Value
48,000,000	The Gillette Company	600.00	4,821.00
23,733,198	Travelers Group Inc.	604.40	1,278.60
1,727,765	The Washington Post Company	10.60	840.60
6,690,218	Wells Fargo & Company	412.60	2,270.90
	Total common stocks	$ 5,029.80	$ 31,780.50

Source: Berkshire Hathaway 1997 Annual Report.

Note: Dollar amounts are in millions.

Table A.22 Berkshire Hathaway 1998 Common Stock Portfolio

Number of Shares	Company	Cost*	Market Value
50,536,900	American Express Company	$ 1,470	$ 5,180
200,000,000	The Coca-Cola Company	1,299	13,400
51,202,242	The Walt Disney Company	281	1,536
60,298,000	Freddie Mac	308	3,885
96,000,000	The Gillette Company	600	4,590
1,727,765	The Washington Post Company	11	999
63,595,180	Wells Fargo & Company	392	2,540
	Others	2,683	5,135
	Total common stocks	$ 7,044	$ 37,265

*Represents tax-basis cost, which, in aggregate, is $1.5 billion less than GAAP cost.

Source: Berkshire Hathaway Annual Report, 1998.

Note: Dollar amounts are in millions.

Table A.23 Berkshire Hathaway 1999 Common Stock Portfolio

Number of Shares	Company	Cost*	Market Value
50,536,900	American Express Company	$ 1,470	$ 8,402
200,000,000	The Coca-Cola Company	1,299	11,650
59,559,300	The Walt Disney Company	281	1,536
60,298,000	Freddie Mac	294	2,803
96,000,000	The Gillette Company	600	3,954
1,727,765	The Washington Post Company	11	960
59,136,680	Wells Fargo & Company	349	2,391
	Others	4,180	6,848
	Total common stocks	$ 8,203	$ 37,008

*Represents tax-basis cost, which, in aggregate, is $691 million less than GAAP cost.

Source: Berkshire Hathaway Annual Report, 1999.

Note: Dollar amounts are in millions.

Table A.24 Berkshire Hathaway 2000 Common Stock Portfolio

Number of Shares	Company	Cost	Market Value
151,610,700	American Express Company	$ 1,470	$ 8,329
200,000,000	The Coca-Cola Company	1,299	12,188
96,000,000	The Gillette Company	600	3,468
1,727,765	The Washington Post Company	11	1,066
55,071,380	Wells Fargo & Company	319	3,067
	Others	6,703	9,501
	Total common stocks	$ 10,402	$ 37,619

Source: Berkshire Hathaway Annual Report, 2000.
Note: Dollar amounts are in millions.

Table A.25 Berkshire Hathaway 2001 Common Stock Portfolio

Number of Shares	Company	Cost	Market Value
151,610,700	American Express Company	$ 1,470	$ 5,410
200,000,000	The Coca-Cola Company	1,299	9,430
96,000,000	The Gillette Company	600	3,206
15,999,200	H&R Block, Inc.	255	715
24,000,000	Moody's Corporation	499	957
1,727,765	The Washington Post Company	11	916
53,265,080	Wells Fargo & Company	306	2,315
	Others	4,103	5,726
	Total common stocks	$ 8,543	$ 28,675

Source: Berkshire Hathaway Annual Report, 2001.
Note: Dollar amounts are in millions.

Table A.26 Berkshire Hathaway 2002 Common Stock Portfolio

Number of Shares	Company	Cost	Market Value
151,610,700	American Express Company	$ 1,470	$ 5,359
200,000,000	The Coca-Cola Company	1,299	8,768
15,999,200	H&R Block, Inc.	255	643
24,000,000	Moody's Corporation	499	991
1,727,765	The Washington Post Company	11	1,275
53,265,080	Wells Fargo & Company	306	2,497
	Others	4,621	5,383
	Total common stocks	$ 9,146	$ 28,363

Source: Berkshire Hathaway Annual Report, 2002.
Note: Dollar amounts are in millions.

Table A.27 Berkshire Hathaway 2003 Common Stock Portfolio

Number of Shares	Company	Cost	Market Value
151,610,700	American Express Company	$ 1,470	$ 7,312
200,000,000	The Coca-Cola Company	1,299	10,150
96,000,000	The Gillette Company	600	3,526
14,610,900	H&R Block, Inc.	227	809
15,476,500	HCA Inc.	492	665
6,708,760	M&T Bank Corporation	103	659
24,000,000	Moody's Corporation	499	1,453
2,338,961,000	PetroChina Company Limited	488	1,340
1,727,765	The Washington Post Company	11	1,367
56,448,380	Wells Fargo & Company	463	3,324
	Others	2,863	4,682
	Total common stocks	$ 8,515	$ 35,287

Source: Berkshire Hathaway Annual Report, 2003.

Note: Dollar amounts are in millions.

Table A.28 Berkshire Hathaway 2004 Common Stock Portfolio

Number of Shares	Company	Cost	Market Value
151,610,700	American Express Company	$ 1,470	$ 8,546
200,000,000	The Coca-Cola Company	1,299	8,328
96,000,000	The Gillette Company	600	4,299
14,350,600	H&R Block, Inc.	233	703
6,708,760	M&T Bank Corporation	103	723
24,000,000	Moody's Corporation	499	2,084
2,338,961,000	PetroChina "H" Shares (or equivalents)	488	1,249
1,727,765	The Washington Post Company	11	1,698
56,448,380	Wells Fargo & Company	463	3,508
1,724,200	White Mountain Insurance	369	1,114
	Others	3,351	5,465
	Total common stocks	$ 9,056	$ 37,717

Source: Berkshire Hathaway Annual Report, 2004.

Note: Dollar amounts are in millions.

Table A.29 Berkshire Hathaway 2005 Common Stock Portfolio

Number of Shares	Company	Cost	Market Value
151,610,700	American Express Company	$ 1,287	$ 7,802
30,322,137	Ameriprise Financial, Inc.	183	1,243
43,854,200	Anheuser-Busch, Inc.	2,133	1,844
200,000,000	The Coca-Cola Company	1,299	8,062
6,708,760	M&T Bank Corporation	103	732
48,000,000	Moody's Corporation	499	2,084
2,338,961,000	PetroChina "H" Shares (or equivalents)	488	1,915
100,000,000	The Procter & Gamble Company	940	5,788
19,944,300	Wal-Mart Stores, Inc.	944	933
1,727,765	The Washington Post Company	11	1,322
95,092,200	Wells Fargo & Company	2,754	5,975
1,724,200	White Mountain Insurance	369	963
	Others	4,937	7,154
	Total common stocks	$ 15,947	$ 46,721

Source: Berkshire Hathaway Annual Report, 2005.

Note: Dollar amounts are in millions.

Table A.30 Berkshire Hathaway 2006 Common Stock Portfolio

Number of Shares	Company	Cost	Market Value
151,610,700	American Express Company	$ 1,287	$ 9,198
36,417,400	Anheuser-Busch, Inc.	1,761	1,792
200,000,000	The Coca-Cola Company	1,299	9,650
17,938,100	ConocoPhillips	1,066	1,291
21,334,900	Johnson & Johnson	1,250	1,409
6,708,760	M&T Bank Corporation	103	820
48,000,000	Moody's Corporation	499	3,315
2,338,961,000	PetroChina "H" Shares (or equivalents)	488	3,313
3,486,006	POSCO	572	1,158
100,000,000	The Procter & Gamble Company	940	6,427
299,707,000	Tesco plc	1,340	1,820
31,033,800	U.S. Bancorp	969	1,123
17,072,192	USG Corp.	536	936
19,944,300	Wal-Mart Stores, Inc.	942	921
1,727,765	The Washington Post Company	11	1,288
218,169,300	Wells Fargo & Company	3,697	7,758
1,724,200	White Mountain Insurance	369	999
	Others	5,866	8,315
	Total common stocks	$ 22,995	$ 61,533

Source: Berkshire Hathaway Annual Report, 2006.

Note: Dollar amounts are in millions.

Table A.31 Berkshire Hathaway 2007 Common Stock Portfolio

Number of Shares	Company	Cost	Market Value
151,610,700	American Express Company	$ 1,287	$ 7,887
35,563,200	Anheuser-Busch, Inc.	1,718	1,861
60,828,818	Burlington Northern Santa Fe	4,731	5,063
200,000,000	The Coca-Cola Company	1,299	12,274
17,508,700	ConocoPhillips	1,039	1,546
64,271,948	Johnson & Johnson	3,943	4,287
124,393,800	Kraft Foods, Inc.	4,152	4,059
48,000,000	Moody's Corporation	499	1,714
3,486,006	POSCO	572	2,136
101,472,000	The Procter & Gamble Company	1,030	7,450
17,170,953	Sanofi-Aventis	1,466	1,575
227,307,000	Tesco plc	1,326	2,156
75,176,026	U.S. Bancorp	2,417	2,386
17,072,192	USG Corp.	536	611
19,944,300	Wal-Mart Stores, Inc.	942	948
1,727,765	The Washington Post Company	11	1,367
303,407,068	Wells Fargo & Company	6,677	9,160
1,724,200	White Mountain Insurance	369	886
	Others	5,238	7,633
	Total common stocks	$ 39,252	$ 74,999

Source: Berkshire Hathaway Annual Report, 2007.

Note: Dollar amounts are in millions.

Table A.32 Berkshire Hathaway 2008 Common Stock Portfolio

Number of Shares	Company	Cost	Market Value
151,610,700	American Express Company	$ 1,287	$ 2,812
200,000,000	The Coca-Cola Company	1,299	9,054
84,896,273	ConocoPhillips	7,008	4,398
30,009,591	Johnson & Johnson	1,847	1,795
130,272,500	Kraft Foods, Inc.	4,330	3,498
3,947,554	POSCO	768	1,191
91,941,010	The Procter & Gamble Company	643	5,684
22,111,966	Sanofi-Aventis	1,827	1,404
11,262,000	Swiss Re	733	530
227,307,000	Tesco plc	1,326	1,193

Table A.32 (Continued)

Number of Shares	Company	Cost	Market Value
75,145,426	U.S. Bancorp	2,337	1,879
19,944,300	Wal-Mart Stores, Inc.	942	1,118
1,727,765	The Washington Post Company	11	674
304,392,068	Wells Fargo & Company	6,702	8,973
	Others	6,035	4,870
	Total common stocks	$ 37,135	$ 49,073

Source: Berkshire Hathaway Annual Report, 2008.
Note: Dollar amounts are in millions.

Table A.33 Berkshire Hathaway 2009 Common Stock Portfolio

Number of Shares	Company	Cost	Market Value
151,610,700	American Express Company	$ 1,287	$ 6,143
225,000,000	BYD Company, Ltd.	232	1,986
200,000,000	The Coca-Cola Company	1,299	11,400
37,711,330	ConocoPhillips	2,741	1,926
28,530,467	Johnson & Johnson	1,724	1,838
130,272,500	Kraft Foods, Inc.	4,330	3,541
3,947,554	POSCO	768	2,092
83,128,411	The Procter & Gamble Company	533	5,040
25,108,967	Sanofi-Aventis	2,027	1,979
234,247,373	Tesco plc	1,367	1,620
76,633,426	U.S. Bancorp	2,371	1,725
39,037,142	Wal-Mart Stores, Inc.	1,893	2,087
334,235,585	Wells Fargo & Company	7,394	9,021
	Others	6,680	8,636
	Total common stocks	$ 34,646	$ 59,034

Source: Berkshire Hathaway Annual Report, 2009.
Note: Dollar amounts are in millions.

Table A.34 Berkshire Hathaway 2010 Common Stock Portfolio

Number of Shares	Company	Cost	Market Value
151,610,700	American Express Company	$ 1,287	$ 6,507
225,000,000	BYD Company, Ltd.	232	1,182
200,000,000	The Coca-Cola Company	1,299	13,154
29,109,637	ConocoPhillips	2,028	1,982
45,022,563	Johnson & Johnson	2,749	2,785
97,214,684	Kraft Foods, Inc.	3,207	3,063
19,259,600	Munich Re	2,896	2,924
3,947,554	POSCO	768	1,706
72,391,036	The Procter & Gamble Company	464	4,657
25,848,838	Sanofi-Aventis	2,060	1,656
242,163,773	Tesco plc	1,414	1,608
78,060,769	U.S. Bancorp	2,401	2,105
39,037,142	Wal-Mart Stores, Inc.	1,893	2,105
358,936,125	Wells Fargo & Company	8,015	11,123
	Others	3,020	4,956
	Total common stocks	$ 33,733	$ 61,513

Source: Berkshire Hathaway Annual Report, 2010.

Note: Dollar amounts are in millions.

Table A.35 Berkshire Hathaway 2011 Common Stock Portfolio

Number of Shares	Company	Cost	Market Value
151,610,700	American Express Company	$ 1,287	$ 7,151
200,000,000	The Coca-Cola Company	1,299	13,994
29,100,937	ConocoPhillips	2,027	2,121
63,905,931	International Business Machines Corp.	10,856	11,751
31,416,127	Johnson & Johnson	1,880	2,060
79,034,713	Kraft Foods, Inc.	2,589	2,953
20,060,390	Munich Re	2,990	2,464
3,947,555	POSCO	768	1,301
72,391,036	The Procter & Gamble Company	464	4,829
25,848,838	Sanofi	2,055	1,900
291,577,428	Tesco plc	1,719	1,827
78,060,769	U.S. Bancorp	2,401	2,112
39,037,142	Wal-Mart Stores, Inc.	1,893	2,333
400,015,828	Wells Fargo & Company	9,086	11,024
	Others	6,895	9,171
	Total common stocks	$ 48,209	$ 76,991

Source: Berkshire Hathaway Annual Report, 2011.

Note: Dollar amounts are in millions.

Table A.36 Berkshire Hathaway 2012 Common Stock Portfolio

Number of Shares	Company	Cost	Market Value
151,610,700	American Express Company	$ 1,287	$ 8,715
400,000,000	The Coca-Cola Company	1,299	14,500
24,123,911	ConocoPhillips	1,219	1,399
22,999,600	DirecTV	1,057	1,154
68,115,484	International Business Machines Corp.	11,680	13,048
28,415,250	Moody's Corporation	287	1,430
20,060,390	Munich Re	2,990	3,599
20,668,118	Phillips 66	660	1,097
3,947,555	POSCO	768	1,295
52,477,678	The Procter & Gamble Company	336	3,563
25,848,838	Sanofi	2,073	2,438
415,510,889	Tesco plc	2,350	2,268
78,060,769	U.S. Bancorp	2,401	2,493
54,823,433	Wal-Mart Stores, Inc.	2,837	3,741
456,170,061	Wells Fargo & Company	10,906	15,592
	Others	7,646	11,330
	Total common stocks	$ 49,796	$ 87,662

Source: Berkshire Hathaway Annual Report, 2012.

Note: Dollar amounts are in millions.

Notes

Chapter One

A Five-Sigma Event: The World's Greatest Investor

1. Carol Loomis, *Tap Dancing to Work: Warren Buffett on Practically Everything, 1966–2012* (New York: Time Inc., 2012), 256.
2. Matthew Bishop and Michael Green, *Philanthrocapitalism: How Giving Can Save the World* (New York: Bloomsbury Press, 2008), 1.
3. Loomis, *Tap Dancing to Work*, 258.
4. Ibid., 261.
5. Bishop and Green, *Philanthrocapitalism*, 75.
6. Loomis, *Tap Dancing to Work*, 149.
7. Ibid., 315.
8. Alice Schroeder, *The Snowball: Warren Buffett and the Business of Life* (New York: Random House, 2008), 51, 55.
9. Roger Lowenstein, *Buffett: The Making of an American Capitalist* (New York: Random House, 1995), 10.
10. Schroeder, *Snowball*, 62.
11. Ibid.
12. Ibid.
13. Adam Smith, *Supermoney* (Hoboken, NJ: John Wiley & Sons, 2006), 178.
14. Ibid.
15. Loomis, *Tap Dancing to Work*, 67.
16. Lowenstein, *Buffett*, 26.
17. Schroeder, *Snowball*, 146. Schroeder references this apt analogy to Plato's cave, which was originally made by Patrick Byrne.
18. John Train, *The Money Masters* (New York: Penguin Books, 1981), 11.
19. John Brooks, *The Go-Go Years* (New York: Weybright & Talley, 1973).
20. Train, *Money Masters*, 12.
21. Berkshire Hathaway Annual Report, 1987, 22.
22. Berkshire Hathaway Annual Report, 2011, 9.
23. Loomis, *Tap Dancing to Work*, 62. The Greek letter sigma is used in statistics to represent standard deviation from the mean, or average. A five-sigma event, measuring five deviations, has a 1 in 3,488,555 chance of happening. Expressed another way, a five-sigma event has a 99.99994 percent chance of being correct.
24. Ibid.

Chapter Two

The Education of Warren Buffett

1. Adam Smith, *Supermoney* (New York: Random House, 1972), 172.
2. *New York Times*, December 2, 1934, 13D.
3. Benjamin Graham and David Dodd, *Security Analysis*, 3rd ed. (New York: McGraw-Hill, 1951), 38.
4. Ibid., 13.
5. "Ben Graham: The Grandfather of Investment Value Is Still Concerned," *Institutional Investor*, April 1974, 62.
6. Ibid., 61.
7. John Train, *The Money Masters* (New York: Penguin Books, 1981), 60.
8. Philip Fisher, *Common Stocks and Uncommon Profits* (New York: Harper & Brothers, 1958), 11.
9. Ibid., 16.
10. Ibid., 33.
11. Philip Fisher, *Developing an Investment Philosophy*, Financial Analysts Research Foundation, Monograph Number 10, p. 1.
12. Fisher, *Common Stocks*, 13.
13. Fisher, *Developing an Investment Philosophy*, 29.
14. Andrew Kilpatrick, *Of Permanent Value: The Story of Warren Buffett*, rev. ed. (Birmingham, AL: AKPE, 2000), 89.
15. Robert Hagstrom, *Investing: The Last Liberal Art* (New York: Columbia University Press, 2013).
16. Remarks made at the 1997 Berkshire Hathaway annual meeting; quoted in Janet Lowe's biography of Charlie Munger, *Damn Right!* (New York: John Wiley & Sons, 2000).
17. Andrew Kilpatrick, *Warren Buffett: The Good Guy of Wall Street* (New York: Donald I. Fine, 1992), 38.
18. Robert Lenzner, "Warren Buffett's Idea of Heaven: 'I Don't Have to Work with People I Don't Like,'" *Forbes*, October 18, 1993, 43.
19. Berkshire Hathaway Annual Report, 1989, 21.
20. Ibid.
21. L. J. Davis, "Buffett Takes Stock," *New York Times Magazine*, April 1, 1990, 61.
22. Berkshire Hathaway Annual Report, 1987, 15.
23. Warren Buffett, "The Superinvestors of Graham-and-Doddsville," *Hermes*, Fall 1984.
24. Berkshire Hathaway Annual Report, 1990, 17.
25. Benjamin Graham, *The Intelligent Investor*, 4th ed. (New York: Harper & Row, 1973), 287.
26. Warren Buffett, "What We Can Learn from Philip Fisher," *Forbes*, October 19, 1987, 40.
27. "The Money Men—How Omaha Beats Wall Street," *Forbes*, November 1, 1969, 82.

Chapter Three

Buying a Business: The Twelve Immutable Tenets

1. Berkshire Hathaway Annual Report, 1987, 14.
2. Robert Lenzner, "Warren Buffett's Idea of Heaven: 'I Don't Have to Work with People I Don't Like,'" *Forbes*, October 18, 1993.
3. *Fortune*, November 29, 1993, p. 11.
4. Berkshire Hathaway Annual Report, 1987, 7.
5. Berkshire Hathaway Annual Report, 1989, 22.
6. Berkshire Hathaway 1995 annual meeting, as quoted in Andrew Kilpatrick, *Of Permanent Value: The Story of Warren Buffett*, rev. ed. (Birmingham, AL: AKPE, 2004), 1356
7. *St. Petersburg Times*, (December 15, 1999), quoted in Kilpatrick, *Of Permanent Value* (2004), 1356.
8. *Fortune*, (November 22, 1999), quoted in Kilpatrick, *Of Permanent Value* (2004), 1356.
9. Berkshire Hathaway 1996 annual meeting, Kilpatrick (2004), 1344.
10. Berkshire Hathaway Annual Report, 1982, 57.
11. Lenzner, "Warren Buffett's Idea of Heaven."
12. Berkshire Hathaway Annual Report, 1989.
13. Carol Loomis, "The Inside Story of Warren Buffett," *Fortune*, April 11, 1988.
14. Berkshire Hathaway Annual Report, 1988, 5.
15. Berkshire Hathaway Annual Report, 1986, 5.
16. Kilpatrick, *Of Permanent Value* (2000), 89.
17. Berkshire Hathaway Annual Report, 1989, 22.
18. Linda Grant, "The $4 Billion Regular Guy," *Los Angeles Times*, April 17, 1991 (magazine section), 36.
19. Lenzner, "Warren Buffett's Idea of Heaven."
20. Berkshire Hathaway Annual Report, 1985, 9.
21. Berkshire Hathaway Annual Report, 1987, 20.
22. Ibid., 21.
23. Berkshire Hathaway Annual Report, 1984, 15.
24. Berkshire Hathaway Annual Report, 1986, 25.
25. Carol Loomis, *Tap Dancing to Work: Warren Buffett on Practically Everything, 1966–2012* (New York: Time Inc., 2012).
26. Berkshire Hathaway Annual Report, 1990, 16.
27. Berkshire Hathaway Letters to Shareholders, 1977–1983, 52.
28. Berkshire Hathaway Annual Report, 1989, 5.
29. Jim Rasmussen, "Buffett Talks Strategy with Students," *Omaha World Herald*, January 2, 1994, 26.
30. Berkshire Hathaway Annual Report, 1992, 14.
31. Berkshire Hathaway Letters to Shareholders, 1977–1983, 53.
32. Lowenstein, *Buffett: The Making of an American Capitalist* (New York: Random House, 1995), 323.
33. Berkshire Hathaway Letters to Shareholders, 1977–1983, 82.

Chapter Four

Common Stock Purchases: Nine Case Studies

1. Mary Rowland, "Mastermind of a Media Empire," *Working Women*, November 11, 1989, 115.
2. The Washington Post Company Annual Report, 1991, 2.
3. Berkshire Hathaway Annual Report, 1992, 5.
4. Berkshire Hathaway Annual Report, 1985, 19.
5. Chalmers M. Roberts, *The Washington Post: The First 100 Years* (Boston: Houghton Mifflin, 1977), 449.
6. Berkshire Hathaway Annual Report, 1991, 8.
7. Ibid., 9.
8. William Thorndike Jr., *The Outsiders: Eight Unconventional CEOs and Their Radically Rational Blueprint for Success* (Boston: Harvard Business Review Press, 2012), 9.110.
9. Carol Loomis, "An Accident Report on GEICO," *Fortune*, June 1976, 120.
10. Although the 1973–1974 bear market might have contributed to part of GEICO's earlier fall, its decline in 1975 and 1976 was all of its own making. In 1975, the Standard & Poor's 500 Index began at 70.23 and ended the year at 90.9. The next year, the stock market was equally strong. In 1976, the stock market rose and interest rates fell. GEICO's share price decline had nothing to do with the financial markets.
11. Beth Brophy, "After the Fall and Rise," *Forbes*, February 2, 1981, 86.
12. Lynn Dodds, "Handling the Naysayers," *Financial World*, August 17, 1985, 42.
13. Berkshire Hathaway Letters to Shareholders, 1977–1983, 33.
14. Andrew Kilpatrick, *Warren Buffett: The Good Guy of Wall Street* (New York: Donald Fine, 1992), 102.
15. Anthony Bianco, "Why Warren Buffett Is Breaking His Own Rules," *BusinessWeek*, April 15, 1985, 34.
16. Berkshire Hathaway Annual Report, 1991, 8.
17. Bianco, "Why Warren Buffett Is Breaking His Own Rules."
18. Dennis Kneale, "Murphy & Burke," *Wall Street Journal*, February 2, 1990, 1.
19. Capital Cities/ABC Inc. Annual Report, 1992.
20. "A Star Is Born," *BusinessWeek*, April 1, 1985, 77.
21. Anthony Baldo, "CEO of the Year Daniel B. Burke," *Financial World*, April 2, 1991, 38.
22. Berkshire Hathaway Annual Report, 1985, 20.
23. Roger Lowenstein, *Buffett: The Making of an American Capitalist* (New York: Random House, 1995), 323.
24. Berkshire Hathaway Annual Report, 1993, 14.
25. Kilpatrick, *Warren Buffett: The Good Guy of Wall Street*, 123.
26. Mark Pendergrast, *For God, Country and Coca-Cola* (New York: Scribners, 1993).
27. Art Harris, "The Man Who Changed the Real Thing," *Washington Post*, July 22, 1985, B1.
28. "Strategy of the 1980s," Coca-Cola Company.

29. Ibid.
30. Berkshire Hathaway Annual Report, 1992, 13.
31. Ibid.
32. John Dorfman, "Wells Fargo Has Bulls and Bears; So Who's Right?," *Wall Street Journal*, November 1, 1990, C1.
33. Ibid.
34. John Liscio, "Trading Points," *Barron's*, October 29, 1990, 51.
35. Berkshire Hathaway Letters to Shareholders, 1977–1983, 15.
36. Berkshire Hathaway Annual Report, 1990, 16.
37. Reid Nagle, "Interpreting the Banking Numbers," in *The Financial Services Industry—Banks, Thrifts, Insurance Companies, and Securities Firms*, ed. Alfred C. Morley, 25–41 (Charlottesville, VA: Association of Investment Management and Research, 1991).
38. "CEO Silver Award," *Financial World*, April 5, 1988, 92.
39. Gary Hector, "Warren Buffett's Favorite Banker," *Forbes*, October 18, 1993, 46.
40. Berkshire Hathaway Annual Report, 1990, 16.
41. Ibid.
42. Ibid.
43. R. Hutchings Vernon, "Mother of All Annual Meetings," *Barron's*, May 6, 1991.
44. John Taylor, "A Leveraged Bet," *Forbes*, April 15, 1991, 42.
45. Berkshire Hathaway Annual Report, 1994, 17.
46. Dominic Rushe, "Warren Buffett Buys $10bn IBM Stake," *The Guardian*, November 14, 2011.
47. Berkshire Hathaway Annual Report, 2011, 7.
48. Ibid.
49. Ibid., 6.
50. Ibid., 7.
51. Rushe, "Warren Buffett Buys $10bn IBM Stake."
52. I am grateful to Grady Buckett, CFA, director of technology at Morningstar, for his tutorial.
53. Steve Lohr, "IBM Delivers Solid Quarterly Profits," *New York Times*, July 18, 2012.
54. Berkshire Hathaway Annual Report, 2011, 7.
55. Quote from Warren Buffett on CNBC, February 14, 2013.
56. Michael de La Merced and Andrew Ross Sorkin, "Berkshire and 3G Capital in a $23 Billion Deal for Heinz," *New York Times*, February 19, 2013.
57. Berkshire Hathaway Annual Report, 1987, 15.

Chapter Five

Portfolio Management: The Mathematics of Investing

1. Conversation with Warren Buffett, August 1994.
2. Dan Callaghan, Legg Mason Capital Management/Morningstar Mutual Funds.
3. Berkshire Hathaway Annual Report, 1993, 15.
4. Ibid.

5. Conversation with Warren Buffett, August 1994.
6. *Outstanding Investor Digest,* August 10, 1995, 63.
7. Ibid.
8. Peter L. Bernstein, *Against the Gods* (New York: John Wiley & Sons, 1996), 63.
9. Ibid.
10. Ibid.
11. *Outstanding Investor Digest,* May 5, 1995, 49.
12. Robert L. Winkler, *An Introduction to Bayesian Inference and Decision* (New York: Holt, Rinehart & Winston, 1972), 17.
13. Andrew Kilpatrick, *Of Permanent Value: The Story of Warren Buffett* (Birmingham, AL: AKPE, 1998), 800.
14. *Outstanding Investor Digest,* April 18, 1990, 16.
15. Ibid.
16. *Outstanding Investor Digest,* June 23, 1994, 19.
17. Edward O. Thorp, *Beat the Dealer: A Winning Strategy for the Game of Twenty-One* (New York: Vintage Books, 1962).
18. I am indebted to Bill Miller for pointing out the J. L. Kelly growth model.
19. C. E. Shannon, "A Mathematical Theory of Communication," *Bell System Technical Journal* 27, no. 3 (July 1948).
20. J. L. Kelly Jr., "A New Interpretation of Information Rate," *Bell System Technical Journal* 35, no. 3 (July 1956).
21. *Outstanding Investor Digest,* May 5, 1995, 57.
22. Andrew Beyer, *Picking Winners: A Horse Player's Guide* (New York: Houghton Mifflin, 1994), 178.
23. *Outstanding Investor Digest,* May 5, 1995, 58.
24. Benjamin Graham, *The Memoirs of the Dean of Wall Street* (New York: McGraw-Hill, 1996), 239.
25. The speech was adapted as an article in the Columbia Business School's publication *Hermes* (Fall 1984), with the same title. The remarks directly quoted here are from that article.
26. Warren Buffett, "The Superinvestors of Graham-and-Doddsville," *Hermes,* Fall 1984. The superinvestors Buffett presented in the article included Walter Schloss, who worked at Graham-Newman Corporation in the mid-1950s, along with Buffett; Tom Knapp, another Graham-Newman alumnus, who later formed Tweedy, Browne Partners with Ed Anderson, also a Graham follower; Bill Ruane, a former Graham student who went on to establish the Sequoia Fund with Rick Cuniff; Buffett's partner Charlie Munger; Rick Guerin of Pacific Partners; and Stan Perlmeter of Perlmeter Investments.
27. Berkshire Hathaway Annual Report, 1991, 15.
28. Jess H. Chua and Richard S. Woodward, "J. M. Keynes's Investment Performance: A Note," *Journal of Finance* 38, no. 1 (March 1983).
29. Ibid.
30. Ibid.
31. Buffett, "Superinvestors."
32. Ibid.
33. Ibid.

34. Sequoia Fund Annual Report, 1996.
35. Solveig Jansson, "GEICO Sticks to Its Last," *Institutional Investor*, July 1986, 130.
36. Berkshire Hathaway Annual Report, 1986, 15.
37. Berkshire Hathaway Annual Report, 1995, 10.
38. The research described here was conducted with Joan Lamm-Tennant, PhD, at Villanova University.
39. K. J. Martijn Cremers and Antti Petajisto, "How Active Is Your Fund Manager? A New Measure That Predicts Performance," Yale ICF Working Paper No. 06-14, March 31, 2009.
40. "Active Funds Come out of the Closet," *Barron's*, November 17, 2012.
41. Buffett, "Superinvestors."
42. Joseph Nocera, "Who's Got the Answers?," *Fortune*, November 24, 1997, 329.
43. Ibid.
44. V. Eugene Shahan, "Are Short-Term Performance and Value Investing Mutually Exclusive?," *Hermes*, Spring 1986.
45. Sequoia Fund, Quarterly Report, March 31, 1996..
46. A Warren Buffett widely quoted remark.
47. Berkshire Hathaway Annual Report, 1987, 14.
48. Ibid.
49. Ibid.
50. Berkshire Hathaway Annual Report, 1981, 39.
51. Benjamin Graham and David Dodd, *Security Analysis*, 3rd ed. (New York: McGraw-Hill, 1951).
52. Berkshire Hathaway Annual Report, 1987, 15.
53. Berkshire Hathaway Annual Report, 1991, 8.
54. Ibid.
55. *Outstanding Investor Digest*, August 10, 1995, 10.
56. Berkshire Hathaway Annual Report, 1991, 15.
57. Berkshire Hathaway Annual Report, 1996.
58. Robert Jeffrey and Robert Arnott, "Is Your Alpha Big Enough to Cover Its Taxes?," *Journal of Portfolio Management*, Spring 1993.
59. Ibid.
60. Brett Duval Fromson, "Are These the New Warren Buffetts?," *Fortune*, October 30, 1989, from Carol Loomis, *Tap Dancing to Work: Warren Buffett on Practically Everything, 1966–2012* (New York: Time Inc., 2012), 101.

Chapter Six

The Psychology of Investing

1. *Outstanding Investor Digest*, August 10, 1995, 11.
2. Benjamin Graham, *The Intelligent Investor* (New York: Harper & Row, 1973), 106.
3. Jonathan Fuerbringer, "Why Both Bulls and Bears Can Act So Bird-Brained," *New York Times*, March 30, 1997, section 3, p. 6.
4. Jonathan Burton, "It Just Ain't Rational," *Fee Advisor*, September/October 1996, 26.

5. Brian O'Reilly, "Why Can't Johnny Invest?," *Fortune*, November 9, 1998, 73.
6. Fuerbringer, "Why Both Bulls and Bears Can Act So Bird-Brained."
7. Larry Swedore, "Frequent Monitoring of Your Portfolio Can Be Injurious to Your Health," www.indexfunds.com/articles/20021015_myopic_com_gen_LS.htm.
8. Shlomo Benartzi and Richard Thaler, "Myopic Loss Aversion and the Equity Risk Premium," *Quarterly Journal of Economics* 110, no. 1 (February 1995): 73–92.
9. Berkshire Hathaway Annual Report, 1984, 14.
10. Graham, *Intelligent Investor*.
11. Ibid.
12. For a comprehensive and well-written historical summary of the development of modern finance, see Peter Bernstein, *Capital Ideas: The Improbable Origins of Modern Wall Street* (New York: Free Press, 1992).
13. Berkshire Hathaway Annual Report, 1993, 13.
14. Ibid.
15. *Outstanding Investor Digest*, June 23, 1994, 19.
16. *Outstanding Investor Digest*, August 8, 1996, 29.
17. Berkshire Hathaway Annual Report, 1988, 18.
18. Ibid.
19. Andrew Kilpatrick, *Of Permanent Value: The Story of Warren Buffett* (Birmingham, AL: AKPE, 1988), 683.

Chapter Seven

The Value of Patience

1. Andrei Shleifer and Robert Vishny, "The New Theory of the Firm: Equilibrium Short Horizons of Investors and Firms," *American Economic Review, Paper and Proceedings* 80, no. 2 (1990): 148–153.
2. Ibid.
3. Keith Stanovich, *What Intelligence Tests Miss: The Psychology of Rational Thought* (New Haven: Yale University Press, 2009). Also see Keith Stanovich, "Rationality versus Intelligence," Project Syndicate (2009-04-06), www.project-syndicate.org.
4. Keith Stanovich, "Rational and Irrational Thought: The Thinking That IQ Tests Miss," *Scientific American Mind* (November/December 2009), 35.
5. Jack Treynor, *Treynor on Institutional Investing* (Hoboken, NJ: John Wiley & Sons, 2008), 425.
6. Ibid., 424.
7. Ibid.
8. Daniel Kahneman, *Thinking Fast and Slow* (New York: Farrar, Straus & Giroux, 2011), 4.
9. The bat costs $1.05 and the ball costs $0.05. It takes 5 minutes for 100 machines to make 100 widgets. It will take 47 days for the lily pad patch to cover half the lake.
10. D. N. Perkins, "Mindware and Metacurriculm," in *Creating the Future: Perspectives on Educational Change*, comp. and ed. Dee Dickinson (Baltimore: Johns Hopkins University School of Education, 2002).

11. Ilia Dicher, Kelly Long, and Dexin Zhou, "The Dark Side of Trading," Emory University School of Law, Research Paper No. 11, 95–143.
12. Carol Loomis, *Tap Dancing to Work: Warren Buffett on Practically Everything, 1966–2012* (New York: Time Inc., 2012), 101.

Chapter Eight

The World's Greatest Investor

1. Roger Lowenstein, *Buffett: The Making of an American Capitalist* (New York: Random House, 1995), 20.
2. John Pratt and Richard Zeckhauser, eds., *Principals and Agents: The Structure of Business* (Boston: Harvard Business School Press, 1985).
3. Carol Loomis, *Tap Dancing to Work: Warren Buffett on Practically Everything, 1966–2012* (New York: Time Inc., 2012), 101.
4. Conversation with Carol Loomis, February 2012.
5. Lowenstein, *Buffett.*
6. Loomis, *Tap Dancing to Work,* 134.
7. Carol Loomis, "Inside Story of Warren Buffett," *Fortune,* April 11, 1988, 34.
8. Berkshire Hathaway Annual Report, 1996, 16.
9. Berkshire Hathaway Annual Report, 1993, 15.
10. William N. Thorndike Jr., *The Outsiders: Eight Unconventional CEOs and Their Radically Rational Blueprint for Success* (Boston: Harvard Business Review Press, 2012), 194.
11. Ibid.
12. Berkshire Hathaway Annual Report, 1933, 16.
13. Ibid.
14. Ibid., 14.
15. Ibid.
16. George Johnson, *Fire in' the Mind: Science, Faith, and the Search for Order* (New York: Vintage Books, 1995), 104.
17. Andrew Kilpatrick, *Of Permanent Value: The Story of Warren Buffett* (Birmingham, AL: APKE, 1998), 794.
18. Ron Chernow, *The Death of the Banker: The Decline and Fall of the Great Financial Dynasties and the Triumph of Small Investors* (New York: Vintage Books, 1997).
19. Berkshire Hathaway Annual Report, 1987, 15.
20. Robert Lenzner, "Warren Buffett's Idea of Heaven: 'I Don't Have to Work with People I Don't Like,'" *Forbes,* October 18, 1993, 40.
21. Berkshire Hathaway Annual Report, 1992, 16.

Acknowledgments

As I have said on many occasions, the success of *The Warren Buffett Way* is first and foremost a testament to Warren Buffett. His wit, integrity, and intellectual spirit have charmed millions of investors worldwide. It is an unparalleled combination that makes Warren Buffett the single most popular role model in investing today and the greatest investor in history.

I first of all thank Warren Buffett for his teachings and for allowing me to use his copyrighted material. It is impossible to improve what Mr. Buffett has already said. The readers of this book are fortunate to be able to read his words rather than be subjected to a second-best paraphrase. My thanks also go to Debbie Bosanek for her kindness and willingness to keep the communication flowing even though I am sure there were a thousand other things that demanded her attention on that day.

I would also like to thank Charlie Munger for his intellectual contributions to the study of investing. His ideas on the "psychology of misjudgment" and the "latticework of mental models" are extremely important and should be examined by all. My appreciation to Charlie also includes thanks for his thoughtful conversations and his kind words of support.

I also have a deeply felt sense of gratitude for Carol Loomis. Two years before Mr. Buffett started his partnership, Carol began her career as a research associate at *Fortune* magazine. Today, she is senior editor-at-large at *Fortune*, a *New York Times* best-selling author, and one of the great American journalists. And as many of you know, she has been editing Berkshire Hathaway's annual reports since 1977. Carol's earliest words of encouragement meant more to me than I can express.

I would like to extend special thanks to Andy Kilpatrick, author of *Of Permanent Value: The Story of Warren Buffett*. Whenever I have misplaced a fact or became fuzzy on a particular event, I would turn to Andy's book. And if I still needed help, I would call Andy, who quickly gave me what I was looking for. Andy is a gentleman, and I consider him to be the official historian of Berkshire Hathaway.

When you have been a member of the Berkshire Hathaway community for 30 years, you have had the privilege of engaging in thousands of conversations, letters, and e-mails. Never once can I recall an unpleasant exchange, which tells you a lot about the Berkshire faithful. With that in mind I would like to thank Chuck Akre, Jack Bogle, David Braverman, Jamie Clark, Bob Coleman, Larry Cunningham, Chris Davis, Pat Dorsey, Charles Ellis, Henry Emerson, Ken Fisher, Phil Fisher, Bob Goldfarb, Burton Gray, Mason Hawkins, Ajit Jain, Joan Lamm-Tennant, Virginia Leith, John Lloyd, Paul Lountzis, Janet Lowe, Peter Lynch, Michael Mauboussin, Robert Miles, Bill Miller, Ericka Peterson, Larry Pidgeon, Lisa Rapuano, Laura Rittenhouse, John Rothchild, Bill Ruane, Tom Russo, Alice Schroeder, Lou Simpson, Ed Thorp, Wally Weitz, and David Winters.

I owe a great deal to a valued friend, Charles E. Haldeman Jr. Ed was there at the beginning. I remember the day I asked him if I should get my MBA or write a book about Warren Buffett. Ed said, "Write the book!" It was good advice. Ed read the original manuscript and made several suggestions that greatly improved the book. Thanks, Ed.

I am grateful to John Wiley & Sons for not only publishing *The Warren Buffett Way* but for their unwavering support and tireless dedication to the book these past 20 years. Everyone at Wiley is a true professional. Let me start by thanking Myles Thompson for taking a chance on a first-time writer. I would also like to thank Jennifer Pincott, Mary Daniello, Joan O'Neil, Pamela van Giessen, and the current team: Kevin Commins and Judy Howarth.

Once again and always, I am greatly indebted to my agent, Laurie Harper at Sebastian Literary Agency. Laurie is the perfect agent. She is smart, loyal, and cheerful, and always acts with the highest level of integrity. Most important, she is willing to go the extra mile to make sure our work together is first rate. In a word, Laurie is special.

Twenty years ago, Myles Thompson sent my first draft of this book to Maggie Stuckey and asked if she would put her skills to work in order to help a freshman writer. Since then, Maggie and I have written nine books together, and I have often wondered what would have happened had she not agreed to be my writing partner. Although we are separated by a continent, I am always amazed at how Maggie is able to connect intimately to the material. She works tirelessly from one chapter to the next, always searching for the best way to structure the material and articulate, in simple language, the work I have forwarded to her. Maggie Stuckey is simply the best in the business.

Anyone who has sat down to write a book knows that it means countless hours spent alone that otherwise could be spent with one's family. Writing requires certain sacrifices from the author, but I assure you much more from the author's family. I dearly love my children and I am forever grateful to my wife Maggie, who never wavers in her support for me and our family. On the first day I told her I was going to write a book, she smiled and convinced me it could be done. Her constant love makes all things possible. Even though my family comes last in this list, they are forever first in my heart.

For all that is good and right about this book, you may thank the people I have mentioned. For any errors or omissions, I alone am responsible

R.G.H.

About the Website

For additional information on applying Warren Buffett's methods in today's markets, please visit www.thewarrenbuffettway.com. The website includes:

- An interactive tool that can be used to value any stock
- A complete and up-to-date list of Berkshire Hathaway's stock holdings
- Warren Buffett news and discussion forum
- Warren Buffett biography, summary of his investment process, and his most famous quotes
- Other Warren Buffett products, including a video and related books

A valuable extension of the book, this website will provide the tools, information, and commentary you need to invest like Warren Buffett.

About the Author

Robert Hagstrom is one of the best-known authors of investment books for general audiences. He has written nine books, including the *New York Times* best-selling *The Warren Buffett Way* and *The Warren Buffett Portfolio: Mastering the Power of the Focus Investment Strategy*. He is also the author of *The NASCAR Way: The Business That Drives the Sport*, *The Detective and the Investor: Uncovering Investment Techniques from the Legendary Sleuths*, and *Investing: The Last Liberal Art*. Robert is a graduate of Villanova University with a BA and MA and is a Chartered Financial Analyst. He lives with his family in Villanova, Pennsylvania. Visit Robert's website at http://RobertHagstrom.com.

Index